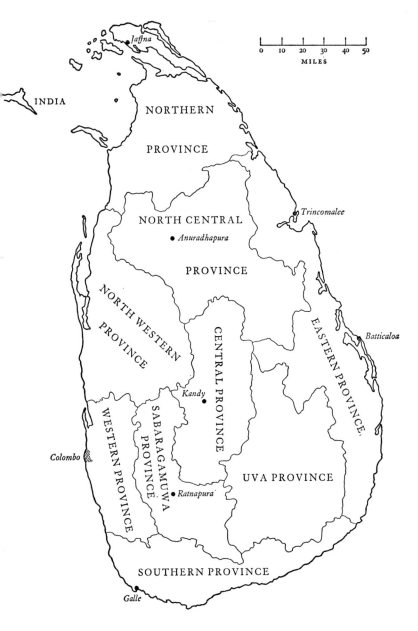

CEYLON

THE GROWTH OF A PARTY SYSTEM IN CEYLON

by Calvin A. Woodward

Brown University Press : Providence

Standard Book Number 87057–115–X
Library of Congress Catalog Card Number 76–89465
Brown University Press, Providence, Rhode Island 02912
Copyright © 1969 by Brown University. All rights reserved
Published 1969
Printed in the United States of America
Designed by David Ford

To my son

CONTENTS

List of Tables   ix

Preface   xi

INTRODUCTION   3

CHAPTER 1   The Pattern of Preindependence Politics   21

    The European Protest   21
    The Indigenous Protest   25
    The State Council   39

CHAPTER 2   The Foundation of a Party System   51

    The Formation of Parties   52
    The Election of 1947   66
    The Formation of a Government   72

CHAPTER 3   The Trend Toward a One-Party System   80

    Government and Opposition, 1947–52   81
    The Election of 1952   87
    Government and Opposition, 1952–56   95

CHAPTER 4   The Emergence of a Competitive Party System   100

    The Election of 1956   100
    The Displacement: Method and Impulse   107
    Government and Opposition, 1956–60   123

CHAPTER 5   Toward Party System Stabilization   134

    The Antidemocratic Trend   135

Contents

The Elections of 1960   140
Government and Opposition, 1960–65   157
Aftermath: The Resurgence of the U.N.P.   164

CHAPTER 6   *Parties as Identifiable Units*   171

The United National Party   172
The Sri Lanka Freedom Party   194
The Marxist Left   211
Communal Parties   230

CHAPTER 7   *The Character of the Party System*   232

Decline of the Independent and Personality Parties   232
The Confirmation of Established Parties   243
Competition and Coalition   249

CONCLUSION   270

From Personal to Social Parties   271
A Replacement Theory of Party Growth   279
Party and the Parliamentary System   286

Annotated List of Major Political Parties and Leaders   293
Notes   297
Bibliography   323
Index   333

TABLES

1 Popular Vote, 1947–56   115

2 Popular Vote for Independent Candidates, 1947–65   234

3 Average Vote for Independent Candidates and Candidates of Major and Minor Parties, 1947–65   234

4 Number of Independent Candidates (Ind.) and of Independent Candidates Who Lost Deposits (Ind. L.D.), 1947–65   236

5 Percentage of Total Vote Won by Independents, 1947–65   238

6 Number of Votes and Percentage of Total Vote Won by Major Parties, 1947–65   244

7 Electoral Strength of United National Party, by Province, 1947–65   246

8 Electoral Strength of Sri Lanka Freedom Party, by Province, 1952–65   248

9 Vote and Per Cent of Total Vote Won by First Two Candidates, 1947–65   250

10 Distribution of Parliamentary Seats among Communal Groups, 1947–65   258

11 Provincial Population and Representation in Parliament, 1947   260

12 Number of Registered Voters per Seat, 1947, 1952, and 1956   260

13 Number of Seats per Province under 1959 Delimitation, and Number of Persons, Citizens, and Voters per Seat   263

14 Distribution of Population by Communal Group   266

15 Distribution of Population by Religion   266

PREFACE

The major part of the research for this book was done in Great Britain and Ceylon in 1963 and 1964 when I was on a research training fellowship from the Social Science Research Council (United States). After I returned from Ceylon, a research grant from the Canada Council made it possible for me to do additional research at Lamont Library, Harvard University. This supplemented my earlier research and enabled me to record the development of a party system in Ceylon beyond the election of 1965, when the United National Party coalition returned to power. This book has been published with the help of a grant from the Social Science Research Council of Canada, using funds provided by the Canada Council. It is a pleasure to record my debt and gratitude to these councils for their invaluable financial help in the production of this book.

I found resource material on Ceylon to be abundant and, for the most part, to be readily available. The British Museum has a fine collection of old books on Ceylon, mostly memoirs and accounts by Englishmen who had lived in Ceylon. The Royal Institute of International Affairs in London has compiled a very useful file of newspaper clippings on affairs in Ceylon, and its library has a number of books, pamphlets, and journal articles on Ceylon. The most complete collection of official documents on Ceylon for the period when it was a British colony is at the Commonwealth Office in London. I am grateful to the staffs of all these institutions for their friendly and efficient assistance to me during my research there. I would also like to express my gratitude to the late Sir Ivor Jennings and to Professor B. H. Farmer, both of whom gave me valuable advice and insights in regard to politics in Ceylon.

In Ceylon I did a great deal of research at the Colombo Museum, which has the best collection of books, pamphlets, articles, and documents on Ceylonese politics of any institution in Ceylon. It has the complete debates of the Legislative Council, the State Council, and the House of Representatives, as well as an extensive collection of Sessional Papers and other government publications. The most complete collection of government documents is at the Government Archives, which was in the process of being moved when I was in Ceylon. Most official documents on Ceylon, including Sessional Papers and the debates of the House of Representatives, were available for purchase at the office of the Superintendent of Documents, Colombo, and this enabled me to obtain documentary material not available at the museum. The Colombo Library and the library of the University of Ceylon at Peradeniya also have good collections of material on Ceylonese politics.

Newspapers in Ceylon are among the finest anywhere and provide the most complete and detailed account of political developments in Ceylon. The archives of the *Times of Ceylon* and the Associated Newspapers of Ceylon are well kept and available to the scholar for research. The *Times of Ceylon* keeps a file of clippings on political and other affairs in Ceylon that draws on other newspapers in Ceylon as well as its own. I found this to be an extremely valuable source of information on political developments in Ceylon since 1947. Another newspaper, the *Tribune,* is a well-written and informative weekly devoted mainly to commentary on political developments in Ceylon. I am very grateful to Mr. S. P. Amarasingham, owner and publisher of the *Tribune,* for allowing me to peruse the volumes of the *Tribune,* and to the *Times of Ceylon* for permitting me to use their archives and clipping file.

Parties in Ceylon have, on the whole, neglected to keep records or to compile literature pertinent to their own affairs. Constitutions, manifestoes, and campaign literature of the various parties is hard to come by, although with the assistance of many party members and other persons, I was able to obtain or consult most of the more important literature of this sort. The University Library at Peradeniya has a useful collection of party and campaign literature, but it is incomplete and sparse. Some of the pamphlets it has, however, especially those that relate to the 1947 and 1952 elections, are invaluable. Both the L.S.S.P. and the C.P. have published brief pamphlets recounting the history of their organizations. All the major parties have newspapers, and these are a good source for official party policy and opinion on various matters. The *Young Socialists,* a journal published by L.S.S.P. intellectuals, contains incisive comment on political affairs in Ceylon. Information about the organization of parties, their membership, the size of their branches and ancillary organizations, the process of decision making within parties, their relation to pressure groups, and matters of this sort has to be gained by interviews and personal contact. I am very grateful to the many party members, journalists, leaders of communal, business, and other pressure groups, and many other informed individuals who gave so willingly to me of their time and knowledge.

Reliable statistical data is sometimes hard to get in Ceylon. In some cases, statistical information is not available or not recorded, in others it is suspect or unverifiable, and in some cases it is incomplete or out of date. This is especially true of statistics relating to trade unions and other private organizations. In the research for this book I have tried wherever possible to use official government sources for statistical information. I have used several sources for election statistics. The *Ceylon Daily News* has published a book of facts on every election in Ceylon since 1931, except that of 1952. The Government published Sessional Papers on the elections of 1960 and 1965, and these contain some statistics on previous elections. I also copied election returns for every election in Ceylon since independence, except that of 1965, from the records kept at the Office of the Commissioner of Elections, Colombo. In some cases there are discrepancies between the voting statistics contained in one source and those contained in another. Such differences, however, are usually minor.

It is indeed a pleasure to see one's work come to fruition. It is equally pleasurable to acknowledge the many personal obligations that one incurs in the course of doing that work. I am particularly grateful to Mr. and Mrs. Clement Mendis, Mr. and Mrs. George C. Marshall, and Mr. and Mrs. Peter Heap for their many kindnesses to my family and myself. Their friendship made our stay in Ceylon more pleasant and full than it would have been without them. I am particularly grateful to Professor Whitney Perkins of Brown University for his guidance and advice during the research for this study, and for his incisive criticism of the initial draft of the book. I would also like to thank Professor Newell M. Stultz of Brown University, who also read and commented upon the initial draft of this book. I am extremely grateful to W. Howard Wriggins who reviewed the manuscript and provided me with a detailed critique of it. It was his fine book on Ceylon that ten years ago first aroused my interest in Ceylonese politics, and I am honored that his wisdom and extensive knowledge of Ceylon have been brought to bear on my study. I would also like to thank Miss Ruth Sanford of Brown University Press for her very careful and detailed editing of the manuscript.

I am of course responsible for its errors.

The Growth of a Party System in Ceylon

INTRODUCTION

In 1947, as Ceylon approached independence, Great Britain looked with pride upon its accomplishments there. Five years later Sir Oliver Goonetilleke, a leader of the independence movement and the first native Ceylonese to be Governor-General of Ceylon, remarked, "Ceylon is the best job the Englishman has done anywhere in the world, almost better than in his own country."[1] Ceylon was prosperous when independence came. It had the highest per capita income of any Asian country until the rapid reconstruction of Japan made it second.[2] Wealth had been accumulated during the war, and Ceylon had built up a sterling reserve of Rs. 1,260 million from British purchases and estate exports.[3] The island seemed like a paradise in contrast to its teeming neighbor India. Coconuts and fruits grew in abundance in the wet areas, and even people with meager incomes had enough to provide for food and the other necessities of life.

But Ceylon has its problems. Prior to independence its population had been increasing at the rate of 1.8 per cent each year. In 1931 the population was 5,306,900. By 1946 it had increased to 6,657,300.[4] Within a few years malaria was brought under control, and by 1953 the population had grown to over eight million.[5] The annual rate of population growth was 2.8 per cent, the highest in Asia except for Taiwan. Many of Ceylon's economic and social problems derive from its high rate of population growth. It has been impossible to satisfy the rapidly growing demand for employment. In 1945 only 21,366 persons were registered as unemployed.[6] Twelve years later this number had increased to 112,758, and by 1961 over 150,000 were registered as unemployed.[7] A decrease in the rate of infant mortality has produced a younger population.[8] As the median age has been lowered, there has been an increase in the size of the working force and a large increase in the school-age population. In 1947 there were 1,004,586 pupils registered in primary and secondary schools in Ceylon.[9] This number had more than doubled by 1961, when 2,313,852 pupils were registered in schools.[10] In addition to meeting the economic strain of school construction and teacher education, Ceylon has had to find ways and means to improve and expand the inadequate health facilities, to provide pensions and care for the old and infirm, and to institute a wide range of welfare programs for its people. In these ways, and others, population increase has tended to absorb the gains made by economic development.

It has also increased the pressure on the already inadequate land. In 1952 it was estimated that nearly 38 per cent of all families in Ceylon were landless.[11] In the central hill area, where large foreign-owned tea estates monopolize the arable land, the problem of landlessness is most severe. One study, for instance, published in 1957, estimated that 66 per cent of the families in this area were without land.[12] It is not so much that land is lacking as that most of the arable land is taken up by tea, coconut, and rubber plantations that are company-owned or individually owned by wealthy foreigners and Ceylonese. There is little room left for the small farm of the peasant. In the eastern region of Ceylon, where there is little rainfall, there stretches a vast dry zone that the government has sought to make arable by irrigation.[13] It was hoped that development of this region would somewhat relieve the problem of landlessness. But the resettlement of people and peasant colonization of the dry zone have not been successful. The pioneer spirit needed for colonization has been lacking in a people reluctant to leave the area of their birth and kinship. Relatively few families have moved into the dry zone, and the development of the area has also been impeded by the financial strain on the government. As it is now, the problem of landlessness can only worsen. It could only be relieved by wholesale nationalization of the foreign-owned estates, which, at present, is not economically feasible. Too much of Ceylon's income depends on these efficiently run estates, and it is understood that if Ceylon were to nationalize them, it would lose its market for tea in both the United States and Great Britain.

Ceylon has remained a predominantly rural and agricultural country. In 1946, 1,023,000 people lived in urban areas, and 5,634,300 people lived in rural areas. By 1953 the urban population had increased to 1,239,100, and the rural population had increased to 6,858,800.[14] Occupationally and economically, Ceylon is bound to its agricultural production. Over half of its gainfully employed workers are in agriculture or forestry, and countless others are engaged in occupations related to the marketing, processing, and distribution of agricultural products.[15] Tea, coconut, and rubber production comprises the bulk of Ceylon's agriculture. Thirty per cent of Ceylon's work force is employed in the production of these three commodities, which provide nearly 40 per cent of the gross national product and up to 95 per cent of Ceylon's foreign exchange earnings.[16] Coconut plantations tend to be small and are almost entirely Ceylonese owned. Rubber plantations are larger. Prior to independence, 45 per cent of capital investment in rubber was British owned.[17] Since then, however, British capital has gradually moved out of this economically uncertain enterprise, and nearly all the rubber acreage is now owned by Ceylonese.[18] While government assistance has encouraged the development of cooperative tea estates, the growing and processing of tea is still dominated by foreign-owned companies. Seventy-five per cent of the tea lands are owned by companies, and over 50 per cent are owned by foreign capital.[19] Because of the domination of the arable land by the export estates, Ceylon must now import over 50 per cent of its food. All its sugar and wheat comes from abroad, and Ceylon has to import over 50 per cent of the rice it needs.[20] Thus Ceylon, like other underdeveloped countries, is heavily dependent upon exports and imports for its very survival.

Economic problems are not the only ones that an independent Ceylon has to face. Foreign invasions and occupations have left a communally plural society that has in various ways affected the political life of the new state. The majority of the people of Ceylon are Sinhalese. Their ancestors came from northern India and were the first important cultural group to settle on the island. They are of the Aryan subrace, and they speak Sinhalese, a language found only in Ceylon. Concentrated in the wet zone of central, western, and southern Ceylon, where the land is arable and productive, the Sinhalese, because of their numbers and long occupation of the island, claim the pre-eminent place in politics. In 1953 there were 5,616,700 Sinhalese in Ceylon, about 70 per cent of the total population. The largest minority group are the Tamils. Both Ceylon Tamils and Indian Tamils live in Ceylon. The Ceylon Tamils came from South India between A.D. 400 and 1200, and are of Dravidian origin. In contrast to the Sinhalese, who are Buddhist, the Tamils are Hindu. In 1953 there were 884,700 Ceylon Tamils, about 11 per cent of the population.[21] While the vast majority of the Ceylon Tamils live in the Northern and Eastern provinces, nearly 90,000 live in Colombo, and another 25,000 live in Kandy. Generally the Ceylon Tamils appear more energetic and more responsive to career opportunities than the Sinhalese. During the British occupation Tamils were more willing to learn English and to seize the job opportunities available in the government service for those who were educated and spoke English. Consequently, Tamils held a majority of the posts open to Ceylonese in the government service. But despite this elite group, the majority of the Tamils in the Northern and Eastern provinces are poor peasants, tenants, and laborers who have much in common, economically and socially, with the majority of the Sinhalese.

In 1953 there were 974,100 Indian Tamils living in Ceylon. Almost all the Indian Tamils work on tea estates inland, although there are Indian merchants and traders in urban areas. There are over 70,000 Indians in the Colombo area, mostly merchants, dock workers, servants, and day laborers. Indians were brought to Ceylon by the British to work on the estates because, as a group, they worked harder and longer than natives of Ceylon. Today Indians are drawn from their homeland by the greater income they can earn on the tea estates. Each year thousands of them enter Ceylon illegally, looking for work, and the situation has strained relations between Ceylon and India. The problem of citizenship for these Indians has been a major issue of Ceylonese politics, especially since their disfranchisement in 1950. The Ceylon and Indian Tamils have never been able to co-operate politically. Both groups are Hindu and of South Indian origin, but the Indian Tamils are generally of lower caste than the Ceylon Tamils, and the longer residence on the island of the latter has produced a cultural distinction between the two groups. The Ceylon Tamils have citizenship, and as a group they have different problems and interests that set them apart from the Indian Tamils. No organization has been able to unite the two groups, and each has its own political organization.

There are also several other cultural or national groups in Ceylon. The Ceylon Moors, who comprise about 5 per cent of the population, are descendants of Arab traders who used Ceylon as a port of call in their trade between the Middle and Far East from the thirteenth to the seventeenth century. Some settled on the island, and today the number of Moors in Ceylon is nearly 500,000. Most Moors are settled in the Eastern Province, where they are mainly small farmers. There are concentrations of Moors, however, in nearly every city and town, where for the most part, they are merchants and shopkeepers. Over 78,000 reside in Colombo, and more than 50,000 live in Kandy. They are Muslims, and, having no language of their own, they tend to speak the language of the area in which they reside. There is also a small Malay population on the island, which, like the

Moors, is Muslim. Brought to Ceylon by the British for police and military service during the preindependence period, the Malays have continued until recently in this occupation. In 1953 there were 25,000 Malays in Ceylon, nearly 16,000 of whom lived in Colombo. Since then many have returned to Malaysia because of Ceylon's policy of recruiting its police and armed forces personnel from the Sinhalese population. There are about 46,000 Burghers and Eurasians in Ceylon. The Burghers trace their ancestry to the Dutch and Portuguese who had occupied coastal areas of Ceylon prior to the British invasion. The Burghers adopted English as their native tongue, and under the British they enjoyed elite status. For the most part they are in the professions and government service. The adoption of Sinhalese as the official language of Ceylon has somewhat limited their career opportunity, and since 1956 many Burghers have migrated to Australia and other countries. In 1953 there were nearly 7,000 Europeans in Ceylon, mainly British engaged in commerce, banking, or the management of tea estates.

The communal pattern in Ceylon is further pluralized by a division in the majority community between the low-country Sinhalese and the Kandyan Sinhalese. The difference between the two groups is more in the attitudes of each than in any outward aspect. Their race and language are the same, and they are both Buddhist. The Kandyan Sinhalese live in the up-country area, which was less exposed to Western penetration than the coastal area where the low-country Sinhalese live. Consequently, more of the traditional social system and culture has survived in the Kandyan area than on the coastal fringe. Western values have modified the values of the low-country Sinhalese to a much greater extent than they have those of the Kandyans, and the caste system is more rigid among the Kandyan Sinhalese. Thus there is a cultural difference between the two groups, and politicians of both areas have sought to emphasize it, in an effort to build a stable base of political support among one or the other of the two Sinhalese groups. The low-country Sinhalese are in the majority. In 1953 there were 2,147,200 Kandyan Sinhalese and 3,469,500 low-country Sinhalese.[22]

Religious affiliation is primarily but not exclusively related to the communal groupings in Ceylon. The Buddhists, who include most of the Sinhalese, are in the majority. In 1953, 5,209,400 people professed the Buddhist faith.[23] Most of the Indian and Ceylon Tamils are Hindus, of whom, in 1953, there were 1,610,500. There are nearly 550,000 Muslims in Ceylon, mostly Moors but including also most of the Malays and some Pakistanis. The 725,000 Christians in Ceylon testify to the success of Catholic and Protestant missionary work. The Burghers and Eurasians are almost all Christian, but they account for only about 5 per cent of the Christian population. As might be expected, the conversion of the indigenous population to Christianity was most effective in the coastal area, which was subjected to progressively greater Western occupation from the sixteenth century to the twentieth. The Catholic population is concentrated on the coastal fringe north of Colombo. It is the result primarily of the Portuguese period of occupation, which lasted from 1517 until 1655, when the Dutch wrested portions of the coast from Portuguese control. Protestant missionary work began under the Dutch and continued under the British. The Catholic population remained firm in its faith, and the Protestant population in the area north of Colombo is not large. For the most part, Protestant missionary work was more successful in the coastal area south of Colombo as far as the city of Galle. Except for Kandy, which is the center of commerce and trade in the hill area, Christianity has not spread into the rural interior of Ceylon, where the traditional culture is strongly embedded. Jaffna, the capital of the Tamil north, and Batticaloa and Trincomalee, in the Eastern Province, also have concentrations of Christians. All three cities were important ports whose long occupation by the Portuguese, Dutch, and finally the British provided the opportunity for missionary work.

The occupation by the British, which began in 1795, has had

a more enduring impact on Ceylon than did the previous occupations. The Dutch and Portuguese had occupied only a limited coastal area sufficient to serve as a trading and export center for the cinnamon trade. Their most lasting impact has been through cultural and religious groups. It was the British who for the first time brought the whole island under the control of a Western power. Their rule in Ceylon lasted for more than a century and a half, and was marked by peace and good relations. Perhaps nowhere else was the movement toward independence accomplished with such good will and compromise. To be sure, the British had exploited Ceylon economically. It was a wealthy land, profitable to the British landlord, and strategically it was one of the bastions of the empire that stretched from Gibraltar to Malta to Port Said, to Aden, Colombo, Singapore, and Hong Kong. But the British occupation resulted not only in exploitation. It provided health facilities, and a communications system that linked the island economically and politically. Also, Great Britain left behind a highly literate population. In 1881 only 394,300 Ceylonese were literate, while 2,362,400 Ceylonese could neither read nor write.[24] Toward the end of the century the British began developing educational facilities that by the time of the transfer of power in 1947 had produced a literacy rate of over 50 per cent. Six years later the proportion of literates was even greater: 4,508,800 persons were literate, while 3,589,100 were illiterate.[25] The proportion is even greater when the 1,208,800 children under the age of five are excluded from the number of illiterates. Thus the British provided well for Ceylon in a number of ways. They left the island in 1947, satisfied that the environment in Ceylon would favor the growth of a democratic political system. No one was more optimistic about Ceylon's future than Lord Soulbury, who had led the commission that recommended independence in Ceylon. "With such natural resources and with leaders of proved experience," Lord Soulbury told the House of Lords in 1947, "I feel that Ceylon can face the future under the happiest auspices." [26]

Ceylon, as Sir Charles Jeffries observes, was in many ways considered "the prototype and model for the new Commonwealth of the latter part of the twentieth century."[27] The British fully expected that the political institutions they had planted would grow well in Ceylon and that Ceylon would exemplify the best traditions of the British political experience. Ceylon has been independent now for over twenty years. It has faced the hardships and strains of its plural society, the challenge of a growing population with rising expectations, the exertions of a painfully slow economic growth, the explosion of a long-contained nationalism, and tensions between divisive political and social elites. In short, Ceylon has encountered all the difficulties of a developing and communally plural nation. But the political institutions planted by the British in 1947 have stood and have grown firm, firmer perhaps than in any other state of the new Commonwealth. No one party dominates, as in India, the parliamentary or political system. Rather, a competitive party system has evolved that is capable of providing alternative governments. On four occasions since 1947 Ceylon has seen the peaceful and democratic transfer of political power from one party or coalition to another in accordance with the preference of the people. Governments have been formed without difficulty, and Ceylon has had none of that political chaos or instability that so often attends multiparty systems in the new states, or even in some of the old states, like the France of the Fourth Republic. The parliamentary system and the parties within it have provided the essential focus and organizations of political life. Ceylon has suffered only a minor and abortive coup attempt and, except for the communal riots of 1958, the political life of the island and the functioning of its political institutions have made great progress toward the maturity of the British model.

But the Ceylon experiment has been a process of evolvement. In 1947 there was novelty and confusion. Parties were new then, and neither their members nor the electorate were familiar with the peculiarities of party contest and operation. It would take time before party politics could replace the politics of personality to which both the masses of people and those involved in politics had for so long been accustomed. The parliamentary system also was new, and all the techniques, customs, and procedures vital to its operation had to be learned and accepted before it could function well. Most of all, the essential roles that Government and Opposition play in the operation of a parliamentary system had to be accepted by the parties and individuals involved. These techniques, understandings, and attitudes would take time to develop, and on their maturation the survival of the parliamentary system in Ceylon would ultimately depend. Twenty years after independence many things had changed. Parties had become more organized and disciplined. To a great extent they had replaced personalities as the primary units of electoral contest and parliamentary action. The parliamentary system had become more stabilized, as parties had learned to co-operate as well as to compete. Gradually relations between the Government and the Opposition improved. It appeared by 1966 that the hopes and expectations that many had had for Ceylon twenty years before were being realized.

Parliament has endured as a political institution in Ceylon because parties have related it to the people, by articulating popular aspirations and transforming them into legislation and law. Parties have thus made the Parliament an effective institution of government, and the people have responded by placing their confidence in both. The parties and the party system in Ceylon have conformed to the operational needs of their institutional environment in the same way as they reacted to the demands of their social environment. If parties were going to operate as efficient and successful units in Parliament, it was soon apparent, both organizational and ideological changes were necessary on their part. At the same time the parties underwent internal changes to adapt to the requirements of effective parliamentary action, they helped confirm procedures that are vital to the smooth operation of a parliamentary system. Thus parties responded to the pressures of both their institutional and their social environment, and much of the success of the parliamentary system in Ceylon is due to this fact.

Parties have come to play an increasingly important role in modern political life, and many observers regard them as essential agents in the social and political development of mass society. The party, in the modern sense of the word, was relatively new when Edmund Burke defined it as "a body of men united, for promoting by their joint endeavours the national interest, upon some particular principle in which they are all agreed."[28] In the century and a half since Burke's classic definition, parties have experienced almost universal growth until, today, as Maurice Duverger observes, "parties function in most civilized nations, and in others there is an attempt to imitate them."[29] Until recently, however, the study of parties has been a relatively neglected area of political analysis. The appearance of Duverger's pioneering work on parties in 1951 and his attempt to develop a theoretical framework for stasiology, or the science of political parties, has had a great deal to do with the many attempts since to use the party as the crucial element in comparative political analysis.[30] In 1954 Sigmund Neumann, noting the work of Duverger and others, observed that only "of late, and at last, has the role of the political party entered the center of our professional concern."[31] To Neumann, "political parties are the lifeline of modern politics" and an essential area of comparative political analysis, because "it is through the nexus of political parties that the manifold character and dynamic life of the different continents can be constantly revealed."[32] David E. Apter argues that "the concern over political parties is central to any comparative political analysis,"[33] while Avery Leiserson maintains that the party has become so important in modern political life that it has replaced, or should replace, the state as the central focus of comparative political analysis.[34]

Most students of political parties relate the origin and growth of parties to the emergence of modern democratic government. Max Weber speaks of the mass parties of today as "children of plebiscitarian democracy," whose organizational growth from "purely personal followings of the aristocracy" to "parties of notables" to "parties of plebiscitarian democracy" was impelled by the extension of the franchise and the need to organize votes.[35] Duverger, like Weber, connects the emergence of parties with the extension of popular suffrage, although he argues that "parliamentary prerogatives" were also a factor. Parties emerged not only "to organize the electors by means of committees capable of making the candidates known and of canalizing the votes in their direction," but also to enable members of Parliament "to group themselves according to what they have in common, so as to act in concert."[36] H. McD. Clokie also relates the rise of parties "to the increasing democratization of life,"[37] and Robert MacIver argues that "the organization of opinion by parties inevitably followed the rise of large-scale democracy."[38] E. E. Schattschneider maintains that "political parties created democracy and that modern democracy is unthinkable save in terms of the parties."[39] Clinton Rossiter shares this view, arguing that "parties and democracy arose together; they have lived and prospered in a closely symbiotic relationship; and if one of them should ever weaken and die, the other would die with it."[40]

As these and other views suggest, political parties are intimately linked to a democratic political order.[41] Sigmund Neumann asserts that "a one-party system is a contradiction in itself" and that "the definition of a party presupposes a democratic climate and makes the term a misnomer when applied to a dictatorship."[42] Neumann's argument rests on the assumption that "the coexistence of at least one competitive group makes a party real."[43] A party, he contends, is united not only on the basis of an identity of view among its membership and followers, but also on the basis of its differentiation from the opinion of other groups. Neumann maintains that existence of a party implies the active participation of a people whose vote it seeks to mobilize in order to obtain the powers of government.

Such a positive view of parties, embracing the assumption that they play an essential role in the growth and vitality of democratic government, was not common at the time parties originated, more than a century ago. Then parties were considered dangerous to democratic government or inconsistent with a popularly controlled political system. George Washington, for example, was concerned about the divisive effect of permanently aligned factions, and Thomas Jefferson once wrote to a friend, "If I could not go to heaven but with a party, I would not go there at all." [44] Even after parties were generally accepted as an inevitable and perhaps necessary aspect of mass democracy, many persons still voiced concern over the oligarchic tendencies revealed by party and the implications that these had for democratic government. Vilfredo Pareto in *The Mind and Society* and Gaetano Mosca in *The Ruling Class* both saw in the party a vehicle for the perpetuation of an elitist, oligarchic rule within a democratic political framework. [45] Such a view had been earlier sustained by M. I. Ostrogorski in his *Democracy and the Organization of Political Parties in the United States and Great Britain* [46] and shortly after by Robert Michels' "discovery" of "the iron law of oligarchy." [47] Thus parties were not always regarded as instruments vital and beneficial to democratic government, and the acceptance of them as such by most people took time.

To an extent, at least, different views on the utility of parties derive from the different perspectives from which parties are viewed—the functions one assigns to parties or the functions one expects them to perform. The tendency now is to emphasize the social functions of parties and the crucial role parties play in the political and social development of states. This view of the party as a social engineer is not entirely new. Anton D. Morse argued at the turn of the century that in any polity, "party is the manifestation of political life, and the indispensable means of its growth." [48] The main emphasis on the social utility of parties relates to the role they play as organizer of the public will and the link they provide between the people and the government. Leslie Lipson, for instance, argues that parties "provide the bridge to connect the groupings of society with the institutions of the state." [49] In similar fashion, MacIver contends that in "every modern democracy the major political vehicle of opinion is the party," [50] and Sigmund Neumann speaks of the party as "the great intermediary which links social forces and ideologies to official governmental institutions and relates them to political action within the larger political community." [51] F. C. Engelmann has a similar view, maintaining that parties "are not only essential mobilizers of the electorate and selectors of candidates for public office; they also form an integral link in the chain of democratic policy making." [52] And Gabriel Almond, while he considers "interest aggregation" to be the main function of the party in modern society, also argues that parties play an essential role in the "recruitment of political elites" and that they are "powerful agents for political socialization." [53] Thus from the perspective of social utility, parties are seen as essential agents in the functioning of the democratic political process.

But the party can be viewed from another perspective and can be considered as an organism that has a life of its own, a role to fulfill, and a function to perform for itself as a unit distinct from the greater social environment in which it operates. This was the view taken by sociologists and the view that led many observers to question the compatibility of parties with democratic government. This view sees the party as a power-oriented organization whose function is the acquisition of power and patronage for its elite. Robert Michels, like Vilfredo Pareto, argued that "the *raison d'être* of the political party is the push for power." [54] Max Weber had a similar view of parties, maintaining that they are "structures struggling for domination." [55] And more recently Maurice Duverger, who also agrees that the objective of the party, as of more primitive organizations in history, is "to win political power and exercise it," has concluded that the "internal structure of parties is essentially autocratic and oligarchic" and that their leadership tends "to form a ruling class."[56] It is this view of parties as oligarchic organizations whose objective is power that has led many critics to question their social utility and operation in democracies.

Although some observers emphasize the social functions of the party and others lay stress on the party as an ambitious unit of self-interest, most parties can and do perform functions both for themselves and for society as a whole. There is no functional dichotomy in the nature of the party, and its performance of one function does not preclude, and in most cases actually enhances or supports, its performance of the other. Max Weber suggested this when he noted that "*all* party struggles are struggles for the patronage of office, as well as struggles for objective goals."[57] Allan P. Sindler, who regards the "power-seeking aspect" of the party as primary, argues that "an emphasis on the power goals of [a] party" does not "foreclose the question of the positive contribution of party to the over-all political system."[58] The party, he continues, "performs certain self-promoting functions which, incidentally but inevitably, affect the over-all system within which party operates."[59] David Apter, while he discerns a "factional and personalistic" orientation in parties, also views parties as "shapers of new communities."[60] That the party performs both a personal and a social function is also the view of S. J. Eldersveld, who maintains that the party "exists as an intermediary group representing and exploiting multiple interests for the achievement of direct control over the power apparatus of the society."[61]

But while parties are power-seeking, socially exploitive organizations that perform social and political functions at the same time they pursue party goals, the primary objective of the party is the satisfaction of its own power ambition. The needs and interests of the party are its primary concern. Men want power, and the function of a party is to obtain it. As both

Duverger and Weber show, the formation and growth of parties resulted from the work of men who sought in the organization of parties a means to advance in and profit from the political vocation. The ideologies and policies that parties adopt are in large measure intended to support the power goals of parties. Sindler, who stresses that he does "not overlook the policy orientation of party," considers it "one of several means to the power end of party: the control of government through the pursuit of election victories." The "material drives of party," he continues, "tend to be more enduring than any commitment in the abstract to ideology or to any particular policy position." [62] A party is the ambitions of individuals organized, and it will respond opportunistically to the demands of its environment because in so doing it can better realize its goal of power.

All parties, totalitarian as well as democratic, perform this self-promoting function. This is basic to the definition and nature of the party. But the degree to which the party will perform functions for the society in which it operates depends in large measure upon its political environment. In one-party states where coercion may be used as a primary means of social control or in states where the political impact of the masses for one reason or another is minimal or restricted, the social function of the party may be limited or not performed. If a party can perform its self-promoting function without also performing a social function, it is under no compulsion to take any other interest than its own into account. It is in competitive party situations that parties are most apt to perform social functions well, because the competition for votes compels them to adopt popular platforms in order to obtain power. As Sindler says, a "party will more often pursue its self-promoting ends in ways beneficial to the public good when each party is forced to operate under a real competitive threat from the other." [63] In this situation parties necessarily and almost unconsciously become socially responsible, because it is the only way they can realize their goal of power acquisition. This is what makes parties engineers of social and political development. They develop organization and they adopt policies in order to mobilize the votes necessary to obtain power, and in so doing they effectively relate the people to their government. In the same process the political institutions of the state are strengthened and the political maturity of the people advanced. As David Apter comments, "Parties that are pluralistic must compete with one another for public favor, thereby strengthening both the electoral and representative mechanisms."[64]

Even in competitive situations, however, the ambitions of parties have to be contained within constitutional limits. The goal of the party is power, and if this can be realized by the adoption of unconstitutional strategies and means, a party may well subvert or circumvent the legal or prescribed political process. The possibility of this is especially real in new states, where the institutions of government are of recent origin and where the political traditions and procedures that support them are not yet firmly rooted in mass opinion. In such situations the survival of the constitutional system and the containment of party ambition and competition within boundaries prescribed by the constitution depend upon the dedication of those involved in politics, power balances among groups in the social environment, and other tenuous and uncertain supports. Such tenuous supports as do exist are liable to collapse at any moment because of economic strains and other problems that new states have to face. The development and maintenance of a viable and competitive party system under such circumstances is a difficult task, and most of the new states have not been able to achieve it.[65] The fact that Ceylon almost alone among the new states has been able to succeed in this endeavor makes the growth of a party system in Ceylon a useful and exciting subject of investigation.

The purpose of this study is to analyze the growth of a party system in Ceylon. Both the parties and the party system have undergone major alterations within the space of twenty years, and it is the task of these pages to record these changes and to relate and analyze the reasons for them. First of all, there has been a change in the relations between parties. They have become less hostile to each other in the course of time, and consequently they are better able to co-operate at the electoral and parliamentary levels. This has facilitated the construction of coalitions, improved relations between Government and Opposition, and moderated the temper of both electoral contests and parliamentary activity. Secondly, the parties have undergone vital transformation in regard to their organization and disposition. And finally, the party system has experienced fundamental structural and ideological changes in the period since independence. My objective is to reveal these changes and examine the extent to which they have resulted from the attempt of parties to perform self-promoting functions.

This study is guided by the assumption that a party is at bottom a group of ambitious men who have chosen politics as a vocation and who seek personal success in that vocation. In societies of the mass franchise, like Ceylon, if a party is to satisfy the personal ambitions of its elite, it must obtain the votes necessary to give it power, and to do this it must appeal to the people on the basis of platform and ideology; thus, while it may originate as an organization designed to acquire power for its elite, it necessarily and perhaps imperceptibly becomes an agent of social development. In this way the two functions of parties are related.

Chapter 1 investigates the preindependence period in Ceylon and analyzes the nature of political struggle prior to the emergence of political parties. Chapters 2 through 5 are concerned with the development of a party system in Ceylon from 1947 to 1965. Chapters 6 and 7 discuss the major changes that have taken place in the parties and the party system in Ceylon in the years since independence. In the Conclusion an attempt is made to analyze the growth of a party system in Ceylon and to examine the reasons for the changes that have taken place in the process of its growth.

CHAPTER 1   *The Pattern of Preindependence Politics*

The British occupation has had greater impact on Ceylon's modern political development than any other. Cultural residues were left by preceding occupations, and these had their effect on politics later, especially in regard to the shape and evolution of a party system. But it was Great Britain that gave Ceylon its political system, and it was during the British period that the politics of a mass society first appeared in Ceylon. Because of this, the nature and organization of politics during the British period needs examination.

THE EUROPEAN PROTEST

The first political contest to occur in Ceylon during the British occupation began to take shape soon after Ceylon became a crown colony in 1802. It was between the Governor and the resident Europeans who had investment interests on the island, and the cause was the Governor's enactment of fiscal and commercial policy that the European residents considered detrimental to their interests. At the time they had no access to any government structure, and thus they had no way directly to influence policy decisions that affected their interests.[1] The Governor had been vested with complete executive and legislative power, although at the time the Secretary of State had advocated the creation of an advisory council in order to give "more satisfaction in the country and to those who are liable to be regulated and affected" by the Governor's policy.[2] But His Majesty's Council, which the Governor set up in pursuance of this suggestion, had no connection with interest groups on the island; it was composed of officials appointed by the Governor from his staff.[3] In any case, its duty was merely "to advise and consult with the Governor only when convoked by him."[4] Because of this, the Governor was effectively insulated from the advice or protests of the commercial interests.

It was not until the financial condition of the island deteriorated that the European interests took direct political action. A European protest movement emerged, sporadic at first and largely unorganized, as resident groups sought to obtain by constitutional reform a government structure in which they could express their claims and influence the decisions that affected their interests. Agitation for reform was carried on in London, and in response to this pressure, as well as to the worsening financial state of the island, a commission was sent to Ceylon in 1829 to investigate the situation. The commission agreed that "the people have had no opportunity of explaining their objections to the passing of regulations which have injuriously affected their interests"[5] and recommended the creation of an executive council and a legislative council, the latter to include members representing indigenous interests. As a result of this recommendation, a new governmental structure was instituted in 1833. The Legislative Council was set up, consisting of fifteen members, all appointed by the Governor. Nine of the fifteen were "official" members; that is, they held posts in the government. The other six were "unofficial" members, or private citizens. The Council was empowered to enact all laws affecting the welfare of the colony, including appropriations. Its power, however, was greatly circumscribed. The Governor had veto power, the Council could discuss only matters proposed to it by the Governor, and the Governor had an official majority sufficient to pass any measures he proposed. Nevertheless, the move was important in that it created an institutional form for the practice of politics. Within this form the European protesters could conduct their struggles with the Governor and press for additional reforms. This was a crucial factor in encouraging the reformist and constitutional orientation of future protests. In addition, the Council provided a rudimentary structure for the evolution of parliamentary government. Colebrooke anticipated its institutional importance, saying that it would "eventually constitute an essential part of any Colonial Legislature for which the Island may be prepared at a future period." [6]

The creation of the Legislative Council was also important in that it allowed an opposition to take shape. Governor Horton, in his first address to the Council, in 1833, did not expect such a development. Instead he anticipated an entirely harmonious relationship, advising the Council that its special province would be "to aid me in the formulation of wise and just laws suited to the circumstances of this important Colony." [7] While in most matters a harmonious relationship did in fact develop, a division in the Council between the unofficial members, on the one hand, and the official members, on the other, did occur. The division was primarily on financial matters, for the unofficial members, representing the commercial and business interests on the island, continually argued against excessive spending on the part of the Governor. In particular, they protested against his financial levies on the colony, the greater part of which bore on them. This issue gave rise to repeated demands by the Council for constitutional reforms that would give it and the unofficial members greater control over financial matters. The unofficial members of the Council demanded both an increase in the number of unofficial members in the direction of a majority and additional powers for the Council, especially in regard to appropriations. Some concessions were made but none satisfied the demands. In 1855 the Secretary of State conferred on the Council the right to propose for discussion and legislation any measure that did not involve a charge on the revenue. In addition, the Governor came to permit the prominent commercial firms on the island to appoint the unofficial members,[8] and in 1889 two unofficial members were added, though the Governor still had an official majority.

These concessions, however, did not satisfy the unofficial members, who by mid-century were the leaders of the European protest. A campaign for greater reforms was carried on both in the Council and in public meetings. In 1863 and 1864 a major clash occurred between the Governor and the unofficial members, the latter being led by George Wall, who represented the plantation interests, and Charles A. Lorenz, who represented the Burgher community. The dispute was over the Governor's decision to levy the entire cost of the military expenditure of the colony on the residents. The unofficial members engaged in a vigorous protest and under the leadership of George Wall attached an amendment to the Council's reply to the Governor's address expressing "dissatisfaction and discontent" with the management of the revenue and the way "the efficiency of nearly every public department has been seriously impaired by the parsimonious policy of the Government."[9] This was tantamount to a vote of no confidence in the Governor, and it is the first instance of such an amendment in Ceylon. But this action was not the end of the protest. The unofficial members sent a memorandum to the Secretary of State, through the Governor, explaining their position.[10] They then resigned en bloc in order to leave it "to the servants of the Crown to assume the whole responsibility of carrying out an unjust and unconstitutional act."[11]

In 1864, after the walkout of the unofficial members, George Wall inspired the formation of the Ceylon League, the goal of which was constitutional reform that would secure for the Council complete control of the financial affairs of the colony. The league was the first comprehensive organization formed to press for constitutional change. It was a cosmopolitan group drawn from among the leading members of society, and it formed an action committee, held meetings, and conducted a vigorous protest and propaganda campaign in both Ceylon and Great Britain. It acquired over 2,000 signatures and sent a petition through the Governor to the Secretary of State.[12] While it failed to reach its objective and lasted only from 1864 to 1869, it nevertheless was important as an organizational experience and as the first reform movement that sought to enlist wide popular support.

This was the last significant action of the European protest movement. Toward the end of the century the politics of protest and reform were to pass to indigenous leadership. The initial period of protest set important precedents and established political techniques and structures that were to influence the organization, action pattern, and temper of the indigenous protest movement. A legislative structure had been established, and precedents had been set for a reformist approach within this structure to constitutional and political change. The gradualist process had been established. Other important precedents were set by the foundation of newspapers as propaganda organs,[13] the formation of an aggregate organization to unite various interests in a common struggle, and the summation of multiple issues into one dominant theme of reform. Some aspects of the reform movement did change, however, as it passed to indigenous leadership. Nationalism became a factor, as it had not been for European residents. The Crown came to be considered a participant in political dispute, rather than a neutral judge from which redress might be obtained.

THE INDIGENOUS PROTEST

Emergence and Organization

The emergence of an indigenous protest movement was gradual, the result of a process of economic and educational expansion that facilitated social mobility and led to the rise of an indigenous elite.[14] The second half of the nineteenth century saw rapid economic expansion, as a prosperous plantation industry developed. Vast new economic opportunities on various levels of enterprise and income opened up, and systems of communications were developed to connect the productive hill area to the commercial life of the sea coast. The expansion of social services and a more pervasive administrative structure provided more opportunity, and toward the end of the century educational facilities underwent massive growth.[15] A small class of wealthy Ceylonese emerged, and, more important, a large indigenous middle class developed that sought entry into the professional, commercial, and public service career system.[16] More and more Ceylonese were attending Cambridge and other British universities, and, especially in the field of law, a Ceylonese professional class was created. Toward the end of the century such men as James D'Alwis, C. A. Lorenz, Muttu Coomaraswamy and, later, Ponnambalam Arunachalam began to compete with Europeans for leadership of the unofficial members of the Legislative Council.

It was the emergence of these groups and leaders that led to the rise of an indigenous protest movement. Protest preceded organization, and at first it was mainly journalistic and culturally oriented. A literary revival found beginnings in the establishment of the Buddhist Theosophical Society in 1880, to develop Buddhist education, and the Sarasavi Sandarasa, to disseminate Buddhist propaganda. In 1889 the *Hindu Organ* was founded, and in the 1890's the *Ceylon Review, The Saree,* and other journals had promising but short-lived careers. At the turn of the century the Ceylon Social Reform Society was formed to encourage the revival of indigenous social customs and "to discourage the thoughtless imitation of unsuitable European habits and customs."[17] In 1906 the *Ceylon National Review* was founded to articulate this cultural revivalism. The renaissance movement was not inspired by an extremely anti-Western mentality, but merely sought to restore a set of social customs that Westernization had brought into disdain and disuse.

The same moderation characterized the early movement for

political reform. One reformer, writing in 1894, admitted that Ceylon was neither prepared for, nor desirous of, self-government. But, he argued, "the ardent desire of every patriot therefore ought to be to hasten the time when self-government shall be granted to Ceylon."[18] In 1907 F. S. De Mel, stressing that "we do not seek self-government," argued for reform of the Legislative Council, to the effect that the unofficial members should be chosen by the people, both native and European, and that the people should be given more control over finance.[19] The movement to make the Legislative Council more reflective of indigenous interests was now gaining momentum and precision. In 1908 James Peiris, soon to become an important leader of the still embryonic reform movement, submitted a memorandum[20] to the Under-Secretary of State outlining a detailed scheme for reform of the Legislative Council to make it "better suited to the present requirements of the Colony." This could be accomplished, he argued, by abolition of "the present system of racial representation and the introduction of the elective principle in the place of nomination."[21] Except for this his scheme did not propose any radical innovations, as he accepted the retention of an official majority. The membership of the Legislative Council was to be increased to twenty-five, consisting of thirteen official and twelve unofficial members. Of the unofficial members, seven were to be chosen on a provincial basis, one by the Planters' Association, one by the Chamber of Commerce, one by the Municipal Council of Colombo, and two through nomination by the Governor to safeguard the interests of minorities.[22] The electorate he proposed was to be a highly "intelligent electorate" consisting of members of the government service, professional men, graduates, landed proprietors, and merchants.

Increasingly the Crown was coming to realize the need for reform. In 1910 the Legislative Council had been in existence for nearly eighty years, and no fundamental reform had been introduced in regard to its structure and power. In India, where a legislative body had been created much later than in Ceylon, several reforms were already being made in response to indigenous protest. In any case, when the Legislative Council was instituted, it had not been intended to endure unchanged for so long; Colebrooke wrote in 1831, "Such a council is not proposed as an institution calculated in itself to provide effectively for the legislation of the island at a more advanced stage of its progress."[23] In 1910, by Royal Instruction, a reform was granted, somewhat along the lines suggested by Peiris[24] and others before him. The Legislative Council was now to include eleven official and ten unofficial members, of whom four were to be elected on the basis of interest-group constituencies. One of these constituencies was to be composed of "educated Ceylonese."

This was the first concession to a direct protest of the indigenous elite. After this the protest was to grow and be sustained by a movement. In 1910, however, the protest of the indigenous elite lacked the organization necessary to unify it and make it into an effective political force. Within the next decade events took place that provided the organizational impetus necessary to galvanize the reform movement and make it a more cohesive and purposeful political force. The riots of 1915 were one factor. Erupting over a religious dispute between Muslims and Buddhists in Kandy, the riots were suppressed by the British; martial law was proclaimed, and Buddhist leaders were imprisoned. The repression was unnecessarily harsh, and the colonial administrators encountered a wave of indignation, both at home and in Ceylon. The episode, besides bringing into prominence several leaders[25] and arousing at least a modicum of popular emotion, convinced leaders of the reform movement of the need for constitutional reforms that would allow them some participation in the rule of the island. Events in India, where the Indian National Congress was now leading the independence movement, also had an impact. India had had more success than Ceylon in gaining reforms, the Morely-Minto reform of 1909 being followed by promises of reform during World War I. In 1919 the Montagu-Chelmsford reform anticipated parliamentary rule and dominion status as future objectives and created an assembly in which two-thirds of the members were elected. Gradually it came to be realized by leaders in Ceylon that these reforms were the product of a well-organized nationalist movement. The Indian National Congress thus provided impetus and example for the Ceylon protest movement.[26]

These factors and events animated discussions among various coteries in Ceylon. The potential nucleus of a protest organization had existed since early in the century. Discussion groups had developed among lawyers who gathered at the Law Library in the practice of their profession.[27] Out of their discussions grew the first nationalist organization, founded in 1916 by a group of lawyers. This was the Ceylon Reform League, an organization similar to the Ceylon League of George Wall. Soon after its formation the Reform League sent a memorial to the Secretary of State requesting reform of the Legislative Council by the abolition of the three main foundations of its structure—the nomination of members by the Governor, racial representation, and the official majority. In their place the league proposed a territorially elected membership with an elected majority that would be permitted to choose its own speaker, or president.[28] In 1917 a parallel organization, the Ceylon National Association, was formed. In his address before its first convention, Ponnambalam Arunachalam demanded reforms to "enable us to share in the actual administration of the country,"[29] reforms that in the end would lead to a "Ceylonese Government."[30]

In December, 1917, a joint conference on constitutional reforms was convened by the Reform League and the National Association. The conference proclaimed self-government as the goal and demanded "a definite measure of progressive advance toward that goal."[31] While programmatically the reform movement was now reaching a point of cohesion and decision, it still had only the rudiments of an organization. One year after the joint conference an attempt was made to remedy this situation. At the Ceylon National Conference held in December, 1918,

Arunachalam, who along with James Peiris had become the leading inspiration of the reform movement, alluded to the usefulness of "these conferences in coordinating public opinion and political thought . . ."[32] At his suggestion the conference passed a resolution "that a permanent organization be formed for the purpose of coordinating public opinion and political thought and work in Ceylon by periodically convoking a representative Congress and carrying out its resolutions."[33] Consequently, in 1919 the Ceylon National Congress (C.N.C.) was formed to co-ordinate the reform movement. At its first session, on December 11, 1919, Arunachalam, in his presidential address, enunciated the moderate, reformist approach of the new organization, whose objective was "only to substitute for one form of British administration, which we have outgrown and which is impeding our development, another form more suitable to our needs and conditions."[34] The new form proposed by the congress was the first that contained provisions for native control of administration. It envisaged a reconstituted legislative council that would contain an unofficial majority elected on a territorial basis by means of a wide male and restricted female franchise, minority representation by nomination, native control of local government, and the introduction of a quasi cabinet system with unofficial members of the legislative council responsible for the administration of some departments.[35]

Thus, by 1919 the nationalist movement in Ceylon was under way. It had a reform program with the ultimate objective of self-government, a cohesive and permanent organization, and a political approach that emphasized gradualism and constitutionalism.[36] The C.N.C. achieved its first success within two years after its formation. In 1921 the Legislative Council was reconstituted to comprise thirty-seven members: fourteen official members and twenty-three unofficial, of whom eleven were to be elected territorially and eight by special-interest constituencies, and four were to be nominated.[37] The reform aroused more discontent than it resolved. Although it granted an unofficial majority for the first time, it greatly increased the Governor's personal powers in order to replace those he had possessed indirectly by his control of an official majority. He did not, for instance, have to consult with the Council on urgent matters, he could reserve bills, he could certify a bill as being of paramount importance, in which case the votes of the official members were sufficient to pass it, and he had veto power. The C.N.C. strongly objected to this power arrangement as well as to the retention of communal electorates. It condemned the reform as "utterly inadequate and reactionary," and argued that it "denies even the beginning of responsible government." [38] The C.N.C. then decided to press for additional reforms that would grant an unofficial majority elected on a territorial basis and that would bestow executive power on the elected representatives. [39] This demand marked a turning point in the nationalist movement, for its immediate result was the defection of minority groups from the C.N.C. The culturally plural texture of Ceylonese society had not, until this point, seriously divided the indigenous protest movement. Tamils and Burghers, as well as Sinhalese, had been at the forefront of the protest, and the Tamils especially had provided leadership for the congress and the preceding organizations. But co-operation had been maintained primarily because representation in the Council was on a communal or combined communal-territorial basis, which ensured the minorities adequate protection against Sinhalese domination in the Council. But now the C.N.C. was pressing for a territorially elected majority, as well as for a transfer of executive responsibility to this majority. This would result in both a Sinhalese-dominated Council and an executive functioning under Sinhalese direction. The Tamil leadership considered the attempt of the C.N.C. to obtain such a system a betrayal of the tacit agreement between the two communities to maintain balanced representation. Consequently, the Tamils withdrew from the congress and, together with other minority groups in the Council, formulated their own communally oriented proposal for reform of the Council.[40] In the end, the Secretary of State granted a reform that was a compromise between the two views, though it was based on the principle that "no single community should be in a position to impose its will on other communities."[41]

The communal rift between the Tamil and Sinhalese elites ended the operation of the C.N.C. as a comprehensive and inclusive nationalist organization. During the 1920's the C.N.C. became not only a Sinhalese organization, but one that was predominantly low-country Sinhalese. Its working-class element drifted to the more radical associations that sprang up toward the end of that decade and during the beginning of the next, and the social composition of the congress became primarily middle class.

Fragmentation and Independence

There were too many cultural divisions and potential sources of communal conflict to allow a united nationalist organization to endure.[42] Cultural pluralism would later have the same impact on parties attempting to attain a mass, intergroup base. The Sinhalese themselves were culturally divided. The Kandyan Sinhalese considered themselves culturally superior to the Sinhalese of the low-country area. Living in the up-country area and protected by impassable mountains and jungles, the Kandyan Sinhalese had held out over two centuries longer against Western penetration. The Westernization of the low-country area, the more rapid breakdown of caste distinctions there, and the infiltration of Christianity into the coastal region accentuated cultural differences between the two communities. The Kandyans considered themselves heirs to the Sinhalese cultural heritage and looked to the future restoration of a Kandyan government. Ever since 1850, communal appointments to the Legislative Council had provided for Kandyan representation. With each successive constitutional change care had been taken to keep proportional representation for the Kandyans, who viewed their up-country area as a separate domain. Once a nationalist organization was formed, tension between the two Sinhalese groups mounted, for the C.N.C., as well as the Reform League and the National Association, was low-country dominated, with its leadership drawn from the Westernized, professional class that resided there. In addition, the drive of the emergent nationalist organization for a self-governed and unified Ceylon ran counter to the aspirations of the Kandyans for a separate state. The fact that in a unified Ceylon the Kandyans would be numerically inferior to the low-country Sinhalese increased their desire for a separate state.

The Kandyans began to organize their own association when the protest movement in the low-country area began to organize and formulate constitutional reforms during World War I. The Kandyan Association was formed in 1918, and one of its first demands was for a separate voice in any postwar reforms that the British might grant.[43] The association was critical of what it termed the "Colombo reformers," and on the basis of "national claims," argued for the recognition of "a distinct political status" for the Kandyan area. This, it felt, could be ensured for the moment by the creation of a minimum of five Kandyan seats in any reformed Legislative Council.[44] The point stressed by the association was that in Ceylon "there is a real complexity of nationality and diversity of interests . . ." Its main issue with the congress was that it had "drawn up a scheme of reforms on the footing of a homogeneity of nationality."[45] Thus, by 1920 the C.N.C. had aroused bitter Kandyan opposition by the nature of its reform program. Because of this reform program, Halangoda, a leader of the Kandyans, concluded that "the Kandyans have not to fight the Government to establish their national claims, but an interested and small section in Colombo . . ."[46]

Until 1924, however, a Kandyan elite formed a small but important segment of the Ceylon National Congress. But the same reform proposal that antagonized the other minorities in the congress at this time also aroused discontent among the Kandyan members. In 1924 the Kandyan wing left the congress and formed its own nationalist organization, the Kandyan National Assembly. This assembly provided a Kandyan voice during the remaining years of the British period, and the congress was never able to regain a foothold among the Kandyan elite, in spite of periodic overtures for reunification.[47] In hearings before the Donoughmore Commission, which was sent in 1928 by the Crown to study constitutional reform, the assembly argued for self-government for the Kandyan area.[48] During the period of the State Council (which replaced the Legislative Council in 1931, as recounted in the next section) representatives of the assembly made repeated references to this claim for self-determination, and before the Soulbury Commission in 1945 the assembly made its final plea for Kandyan autonomy. An attempt to bridge the schism between the Sinhalese communities was made by S. W. R. D. Bandaranaike in 1934, when he founded the Sinhala Maha Sabha (S.M.S.). In fact, it is possible that at first Bandaranaike anticipated the growth of the S.M.S. into a comprehensive nationalist organization embracing all communities, for while he defined its primary objective as Sinhalese unity, he also said it would "work for the higher unity, the unity of all communities."[49] In any case, it was partially successful in uniting Sinhalese, as Bandaranaike was able to attract members of the Kandyan elite to it. Although Bandaranaike was secretary of the C.N.C., his leadership of the S.M.S. did not help the congress regain Kandyan support, which, in any case, was not Bandaranaike's intention. It merely established another rival to the congress and further diminished its universalist, or at least pan-Sinhalese, pretensions. So far as the two Sinhalese communities were united at all during this period it was primarily through the personal symbols of the S.M.S. leadership, especially Bandaranaike and B. H. Aluwihare. Neither the S.M.S. nor the C.N.C. was able to develop organizational symbols of Sinhalese unity.

The failure of the C.N.C. to maintain its Tamil base was the first and most serious obstacle to its nationalist ambition. The rift that began at the Sravasti conference in 1921 and led to the Tamil withdrawal from the C.N.C. was never healed. In fact, in time it grew wider. Tamil organizations, such as the All-Ceylon Tamil Conference, sprang up to unite Tamil resistance to the territorial principle of election and to agitate for communal representation. They argued in vain for this before the Donoughmore Commission,[50] and in protest against the reforms it instituted, they boycotted the elections of 1931. As a result there was no Tamil voice in the State Council from 1931 to 1936. In the second State Council, lasting from 1936 until 1947, G. G. Ponnambalam quickly arose as the most eloquent voice of Tamil protest. His main theme in the Council was that the only way minority interests could be protected was through communal electorates that would assure a "balanced representation" in the legislature. He feared a self-governed Ceylon run by a majority elected on a territorial basis, for he felt this would only result in the growth of a racialist party system and Sinhalese oppression of the minorities.[51] In 1944 he founded the All-Ceylon Tamil Congress (T.C.) in order to argue before the Soulbury Commission for his scheme of "balanced representation." The substance of his reform scheme was an electoral system that would assure the minorities equal representation with the Sinhalese. Realizing the unacceptability of this scheme, many Tamils came to favor retention of British rule over independence and the consequent transfer of political control to the Sinhalese. When independence was finally granted, the Tamil community was divided over its implications. Some accepted it reluctantly as the will of the majority and offered their co-operation.[52] Others, such as S. J. V. Chelvanayakam, argued that freedom had "been won for only one community on this island." [53]

At the same time that the Kandyans and Tamils withdrew their support from the C.N.C., the Burghers and Europeans came out in opposition to any further reforms that would lead to the transfer of political power to the Sinhalese. The Europeans formed the European Association in 1927 to protect their interests,[54] and together with representatives of the Burgher community they used their seats in the legislature to oppose reforms. Neither group provided any support for the C.N.C. The Muslim element in Ceylon was more favorable toward constitutional reform. In 1932 the Ceylon Muslim League adopted a revised constitution that pledged the league to "work for full Responsible Government in Ceylon."[55] Unlike the Tamils, the Muslims recognized, as self-government approached, that in any native-controlled legislature the majority Sinhalese should have "major representation." They therefore opposed Ponnambalam's scheme of "balanced representation" and asked only for "adequate representation" for the Muslims.[56] But while the Muslims supported the movement toward self-government, they did not join the congress. The Muslim interest was expressed through Muslim organizations, primarily the Muslim League and the All-Ceylon Moors' Association.

Because of these developments the C.N.C. inevitably expressed and symbolized an ideology that was more racialist than nationalist. The Donoughmore Commission had seen this bias in 1928; it noted that the "conception of patriotism in Ceylon is as much racial as national, and that the best interests of the country are at times regarded as synonymous with the welfare of a particular section of its people."[57] The congress had done nothing to change this, and if anything, it had contributed to the growth of communal awareness and intercommunal tension. In any case, it had become, within a decade of its formation, a low-country Sinhalese organization. It was never able to extend its cultural base beyond this.

Its social base was to become just as narrow within the same period. Although its founders and leaders had been middle class, members of the Westernized, professional elite, its membership had also included more radical elements, drawn partly from the Young Lanka League. This group, led by A. E. Gooneshina, was more militant and advocated direct action in order to accelerate the movement toward self-government.[58] The C.N.C. had organizational connections with the working class through its leadership of the emergent trade union movement, and these connections provided the social extension necessary for development into a mass movement. But this association came to an end toward the close of the decade.

In the hearings before the Donoughmore Commission the C.N.C. adopted a conservative position in regard to the extension of the franchise, one of its leaders arguing that "ignorance must not be put on the same level with knowledge."[59] Gooneshina, on the other hand, who now led the Labour party, which had a trade union base, argued for universal suffrage. After this, Gooneshina actively promoted his own organization, and the congress lost its primary link with the working class. In addition, the universal franchise spurred the organization of Marxist unions and parties, and the working class drifted from the C.N.C. to these other organizations, which were more active among them and more articulate in support of their interests.

During the 1930's the leadership of the C.N.C. became more conservative in spite of the fact that some radical elements were attracted to its ranks. This was especially so after the death of W. A. de Silva and the passing of the leadership of the C.N.C. to D. S. Senanayake, who also became leader of the State Council. By this time the C.N.C. had become so torn with internal dissension that it was practically inoperative. The wing led by Bandaranaike was, for all practical purposes, in opposition to the Senanayake wing. The Sinhala Maha Sabha passed resolutions that conflicted with the official policy of the C.N.C., and in the State Council Bandaranaike led a radical bloc that frequently was in opposition to both Senanayake and the other ministers.[60] In 1945, for instance, when Senanayake went to London to engage in negotiations for dominion status, the State Council refused him a mandate to speak in its name.[61]

The lack of unity in the C.N.C. thus made it difficult for it to function as a cohesive and energetic organ of nationalist opinion. In the last years before independence it actually became an almost functionless and impotent organization, since it had lost any pretension to leadership of the independence movement. Leadership in this movement became completely personal, as D. S. Senanayake and Oliver Goonetilleke became the agents of negotiation for reform. Neither heeded the advice or the resolutions of the State Council or the C.N.C., both of which had become restive and more demanding in respect to reform. In 1942, for instance, when the C.N.C. at its annual sessions at Keleniya passed a resolution demanding full independence, D. S. Senanayake, who was more moderate, resigned from the Executive Committee of the C.N.C.[62] After this, negotiations for reform became a personal affair between D. S. Senanayake and the British, who preferred to work with a moderate.[63] In the end, D. S. Senanayake, who was in effect not the spokesman for either the C.N.C. or the State Council, succeeded in persuading the British to grant reforms and independence largely because if they had not, leadership would have passed into more radical hands.[64] At the same time, it was British willingness to work with Senanayake and British disregard for the C.N.C. and the State Council that enabled Senanayake to retain his position of national leadership. It was thus a mutually beneficial arrangement.

With its popular base confined racially to the low-country Sinhalese and socially to the Westernized middle class, the Ceylon National Congress came to have no connection with the working class and only minimal personal linkage to the peasantry.[65] This confinement, combined with the competition of other organizations, weakened its authority and vitality. After 1930 the State Council, as the institution that incorporated the multiple voices of dissident factions, became a much more energetic center for reform formulation and agitation, and national power and influence was directed not to organizations but to personalities. Because of this, no organizational symbols of nationalism developed in Ceylon. On the contrary, the whole reform experience personalized nationalist symbols among a number of leaders. One result of this was that the C.N.C. did not survive the grant of independence. In addition, the movement toward independence failed to involve a mass experience and did not evoke much nationalist emotion among the people. This was due to the communal texture and tension of Ceylonese society, the absence of a monolithic nationalist organization, and the quiet, constitutional, and reformist character of the evolution toward independence. No riots or bloodshed marred the evolution. Politics was never simply a matter of native versus British interests, for often this contest was overshadowed in the heat of communal antagonism. It was in the framework of the State Council that the issues of independence, communalism, and other political contests were joined in the decade before independence. After independence, many of the same issues would provide the substance of politics.

THE STATE COUNCIL

The organization of the indigenous protest introduced a period of active interest-group formation in Ceylon. Throughout the 1920's the various cultural and racial streams of Ceylonese society founded political and social extensions in an effort to articulate their interests and to unite their forces for the coming confrontations over reforms.[66] Economically and professionally based pressure groups also formed with vigor during this period, and labor unions emerged to contest the well-entrenched business organizations and the government. Prior to 1920 James Peiris, Ponnambalam, and Arunachalam had formed the Ceylon Social Services League and the Ceylon Workers Welfare League, which briefly linked the C.N.C. to the working class.[67] But these faded as the 1920's advanced and leadership in the trade union movement shifted to other hands. Under K. Natesa-Aiyar, trade union organizations were begun among the Indians on the tea estates, and militant unions were formed in the industrial and commercial sectors in Colombo under the energetic and aggressive direction of

A. E. Gooneshina. Labor unrest and militant strike action persisted through the remainder of the decade and into the 1930's.[68]

While these and various other associations provided a suborganizational base for potential party construction, no parties emerged until just prior to the reform hearings of the Donoughmore Commission in 1928. Personnel from the C.N.C. and other such organizations sat in the Legislative Council, as either elected or nominated members, but their behavior was not determined by the association to which they belonged. Often the actions of a member of the Legislative Council coincided with the policy of the association of which he was a member, but this was due to a common attitude or interest rather than to the type of organizational commitment characteristic of political parties. Here were the beginnings of parties, perhaps, the primordial conditions out of which they grow, but certainly nothing resembled at this time the disciplined and co-ordinated action of parties.[69]

The main reason that no parties emerged during the entire period of the Legislative Council was the fact that the Council had no responsibility for government. To be sure, after 1924 the Ceylonese-dominated Council had power, but it was pre-eminently negative power. The Council could kill or delay legislation, but it could not promise the implementation of legislation, for executive responsibility resided in the Governor and his Executive Council. It was this separation of power from responsibility that eventually led to the breakdown of the whole system. The whole government structure had been premised upon co-operation between the Legislative and Executive councils, a condition that was originally assured by the Governor's possession of an official majority in the Legislative Council. When constitutional alterations ended this majority and power in the Council passed to the Ceylonese, antagonisms between the Governor and the Ceylonese prevented the co-operation necessary to the functioning of the system. As the Donoughmore Commission noted in 1931, "the unofficials came gradually to regard themselves as a permanent Opposition," [70] and the Governor was like a prime minister trying to run a government with a minority in the House.[71] Francis De Zoysa, in his presidential address to the C.N.C. in 1925, observed that the only way the system could function was to place "the Executive in a position to command a majority of votes in the Legislative Council." This meant giving a predominant voice in the executive to the elected representatives "who enjoy the confidence of the Majority of members in the Legislative Council." [72] Thus it was generally recognized, as the Donoughmore Commission noted, that the major problem in the structure of the government system was the "divorce of power from responsibility." [73]

Great Britain came to the conclusion that a new government structure would have to be devised that would permit a measure of responsible self-government. It was not, however, prepared to accept the proposal for full self-government that the C.N.C. had advanced. Its own interests were sufficient warrant for it to deny this request, and the opposition of minorities in Ceylon to self-government [74] only provided more justification for the denial. As it worked out, a traditional parliamentary system was refused primarily on the grounds that it would encourage the growth of a racialist party system. This conclusion was based on three observations of the Donoughmore Commission. First, the commission noted the recent growth of communal patriotism and the lack of any intercommunal patriotism or national feeling.[75] Second, it observed that circumstances had "not been such as to cast political activity in the form of a balance of parties in the Legislative Council." [76] It noted, but did not fully share, the opinion that the lack of parties was due to the denial of responsibility to unofficial members and that "the growth of responsibility would result in the immediate development of a party system." [77] Third, while the commission did not deny that the grant of responsible government might result in the development of a party system, it contended that it was "difficult to discover any clear cut lines of division on political, constitutional or economic issues which would form the basis of a party system suited to the conditions and forms of British Parliamentary government as that has generally been understood."[78] It argued that it saw few signs that if parties formed they "would owe their origin to economic or political differences in national policy rather than to racial or caste divisions."[79] Much of the dissension in the Legislative Council had involved communal differences, and by the end of the 1920's each of the communities had built its own organization. No comprehensive, intercommunal organization was by then functioning. Thus it appeared to the commission that if parties formed, they would naturally organize on a communal basis, and, therefore, communalism would provide the framework for the emergent party system. Its conclusion was that such cleavages and such a party pattern were not conducive to the healthy functioning of a parliamentary system. Thus it recommended that a traditional parliamentary structure should not be instituted.

The legislative structure that was finally devised was unique and was intentionally shaped to inhibit the growth and operation of a party system.[80] Executive power was conferred jointly upon the Governor and a State Council. The Governor's power was intended to be supervisory rather than executive, as he was to act on the advice of the State Council. However, he was allowed to use his "own deliberative judgement" on whether or not to accept this advice, though refusal was only supposed to be resorted to if the Council's advice was contrary to certain constitutional principles, such as minority rights. In addition to this, the Governor had other powers,[81] such as a veto and emergency power, and such areas as defense and foreign affairs were beyond the authority of the Council. With the limitations noted above, the State Council was to be responsible for domestic policy and management, the departments concerned with the administration of the island being under its direct control.

While the Council thus had a good measure of governmental responsibility, it had none of the political responsibility usual in a parliamentary system and conducive to the operation of a party system. This was due to the structure of the Council and the manner in which its executive was organized. Seven executive committees were to be elected by secret ballot by the fifty elected and eight nominated members of the Council. Each committee would then meet and by secret ballot choose a chairman. Each committee was to be responsible for the policy and administration of the department under its control.[82] The chairmen of these committees, together with the three official members appointed by the Governor,[83] formed the Board of Ministers. Except in regard to appropriations, the Board of Ministers had no collective responsibility. Proposals to the Council were made by a committee chairman on behalf of the committee, and the Board of Ministers was not charged with the responsibility of presenting programs or bills. Defeat of a proposal did not involve a question of confidence, in either the chairman or the Board. Thus the Board of Ministers was not a cabinet of the Westminster type, and it was expected that this deficiency in regard to a cabinet system would be the major obstacle to growth of a party system. Since there was no cabinet responsibility, it was felt, there would be no encouragement to divisions on party lines. This situation was also expected to discourage the solidification of those pre-party formations that elsewhere gave rise to the growth of parties. As Sir Ivor Jennings later observed, the State Council "was designed to suit a legislature without parties and therefore actively discouraged them."[84]

In spite of the fact that the State Council was not designed to encourage or accommodate party government, several parties had recently been formed, stimulated mainly by anticipation of the coming reform and the need to organize the social element they sought to represent. In 1928 the Unionist party was founded by Sir Solomon Dias Bandaranaike in an attempt to unite the minorities for political action. The Labour party was organized by A. E. Gooneshina in 1927 as the political extension of his trade unions, and the Liberal League was started by E. W.

Perera in 1931 in order to press for constitutional reform. Of these, only the Labour party would survive. The election of 1931, held under a universal adult franchise and on the basis of territorial constituencies, provided the first opportunity for party contest. One hundred candidates ran for the 50 elective seats on the Council,[85] half of them running under a party label. Of these, 22 were from the C.N.C., 20 from the Liberal League, and 6 from the Labour party. In addition, there was one candidate from the Unionist party and one from the Independent Labour party, a personality party formed by a dissident who broke from the Labour party. As a party contest, however, the election was a farce, for while there were parties in the field, as one observer noted, the election was "not fought on party lines." [86] In the first place, the election was a highly personal affair and "was not fought on a particular plank or platform." [87] Almost every candidate expressed his displeasure at the nature of the new system and promised his constituents that he would press for its revision if he were elected. Sir John Kotelawala, for instance, who made his first entrance into politics in 1931, recalls that in his campaign he repeatedly said he would seek a revision of the State Council "to make it an effective instrument of responsible government." [88]

No party issued a manifesto or organized a campaign, and party candidates did not run on a common platform, although the candidates of the Labour party all discussed a proposed income tax. The parties did not themselves nominate candidates. Almost all who ran were local notables, and their membership in a party was irrelevant to their candidacy. Consequently, candidates running under the same party label often competed against each other. Moreover, party leaders did not restrict their support to members of their own party, and several spoke for the election of "opposition" candidates. Local and personal issues appear to have been decisive. Caste, race, and religion were definite factors, and the personal wealth of the candidate was a factor of local influence and campaign assistance.[89] But the local prestige and standing of the candidate among his constituents was most important.[90] The election was an affair of personalities, rather than of national, party, or social issues. While a few national leaders attempted to influence voting, the results of the election "indicate that the electors did not allow themselves to be influenced by such leaders to any considerable extent. The local candidate generally enjoyed an advantage over others." [91]

The nature of the election and the voting behavior of the electorate, therefore, were not encouraging to the growth of parties. The experience of the first State Council was further damaging. As one local newspaper had anticipated, the struggle of the councilors to obtain positions and influence in the executive committees was an immediate and recurrent obstacle to party unity.[92] Party affiliations meant little in the scramble for assignments, as personal deals, wealth, and influence were primary factors in a candidate's success in regard to committee appointment. Only the C.N.C. returned an appreciable number of candidates, but there was so much wrangling for office among them that any unity on a party basis was prevented.[93] Thus hope that the parties would act as power or voting blocs quickly faded. Even the Labour party could not act as a cohesive or disciplined unit, and it was soon disrupted by personality and power conflicts. Candidates had been elected, not because of the party to which they belonged, but because of their personality. The parties possessed no means to enforce discipline even if they wanted to, and the importance of personality to election would have militated against party discipline anyhow. Party members were not even linked by an ideology that would have given them a common reference in distinction to other members of the Council. Communalism cut across party lines and was a stronger unifying force than any party affiliation. In addition, demands for constitutional reform were universally shared. The one possible source of party unity and discipline, the use of party association as an instrument of personal power advancement, had been effectively negated by the structure of the State

Council.[94] As time passed, each member came to view his own committee as his primary constituency and source of power. Thus, further obstacles were put in the way of party unity and growth. Committee interests also fostered a parochial attitude toward policy; the development of a comprehensive policy outlook, vital to the formation of party identity, was thus inhibited.

The effect of all this was the decline of political parties by 1936. In the election of that year, according to the official report, "there was no evidence of the establishment of any political party with a definite program of legislative activity."[95] As in 1931, the election was mainly a personal affair, although there was greater organization on a candidate's behalf. Flags and posters were displayed, "pamphlets [were] widely distributed throughout the constituency," and friends and relatives of candidates undertook extensive campaigns of canvassing.[96] The wealth of a candidate was again a prime election factor, not only as a means to finance the campaign, but also because contributions to public charities were prestige items in the build-up of a candidate's public image.[97] Incumbent candidates stressed their activity in the State Council, and their ability to secure funds for schools or local development was a definite electoral advantage. Policy does not seem to have been of much importance, one observer noting that "everywhere personalities take the place of policies."[98] Pertinax, a columnist of the *Times of Ceylon,* noted that no candidates "have any definite policy or plan of action which they intend adopting in the event of being returned."[99] Later, in a statement before the Soulbury Commission, another observer noted that a candidate was "elected almost entirely on his personal prestige, his family of influence, or the liberality of his charity."[100] Race, caste, and religion were again involved in the campaign. Most candidates, both successful and unsuccessful, were members of the dominant caste or community in their constituencies. In some instances, however, caste or religion was a decisive factor. It was believed that E. W. Perera, an outstanding member of the first State Council, was defeated in

1936 primarily because he was a Christian. The campaign literature of his Buddhist opponent is said to have alluded to virtues of Buddhism that are lacking in Christianity. It also laid stress on the fact that "the contestants on this occasion are a Buddhist from your district and a Christian from outside." [101] In his address to the newly formed second State Council in 1936 the Governor criticized such occurrences as this. He deplored the "introduction of the religious element" and decried "the tendency which has been manifested in many, perhaps in most, constituencies to pay regard not to the merits of candidates, but to considerations of race, religion or caste." [102]

Thus the election of 1936 was not fought in any way that was conducive to party contest. No party was prepared or anxious to contest the election anyway, and this was an indication of regression in the growth of a party system since the appearance of parties at the turn of the decade. The Liberal League and the Unionist party had died out, and the Labour party had declined from hopeful beginnings into little more than a personality party revolving about A. E. Gooneshina. The C.N.C. was still functioning, though it was much more dependent now upon its prominent personalities than were they upon it as a meaningful and popular organization. Some new parties had emerged. The S.M.S. of Bandaranaike counted several members in the State Council, but none owed their election to the S.M.S., and the party made no attempt to form them into a cohesive unit. The Lanka Sama Samaja party (L.S.S.P.) was launched in 1934, and it elected two of its leaders in 1936, both of whom were local notables in their constituencies. Thus the second State Council, which lasted until 1947, was in effect a legislature without parties. The electoral experiences of 1931 and 1936, together with the antiparty structure of the State Council, had effectively discouraged the growth and operation of parties.

While no significant party units operated in the State Council, there were a number of blocs and tendencies of a more or less fluid nature. The nominated members came to be known as the "Governor's party" because of their appointment by him and their tendency to vote according to his opinion and the interests of the Crown. They formed a rather solid voting unit and were often joined by the Tamil members in opposition to resolutions on constitutional reform proposed by the Sinhalese majority. The Board of Ministers usually voted as a bloc, and occasionally they found themselves in opposition to the rest of the members of the Council, especially as negotiations on independence progressed. In both State Councils there was what might be called a radical bloc that worked for reform in the name of social justice. In the first State Council the bloc included A. E. Gooneshina, S. A. Wickremasinghe, A. Ratnayake and E. W. Perera. In the second State Council it consisted of N. M. Perera, P. Gunawardena, A. E. Gooneshina, A. Ratnayake, B. H. Aluwihare, W. Dahanayake, and Dudley Senanayake, the son of D. S. Senanayake. In their more urgent and radical proposals for political reform they were joined later by Bandaranaike and most of the members of the Council. Communalism also provided a basis for the formation of blocs, the most notable of which was the Tamil bloc led by Ponnambalam. In many instances this bloc found support among other minority representatives in the Council. No unified reform bloc developed, at least not until after 1940, when anxiety for dominion status united all the members of the State Council except the nominated members and most of the minority groups. While most of the members disliked the State Council system from its inception, no unity in regard to the nature of reform was reached until after 1940. The Sinhalese were split into conservative and radical wings, and the others were not at all enthusiastic over any progressive reforms. The most inclusive unity forged in the State Council came from the effort of the Council to guard its prerogatives and authority from encroachment by the Governor. It gave notice of this at almost its first meeting, when it notified the Governor that it would regard his veto, or refusal to accept its advice, as tantamount to a vote of no confidence in the Council.[103] While there were instances of tension between the Governor and the Council after this, no serious conflict occurred until 1937. In that year the Governor ordered the deportation of a suspected Communist without consultation with the Acting Minister of Home Affairs. By a vote of 34 to 7 the State Council censured the Governor for having "violated the Constitution and the express conditions of his appointment by ordering the deportation of Mr. Bracegirdle without the advice of the acting Home Minister."[104] Later the Council passed a vote of confidence in the Leader of the House because of his stand against the Governor.[105] The most serious clash occurred in 1940. A riot had occurred on the Mooloya tea estate, and the police had made several arrests. The Home Minister ordered a postponement of the trial, but the Inspector-General of Police refused to accede to his demand. The Governor intervened and supported the police. Led by D. S. Senanayake, the Board of Ministers resigned in protest. The issue was finally resolved by the appointment of a select committee. But, at least until 1940, such incidents were rare. There never was a clear and stable opposition to the Governor and the Crown. The conservatism of the Board of Ministers and communal differences were primary in preventing such a division.

There were several blocs, and for the most part they were fluid. The lack of stable blocs accentuated the role of the individual candidate, who was free to determine his own behavior without either organizational or bloc dictation. Each was motivated by his personal evaluation of issues, as well as by an appraisal of situations in terms of self-interest and personal power advancement.

The whole experience of the State Council was, therefore, antiparty. Not only was the activity of parties inhibited, but the experience left a tradition of individualism and independent action that militated against the growth of the disciplined behavior necessary for party operation. In fact one member of the State Council argued against the growth of a party system because of "the tyranny of party discipline, the sine qua non of a party system." [106] When a party system was finally instituted in Ceylon, one of its major problems was developing the cohesion and discipline necessary for its operation.

CHAPTER 2   *The Foundation of a Party System*

The reforms that brought about dominion status and then independence for Ceylon form the constitution on which the governmental framework is based.[1] The parliamentary system thus
created is structurally bicameral, consisting of the House of
Representatives and the Senate. Functionally, however, it is uni-
cameral, for the lower chamber, as in Britain, is effectively unchal-
lenged by the upper. Originally the House of Representatives
consisted of 101 members, of whom 95 were elected from territorial constituencies and 6 were appointed by the Governor-
General. Provision was also made for a cabinet that would be
responsible to the parliament for the exercise of executive functions. Thus a parliamentary system under cabinet direction was
created, specifically designed to operate according to the procedures evolved from the British experience.

It was fully understood, therefore, that the development of a
party system would be both essential and inevitable. It was the
fear that a racialist party system would emerge that had rationalized the denial of a parliamentary system in 1931. The
commission that studied constitutional reform in 1945–46 was
well aware that if its recommendations for a responsible parliamentary system was instituted, the formation of a party system
within a racialist or communal framework would most probably
occur. The commission, however, was not convinced that this
would inevitably result in minority persecution. It had observed
that during the period of the State Council there was "no substantial inclination of a general policy on the part of the Govern-

ment of Ceylon of discrimination against minority communities." [2]
In addition, the constitution it recommended incorporated safeguards for the rights of minorities,[3] and the electoral system was
so structured as to ensure a minimum of communal representation. The British also expected D. S. Senanayake to be Ceylon's
Prime Minister, and they had faith in his good will toward
minorities.

While its concern over possible minority persecution was thus
allayed, the commission did anticipate the temporary exclusion
of the minorities from effective political participation. It recognized that "unless and until parties in Ceylon become divided
on social and economic, in place of racial, lines, a minority will
have no reason to rely on the swings to the right or left that
occur in Western Democracies and, consequently, will have little
expectation of taking over the reins of government." [4]

THE FORMATION OF PARTIES

The election of 1947 was the first held in Ceylon since 1936.
The State Council had decided in 1940 to postpone elections and
extend its life because of the exigencies of war. After that,
negotiations over reform led to further delay, and, in all, nearly
twelve years passed without an election. The Soulbury Constitution had gone into force in the meantime, and consequently the
election of 1947 was to determine Ceylon's first responsible
government. Some of the parties that contended in 1947 were
formed in anticipation of the election, and others owed their
origins to an earlier time and situation. Each party was based on
either communal or social divisions, though some were little
more than cliques led by dominant personalities. The Marxist
Left parties and the United National party were the only ones
formed on an intercommunal basis, and each represented an
extreme of social division. Only the U.N.P., however, had any
possibility of becoming the Government, for no other party con-

tested a sufficient number of seats to attain a potential majority. For this reason, the U.N.P. was central in the election.

The United National Party

The United National party was formed in 1946 in anticipation of the coming grant of independence. It was a combination of several associations and included prominent members of the State Council, whose shared objective was the construction of an organization sufficiently comprehensive to win an electoral majority and provide a government. The lack of a cohesive nationalist movement and the political fragmentation evidenced by the many group-oriented associations that had formed prior to independence, left Ceylon without an organization capable of drawing mass support. The Ceylon National Congress lacked both vitality and comprehensiveness, and was incapable of developing a mass identity. The choice before the ruling elite, therefore, was either the creation of a new comprehensive organization or the perpetuation of the group-based associations. The latter alternative was less appealing for several reasons. In the first place, personal opportunism advised against it. Competition between separate organizations would inevitably result in a multiparty situation so fragmented as to make the construction of a coalition government extremely difficult.[5] No organization then in existence was sure of its popular strength, and all were so dependent upon the local popularity of their elite nucleus that none could be certain of controlling the parliamentary behavior of its elected members. If the parties proved unable to contain the personal maneuvering of their members in their struggle for power and position in Parliament, the result might be an organizational decline similar to that which occurred in the State Council after 1931.

But the most compelling factor dictating the formation of a comprehensive organization was the power and threat of the

Marxist Left. In spite of their disunity, the Marxist parties appeared to be a formidable political force with a solid base of popular support through their trade union connections with the working class. In addition, the Marxist parties possessed leaders of wide popular appeal who were capable of evoking a nationalist response almost as strong as that aroused by any party in Ceylon. At the time, no one knew the extent of Communist strength, but it was obvious that a multiparty situation and the fragmentation of the non-Communist elements would definitely contribute to that strength. A common interest in preventing such an outcome was sufficient to cut across communal and organizational divisions and to lay the basis for non-Communist unity.

It was D. S. Senanayake and his faction in the Ceylon National Congress who took the initiative in urging the formation of a comprehensive party. Discussions to this end took place in 1945 and 1946, and were attended by leaders of all the communal groups in Ceylon. The primary organizations represented in the discussions were the Ceylon National Congress, the Sinhala Maha Sabha, the All-Ceylon Muslim League, and the Moors' Association. The Tamil community was represented by a few of its notable leaders, such as A. Mahadeva and S. Nadesan. Those who attended the discussions included almost all the more prominent members of the State Council. On the whole, it was not difficult to reach agreement, and in 1946 these groups and leaders combined into the United National party.

The most crucial and most difficult task of the discussions had been to bring Bandaranaike and his S.M.S. into the proposed party. Bandaranaike had his own leadership ambitions, and as head of the S.M.S. and the radical bloc in the State Council and Minister of Local Government on the Board of Ministers, he had developed an impressive popular, political, and organizational base of power. But he knew his limitations, he was a keen political observer, and he was aware that some combination of forces would be necessary to form a government. He told the annual convention of the S.M.S. in 1945 in his presidential address that the S.M.S. "must contemplate some sort of coalition for government purposes."[6] In pursuance of this aim, the S.M.S. adopted a resolution that permitted Bandaranaike, in consultation with the Executive Committee, "to come to any reasonable arrangements with any other Party or Parties and with any other sections as well for the formation of a government thereafter."[7] On the basis of this resolution Bandaranaike entered into discussions with D. S. Senanayake and other leaders. It is widely believed that before he accepted D. S. Senanayake's leadership in the U.N.P., Bandaranaike exacted the promise of a governmental and party post that would assure him leadership succession when Senanayake retired, and that only after this assurance did he bring the S.M.S. into the U.N.P. as a founding member. Both then and later, however, Bandaranaike explained his decision to join the U.N.P. on the basis of a desire to contribute to national unity and stability.[8]

The formation of the U.N.P. was not accomplished without a price. The U.N.P., as Bandaranaike stressed in his address to the S.M.S., was "a coalition party."[9] As such, the maintenance of its unity required a decentralized organization and a programmatic emphasis limited to objectives that were consensual. As an essential concession to the associations that founded the U.N.P., its constitution expressly permitted them to retain their separate organizations provided they accepted the program and principles of the U.N.P. and acted in accordance with its constitution and the decisions taken by the party.[10] Thus the founding associations of the U.N.P. were not dissolved upon its formation, and they persisted as organized blocs of power and interest alongside the party. Because of this, the union obtained in the U.N.P. was largely personal, and to a significant degree the U.N.P. was held together by personalities rather than organization. The Working Committee of the party included the leaders of the organizations that founded the party. D. S. Senanayake was made president, and vice-presidencies were given to the leaders and prominent members of the S.M.S., the C.N.C., the Muslim League, and the Moors' Association, as well as to the leaders of the Tamil community.[11] These men composed the ruling hierarchy of the U.N.P., and policy-making was pre-eminently a function of this group. Other than this, the U.N.P. had no extensive organization. It was in no position to exercise discipline over its members, and it had to operate by means of consensus rather than organizational dictation. The Executive and Working committees were centers for the expression and compromise of views, but after a decision was made, there was no way to be sure that dissenting leaders and associate organizations would adhere to it.

Unified action by the U.N.P. was facilitated, at least initially, by the fact that the groups and personalities that founded it participated in a broad ideological consensus. They all believed in progressive capitalism, private enterprise, and the validity of middle-class democracy and the parliamentary system. In addition they believed in a moderate approach to the solution of social problems. But there were latent divisive tendencies, and consequently the U.N.P. had to avoid programmatic precision. The potential mass base of the U.N.P. was approached by integrating the leaders of various social groups rather than by devising a program designed to appeal to the popular base of the groups themselves. Each group had special problems, related to its own interests, that in some respects brought it into conflict with other groups. Potential conflict was inherent in differences over language policy, the economic role of the state, social reform, and religious, cultural, and social issues. Because of this, the U.N.P. had to limit its commitment to vague generalizations in regard to policy and seek refuge in the broad ideological consensus upon which it was built. On the negative side this consensus involved anticommunism, and on the positive side, a faith in liberal, middle-class democracy. The U.N.P. constitution stated simply that membership was open to all who stood for maintenance of "the present economic system with an ample measure of progressive social reform." [12] Its platform in 1947 did not specify any program that it intended to implement, but instead stressed that the goal of the U.N.P. was the attainment of Five Freedoms—freedom from want, foreign control, unemployment, ignorance, and disease.[13] Had it gone into detail in any of these areas it would have aroused antagonism in both its leadership and its social base.

Thus the U.N.P. was forged largely on the basis of opportunism: a common ambition on the part of its leaders for power and a need to prevent the development of a multiparty situation beneficial to Communist parties. On the positive side it was formed to help make a new government and a new political system work; to give Ceylon, as Bandaranaike later remarked, "that stability of Government which was needed particularly at the beginning of a new era of freedom." [14] Because of its intercommunal base and because collectively its leaders symbolized national unity, it offered Ceylon the best chance it had at the time for a stable government.

The Marxist Left

Marxist parties had a much earlier origin than the U.N.P. The Marxist movement in Ceylon emerged during the depression of the 1930's, when unemployment and discontent led to great social tension. The worsening economic condition made the working classes ripe for organization and action, and they became increasingly responsive to more militant leadership than that provided by A. E. Gooneshina, who had become more conservative over the years, especially after his entry into the State Council.[15] It was here, though, that Gooneshina made a significant contribution to union development in Ceylon, for in 1934 he secured passage of the Trade Union Act, which permitted an increase in trade union organization and activity. Both the legal and the social environments were thus conducive to renewed labor agitation. Leadership for such agitation came from an intellectual elite, educated mainly at British universities, who had been unable to find employment. The lack of career opportunities in Ceylon for these persons led many of them to seek leadership and responsibility in more radical careers. Among the discontented was a group of intellectuals who had studied at the London School of Economics under Harold Laski. It was predominantly this group that provided the leadership core for the Marxist movement.

The first Marxist trade union was the Wellawatte Mill Workers' Union, organized by Colvin R. de Silva in 1932 upon his return from studying at the London School of Economics.[16] Other Marxists, such as Dr. S. A. Wickremasinghe, N. M. Perera, M. G. Mendis, Philip Gunawardena, and Leslie Goonewardene, were active in forming socialist meetings. In 1933 most of these combined to direct the Suriya Mal movement in a protest against the British.

It was out of such joint enterprises and shared views that the Lanka Sama Samaja party (L.S.S.P.) was formed on December 18, 1935. Initially the L.S.S.P. sought to achieve a mass organization, and membership in the party was open to all who paid a monthly subscription of twenty-five cents. Later, after its adoption of a revolutionary strategy, the L.S.S.P. became an elitist organization, and its membership was limited to those "who engaged in party activity as members in a party group or local organization." The purpose of the organizational change was "to convert the party from a loose body of individuals into a fighting organization."[17] But while it adopted a closed, militant organization, the L.S.S.P. continued to develop a mass following through agitation and the creation of ancillary organizations, such as trade unions and youth groups. It moved quickly into the trade union movement, organizing workers in the industrial, commercial, communication, and harbor areas. Toward the end of the decade it moved into the economically critical estate sector with the formation of the Lanka Estate Workers Union. It was this union that led the Mooloya Estate strike of 1940. The L.S.S.P.

further attempted to spread its influence by the establishment of newspapers. In 1936 it founded the *Samasamajist,* a Sinhalese paper, and in 1938 the *Samatharurau,* a Tamil paper.

In spite of a widening popular base among workers, peasants, and the middle-class intelligentsia, the L.S.S.P. was considerably weakened by internal tensions and competition for power among its leaders. It had a highly pluralistic and articulate leadership, and divisive tendencies in the party were heightened by the wide range of the ideologies embraced by its members. As Pieter Keuneman later remarked, the L.S.S.P. "was not an ideologically consolidated or homogeneous socialist party. It was a loose organization that united different anti-imperialist trends from petty-bourgeois radicals to communists."[18] This made the initial period of self-definition difficult for the L.S.S.P. Its first manifesto contained ideological contradictions on such subjects as internationalism and nationalism, and reformist and radical socialism, which in sum represented the sentiments of the party's disparate elements.[19] It was to be expected, therefore, that the history of the L.S.S.P. should be marred by factionalism and ideological feuds. The most serious split came in 1939 when the Executive Committee of the L.S.S.P. passed a motion of no faith in the Third International and expelled the Stalinist minority from the party.[20] While Stalin's manipulation of the Third International and other events such as the purges, the Nazi-Soviet pact, and the conflict between Trotsky and Stalin provided the immediate cause, the split had deeper roots in a growing ideological schism and personal struggles for power within the party. As a result of the split, the L.S.S.P. became a Trotskyist party, reformed its constitution, and adopted a revolutionary program inspired by the platform of the Fourth International.

The revolutionary ideology adopted by the L.S.S.P. at this time included a policy of "revolutionary defeatism" toward the war. This led to suppression of the L.S.S.P. by the Government and detention of its leaders. After the escape of some of them, the L.S.S.P. was proscribed, in April, 1942. Those who escaped fled to India, where they helped to form the Bolshevik-Leninist party of India (B.L.P.I.) as a section of the Fourth International. As a result, the entire organization of the L.S.S.P. was disrupted. After the war the restraints imposed on the L.S.S.P. were removed, and its leaders quickly set about reconstructing the party. They organized the All-Ceylon Peasant Congress in an attempt to establish a peasant base, and in league with the Workers and Peasants Union of A. Gunasekera, who led the Radical party, they strove to rebuild their trade union connection. In order to bring the various unions into a more centralized organization, the Ceylon Federation of Labour was formed. But in 1945 competition for leadership of the L.S.S.P. broke out between the leaders of the B.L.P.I. who had returned to Ceylon and the remainder of the original L.S.S.P. elite who had spent the war years in detention in Ceylon. Rival factions formed about the two centers of leadership, and an internecine struggle developed to gain control of trade unions and the organization of the L.S.S.P. The result was another split, and a separate party was set up, the Bolshevik-Leninist party (B.L.P.), led by Colvin R. de Silva, while the L.S.S.P. was led by N. M. Perera and Philip Gunawardena, both of whom espoused Trotskyist Marxism. Ideologically the parties were therefore alike, and the split did not represent an ideological schism but rather a personal struggle for power. In the 1947 election the two parties ran on essentially the same platform.

In addition to the B.L.P. and the L.S.S.P., a third Marxist party, the Ceylon Communist party (C.P.), also competed in the 1947 election. The Communist party was the creation of the Stalinist faction that had been expelled from the L.S.S.P. in 1939–40.[21] After their expulsion the Stalinists held a conference at Peliyagoda, and in November, 1940, they formed the United Socialist party (U.S.P.). The U.S.P. used the opportunity provided by the detention of the L.S.S.P. leaders to penetrate trade unions previously controlled by the L.S.S.P. In December, 1941, it founded the Ceylon Trade Union Federation to co-ordinate the increasing number of trade unions coming under its management. It also sought to widen its intellectual base by the organization of Marxist study circles and the establishment of Sinhalese, Tamil, and English newspapers, the latter in an attempt to build a base of support among the English-speaking intelligentsia. Although police raids interrupted its activity, the U.S.P. was not at first proscribed, since it did not oppose the war. However, its increasing use of the strike was considered dangerous to the war effort by the Government, and in March, 1942, the party was declared illegal. This broke up the organization of the U.S.P. and sent it into clandestine activity. In July, 1943, a secret conference of U.S.P. leaders was held, which decided to dissolve the U.S.P. and form the Ceylon Communist party. The reason for this decision was Stalin's dissolution of the Third International and the resulting more lenient attitude toward Communist parties taken by the British government. On its promise not to engage in strike activity detrimental to the war effort, the Communist party was legalized in 1943. It bent its efforts to building a strong organization and a firm trade union base, and was accepted into the Ceylon National Congress, where it joined with the radical elements to press for the immediate granting of independence. Upon the conclusion of the war it led a general strike for increased benefits for the working class and in protest against what it considered the meaningless reforms granted by the British. Its belief was that the grant of political freedom was of little value unless accompanied by a corresponding social revolution, which, at the minimum, required the liquidation of British control over Ceylon's economy. While the general strike was unsuccessful, it served as an indication of the great strength the Communist party had developed among the working class and so was one of the prime factors persuading elements of the non-Communist elite to unite and form their own party.

This was the shape of the Marxist Left in 1947. It was divided into three parties whose leadership had undergone a history of struggles for personal power. Ideological differences existed, partly because of various doctrinal interpretations and different responses to the needs of international Communism, but primarily because they served to rationalize personal disputes among the leaders. Intense conflict existed in the trade unions also, where the Marxist parties and their leaders competed in the organization of the working class. Rival unions were set up, invasions of the union complex of one party were undertaken by the leadership of another, and attempts were made to prevent a party's consolidation of its trade union base. In addition, within each of the Marxist parties each leader tried to construct his own trade union connection in order to stabilize and extend his personal power base within the party. Other, ancillary organizations of the parties, such as youth leagues, were also under the personal control of party leaders and were used as bases of personal power. All of these factors prevented any united action by the Marxist Left in 1947, and it competed in the election not only with capitalist elements but also with itself. The result was the weakening of its appeal, the fragmentation of the Leftist vote, and the consequent strengthening of the non-Communist position.

Communal Parties

In contrast to the U.N.P. and the Marxist parties, with their predominantly social orientation, two parties emerged with a purely communal basis. Both originated in the communal fears and tensions of the declining years of colonial rule, and each was formed to consolidate the political effect of the minority group on which it was based. Their survival into the period after independence was assured by the territorial concentration of communal groups and the designing of electoral constituencies to correspond to these concentrations. The Indian population of Ceylon is settled in the tea estate area in the central highlands of Central and Uva provinces, while the Ceylon Tamils, except for a minority located in the Colombo area, inhabit the coastal fringe of the north and east within the administrative areas of the Northern and Eastern provinces. The existence of these two communities, the Tamils and the Indians, therefore, encouraged the formation, and made possible the operation, of communal parties.

The All-Ceylon Tamil Congress was founded by G. G. Ponnambalam in 1944 in order to present an organized Tamil front in the hearings before the Soulbury Commission on constitutional reform. Ponnambalam's argument before the commission called for a system of "balanced representation" in any new governmental structure to be devised for Ceylon. He advocated the so-called 50–50 scheme, by which the minority groups in Ceylon, considered as a unit, would be guaranteed representation on an equal basis with the Sinhalese. When his proposal was rejected, Ponnambalam continued the Tamil Congress in order to organize the Tamil vote and return a consolidated Tamil bloc in the House of Representatives. When dominion status was granted in 1947, there were three streams of Tamil thought as to the best strategy for protecting Tamil interests. One group felt that it was best to combine with an intercommunal party and work within its organization as a disciplined voting unit essential to the party's electoral and parliamentary success. Another group, whose most articulate spokesman was N. Suntharalingham, argued that the Tamil community should return independent, unattached candidates, who would be free to appraise the political situation in Parliament after their election and adopt an appropriate course of action geared to maximizing Tamil influence. The third group included Ponnambalam and the Tamil Congress, and believed that an organized vote and party could best fight for Tamil rights in Parliament. In 1947 all three groups competed for the Tamil vote. The fact that the Tamil Congress was led by Ponnambalam, who had become the most eloquent Tamil spokesman, greatly strengthened it as a political force among the Tamils.[22]

Many Indians had come to Ceylon toward the end of the nineteenth century to supply labor for the coffee and tea plantations.[23]

A second wave of immigration came in the 1930's and during World War II in order to help in the war effort. By 1945 there were over 500,000 Indians in Ceylon, almost all of whom worked on the tea estates in the Central Province. The first attempt to organize the Indians was undertaken by K. Natesa-Aiyar in the late 1920's, when he founded the Ceylon Indian Workers Federation and the All-Ceylon Indian Estate Labourers' Federation. After this, other organizations, like the Ceylon Indian Association, were formed under the inspiration of such men as I. X. Pereira, who became a nominated member of the State Council, and G. R. Motha. However, the Indians were still ineffective as a pressure group, largely because their strength was dispersed and fragmented among a number of organizations, including Marxist unions. No comprehensive organization existed to articulate the interests of the Indians as a distinct communal group. The impulse to the formation of such an organization came from Nehru. In 1939 the Minister of Transport dismissed 8,000 Indian railroad workers, and Nehru was sent from India to protest to the Board of Ministers. While in Ceylon, he talked with Indian leaders and suggested the formation of a comprehensive organization to protect Indian interests. As a result, the Ceylon Indian Congress (C.I.C.) was formed on July 15, 1939, under the leadership of Motha and Pereira. One year later the Ceylon Indian Congress Labour Union was organized to confirm the popular base of the C.I.C. among Indian workers.

The C.I.C. became the main political spokesman of Indians in Ceylon. Its main objective was to obtain political and legal rights for Indians. As one of its leaders later remarked in explanation of the formation of the C.I.C., the Indians were denied certain rights and so they "joined together to achieve those rights." [24] The C.I.C. presented the case for the Indians to the Soulbury Commission in 1944 and argued that numerically they deserved at least fourteen seats in the new legislature. As it turned out, there were seven constituencies where the Indian vote was in the majority and a few others where it could be a decisive electoral factor. The C.I.C. came forward in 1947 to contest the seats in constituencies where the Indian vote was heavy in an attempt to elect an Indian bloc to the House of Representatives. While its platform enunciated solutions to the various problems of the Indians in Ceylon, the main stress of its campaign was a promise to fight for the attainment of citizenship rights for Indians.

Minor Parties

A number of what might be termed personality parties were also active in the 1947 election. Nine candidates ran on the label of the Labour party, though only A. E. Gooneshina, who ran first in the Colombo Central district, was returned. The decline of the Labour party was related to its failure to develop a trade union base and its confinement to the Colombo area. Gooneshina, as mentioned, was a pioneer in union development in Ceylon, and his Ceylon Trade Union Congress had led a number of militant strikes in the 1920's. He was invited to London by the British Labour party in 1927, and upon his return he formed the Labour party. Gooneshina spent little effort in developing the organization of the Labour party, and it relied upon its trade union base for its influence. The emergence of Marxist unions challenged Gooneshina's power among the working class, and competition with them turned Gooneshina toward a more conservative attitude in regard to business and the government. The more energetic L.S.S.P. began to capture unions from him, the most significant being the Ceylon Mercantile Union. By 1947 the Labour party had only a small union base, in the Colombo area, and it was this that gave Gooneshina his victory in 1947. Other candidates of the Labour party had no union support or personal strength, and as a result all were defeated. The ideology of the Labour party was similar to that of its British counterpart, though it was less socialistic. Its creed, which it described as "political democracy," incorporated a number of political, legal, and constitutional rights that have come to be traditional in Western democracy.[25] It declared itself opposed to the Marxist concept of class struggle and hatred, proposed the establishment in some areas of public corporations in which 60 per cent of the stock would be government controlled, and stood for moderately progressive social reforms. Much of the program of the Labour party was to be adopted after 1956 by the U.N.P. when it sought an ideological revision that would place it somewhere between the antipodes of capitalism and socialism.

Two other minor parties are worth mention. The Swaraj party was founded by Dr. Nell and others in 1946. At its inception it had ambitions of attaining the comprehensive and mass character that the U.N.P. also sought. Nell negotiated with Bandaranaike and other prominent men in the State Council in the hope of developing the Swaraj party into a party of notables. Its failure in this regard and the consequent formation of the U.N.P. frustrated its ambition, and by the time of the election it was little more than a personality clique. It ran three candidates in the election, all of whom were defeated. The United Lanka party was organized by Darrell Peiries and K. A. Dalpatada. It, too, came to nothing, as both its candidates lost by large margins. After the election the two parties and their leaders retired from politics.

THE ELECTION OF 1947

No party ran a co-ordinated campaign in 1947, and candidates did not depend on party organization to any great extent. The U.N.P. had electoral associations operating in a limited number of constituencies and a central organization that it later described as "tolerably well-equipped."[26] The propaganda office was the most active section of the U.N.P. organization. In 1947 it had two trucks, a number of loudspeakers, nine assistants who went on speaking tours, and two assistants who directed activities from the central headquarters.[27] Other than this the U.N.P. organization was primitive, and Sir John Kotelawala explained that it would not be fair to "expect a faultless organization from the United National Party so early in its record of service to the Nation."[28] Except in the Colombo districts and a few other areas of the Western Province, U.N.P. candidates had to rely upon their own organization. The reported $40,000 spent by the U.N.P. on the campaign[29] went for advertising and pamphlets, some of which were sent to U.N.P. candidates for distribution. For the most part, candidates had to use their own funds and organize their own campaigns. As a consequence of this, the central organization of the U.N.P. could exert little control over those who ran under its label. Over 200 potential candidates sought nomination by the U.N.P., and of these, several wanted to run in more than one constituency.[30] The Executive Committee of the U.N.P. was responsible for nominations, but the primitiveness of the U.N.P.'s organization and its reliance on local notables prevented it from exercising firm control over members who sought candidacies. As a result, in many constituencies two or more U.N.P. candidates competed against each other. Of the six candidates who ran for the Polonnaruwa seat, for instance, five ran under the U.N.P. label.

The amorphism of the U.N.P. was both cause and consequence of the persistently personal nature of politics in 1947. The party offered no detailed manifesto that linked its candidates on a common platform, and its candidates, for their part, stressed their personal qualities in their campaigns. There were, however, some common elements in the campaigns of U.N.P. candidates. In the Tamil areas where the U.N.P. had to compete with the Tamil Congress and independents, its candidates stressed the need to return candidates of a potentially major party in order to share in the government of the country. In those areas where competition was mostly provided by independents, U.N.P. candidates emphasized that stable government could only be ensured by returning party candidates. R. A. De Mel, for instance, who competed against a number of independent candidates, told his electorate to vote for the party candidate because under the new system "the independent politician will be an anomaly."[31] But it was in those areas of the Southern and Western provinces where competition came mainly from Marxist parties that the central organization of the U.N.P. was most active and a more definite campaign and ideological linkage existed between the U.N.P. and its candidates. Almost the entire output and campaign of the central organization was directed to these provinces, and almost all its output included denunciations of the Marxist parties for the danger they posed, not only to the new political system but also to the cultural-religious values cherished by the Ceylonese. Sir John Kotelawala, who directed the propaganda office of the U.N.P., said that the main function of U.N.P. propaganda was to expose the destructive policy of Marxists and their opposition to religion.[32] In pursuit of this aim, anti-Communist and anti-L.S.S.P. booklets, such as *Sama Samajist Bhikkhu,* were printed, and some 20,000 letters were sent out explaining the antireligious nature of Communism.[33] So intense was this effort of U.N.P. propaganda, that a columnist of the conservative *Times of Ceylon* accused the U.N.P. of stirring up "religious fanaticism."[34] The U.N.P. also played upon the anti-Indian sentiment of many Sinhalese and sought to link the Marxist parties with the Indian community. D. S. Senanayake, for instance, warned the Sinhalese that Communist parties intended to give land to Indian residents.[35] Throughout the campaign D. S. Senanayake and other prominent leaders of the U.N.P. toured constituencies in the Southern and Western provinces making speeches for U.N.P. candidates against their Marxist opponents.

The Marxist parties lacked funds, and only a few of their candidates had personal wealth to compare with that of U.N.P. candidates. Each party, however, had a stable social base through its trade union extensions, and for the most part, each restricted its competition to those areas where it had a trade union or where it had a locally prominent candidate. Of the 52 candidates of the Marxist parties, 29 ran in the Western and Southern provinces, where Marxist trade union development was at its height. But while collectively the Marxist parties were to receive over 20 per cent of the total regular vote, they were considerably weakened by competition among themselves. The Ceylon Communist party and the L.S.S.P. were bitterly opposed to each other, and the L.S.S.P. itself split into rival factions.[36] During the May Day rallies the various Marxist leaders made speeches against each other, and by the time the campaign opened in July, the Marxist parties were as much opposed to each other as they were to the U.N.P. While the two Trotskyist parties, the L.S.S.P. and the B.L.P., avoided competition, both clashed with the Ceylon Communist party, and the split vote cost them several seats.

Unlike the U.N.P., the Marxist parties presented definite manifestoes that formed the main platforms upon which their candidates ran. All expressed dissatisfaction with the Soulbury Constitution, the L.S.S.P. claiming that it merely transferred the "reins of government to an aristocracy of capitalists."[37] The manifesto of the B.L.P. demanded complete independence, outside the empire, and listed a number of social and economic reforms that it wanted implemented. These included nationalization without compensation of all insurance companies, all plantations of over 500 acres, all transport and public utility companies, and foreign trade. It also called for abolition of "all indirect taxation on essentials" and distribution of land to the landless.[38] The manifesto of the Ceylon Communist party was similar in regard to nationalization and land distribution, but, more specifically, it called for Ceylonization of the armed services, the closing of British bases in Ceylon, and control of Indian immigration. Like the L.S.S.P., it wanted Sinhalese and Tamil made the official state languages.

The election of 1947, therefore, involved competition among organized parties on a greater scale than ever before. But personality was again a prime electoral factor, and while parties conducted campaigns, campaigning was more of an individual than a party effort. Most of the initiative came from the candi-

dates themselves, and all candidates stressed their personal qualities. In general, particular issues do not appear to have been a
major factor. Sir Ivor Jennings, who witnessed the election, suggests that local prominence was a prime electoral factor and that
caste played a "considerable part in the election."[39] In spite of
this, Sir Ivor discovers a definite party alignment in the election
and concludes that it was a contest between the U.N.P. and a
variety of opposition forces. The U.N.P. included all the retiring
ministers of the State Council and a majority of the councilors.
They were all from the middle class, most were English educated
and proponents of the Western political tradition, and they shared
a "common political philosophy favoring social reform" on conservative lines.[40] According to Jennings, since many of the U.N.P.
candidates had been active in the State Council, the electorate
was aware of the kind of policy they would implement if they
were returned. Frank R. Moraes, who went on a pre-election
tour of the island, suggests that the Leftist-led strikes in the spring
and the stringent retaliatory action taken by the State Council
may have polarized voters in the Sinhalese areas.[41] S. J. K. Crowther, a columnist of the *Times of Ceylon,* also felt that the election in the Sinhalese area was to be mainly a battle between the
U.N.P. and its Leftist opponents.[42] And Moraes, like Jennings,
observed that in the Tamil areas it was largely a contest between
the U.N.P. and the Tamil Congress.[43]

It appears, therefore, that party contest was definitely a factor
in the election and that significant progress in the growth of a
party system is reflected in the nature of the 1947 election. But
the results of the election and the number of independent candidates suggest that the party system was still relatively immature.
Over half of the 360 candidates either ran as independents or
were affiliated with minor parties. Except for communal parties,
no party returned over half its candidates. The U.N.P. elected
42 of its 98 candidates, the L.S.S.P. 10 of its 28, the B.L.P. 5 of
its 10, the Ceylon Communist party 3 of its 13, the Ceylon Indian

Congress 7 of its 8, and the Tamil Congress 7 of its 9, and of
the 181 independents who ran, 21 were elected. Several factors
account for the large number of independents. Many of them
had sought U.N.P. nomination and, failing that, ran on their
own. In many areas there was no organized opposition to the
U.N.P., and thus independents arose to take advantage of whatever popular antipathy to the U.N.P. or its candidate existed. In
the Sinhalese areas the independents provided the only non-
Marxist opposition to the U.N.P.

The results of the election were particularly disappointing to
the U.N.P., as it had hoped to obtain a majority. In view of the
prominence of its candidates and its other advantages, the results
are surprising, especially because through its control of the State
Council the U.N.P. was in a position to manipulate the election
machinery in its own favor. N. M. Perera, a leader of the L.S.S.P.,
later condemned the election as "one arranged to suit a particular
Party."[44] He claimed that electoral lists were manipulated to
prevent people of a "progressive age," from 21 to 30, from voting,
that election districts were gerrymandered, and that "thuggery"
was used to keep anti-U.N.P. people from voting.[45] Moraes observed that there was a great deal of corruption evident in the
campaign, that the U.N.P. made use of the administrative services
in its campaign, and that posters were displayed by the U.N.P.
on public buildings.[46] The fact that voting was spread over several weeks, from August 22 to September 20, gave the U.N.P. an
opportunity to stagger local election days to its own advantage.
By scheduling the contests in which its prominent men were
involved for the first few days of the election period, it released
them to speak in other constituencies on behalf of U.N.P. candidates. Contests involving opposition leaders such as N. M. Perera
were scheduled near the end of the period, and thus these leaders
were more confined to their own constituencies. Sir Ivor Jennings
concluded that the U.N.P. was definitely helped by the staggering
of the election schedule, arguing that an early anti-U.N.P. trend

was later reversed because of popular fear that a Marxist government was in the process of being elected.[47]

THE FORMATION OF A GOVERNMENT

The election produced a party pattern that was fragmented and that required the construction of a coalition for the formation of a government. While the U.N.P. had less than the 52 seats required for a majority, the organized strength of the party made it likely that it would form the pivotal group in the coalition. The Marxist parties had a total strength of 18 seats, and with support from the Ceylon Indian Congress and a number of independents they had a potential voting bloc of 28 seats. However, the leadership of the parties was so torn by disputes that unity was impossible. By themselves, the independents formed a potentially powerful bloc of over 20 seats, but the broad ideological range that they covered inhibited concerted action. Even the attempt by Wilmot Perera to unite the independents in his proposed Lanka Swadhina party, described by Bandaranaike as "Protean in its variation,"[48] came to nothing. The only other organized group was the Tamil Congress, and for the moment it was hesitant about any coalition with Sinhalese groups.

It had been realized before the election that the U.N.P. probably could not attain a majority.[49] As early as its inception there was tension in the U.N.P. in regard to the admission of Communists in order to make it more ideologically cosmopolitan and stronger. The Bandaranaike wing favored this move, but the opposition of D. S. Senanayake and the U.N.P. right wing prevented it. During the election period the Ceylon Communist party again offered support to the U.N.P., but it was rejected.[50] There was thus no possibility of a coalition between the U.N.P. and the parties of the Left. The U.N.P., in spite of this, found it comparatively easy to form a coalition. It was aided immeasurably in this endeavor by the constitutional provision allowing the appointment of six members by the Governor-General. This provision had been included in the constitution to ensure or increase minority representation, but its value in augmenting the strength of a possible government party was immediately recognized. Assured of the support of the six nominated members, the U.N.P. needed only four more votes to obtain a majority. The independents were the natural reservoir from which to draw support, and initially the U.N.P. succeeded in attracting twelve of them, eight of whom eventually joined the U.N.P. With the inclusion of A. E. Gooneshina, the U.N.P. had a voting bloc of sixty. Within a year, Ponnambalam brought five of his Tamil Congress members over to the Government, on the basis of "responsive cooperation."[51]

To a considerable extent the U.N.P. government was knit together by a common interest in holding office. Positions in the Cabinet and Government were used by the U.N.P. to attract support and to forge unity among its leaders and the various social and cultural strata whose interests it articulated. Fourteen ministerial posts were distributed as well as twelve posts as parliamentary secretary. In the Cabinet there were four members of the S.M.S., four from the C.N.C., one from the Muslim League, two Tamil independents, and A. E. Gooneshina.[52] When the Tamil Congress supported the Government, Ponnambalam was given the post of Minister of Industries, Industrial Research, and Fisheries. Thus the Cabinet included the leaders of important groups in both the Government and the U.N.P. in an attempt to confirm their support. N. M. Perera criticized this method of recruiting a government. He condemned the U.N.P. for forming a government that was a "minority Party Government,"[53] and accused the U.N.P. of creating ministerial posts in order "to maintain a secure majority in Parliament."[54] He criticized the independents who joined the Government, most of whom had won their seats by defeating U.N.P. candidates. By joining the Government, Perera argued, they were negating the verdict of the people who had voted against the U.N.P. Two independents, C. Suntharalingam and C. S. Sittampalam, both of whom had been made ministers, justified their action by citing precedents among European party systems, arguing that coalition government was normal procedure in multiparty situations.[55]

Both the U.N.P. and the government party that it constructed were built largely on opportunism. The same factors that led to the formation of the U.N.P.—a fear of the Marxist Left and a common ambition for power—had been the impetus to the formation of the Government. The U.N.P. and the Government found ideological consensus in their ranks only in the imprecision of generality; and the added comprehensiveness that the U.N.P. sought by the creation of a coalition increased centrifugal tendencies. It also multiplied the number of leaders and thereby increased the potential for divisions arising from personal ambition and competition for power. In spite of this, the government party maintained remarkable cohesion. This was due chiefly to two factors: the nature of its program and the personality of its leader. In the first place, the Government refrained from introducing potentially divisive legislation that would strain the tenuous cohesion that kept it together. The U.N.P. took office without any detailed plans concerning policy, a fact that led N. M. Perera to conclude that the U.N.P. presumed a "Divine right to rule."[56] In his speech on appropriations, Finance Minister J. R. Jayewardene admitted that "the time at our disposal for the formulation of long term proposals was totally inadequate."[57] The intention of the U.N.P. was to study the problems facing Ceylon and seek solutions within the context of a vague ideology described as "constitutional socialism." The objective of this socialism was "a new order of society . . . based on principles of social justice giving equal opportunity to all avenues of life."[58] Later, the Finance Minister went on to clarify the policy objective of the U.N.P. as an "attempt to close from both ends the gap which separates the standard of living of the great mass of our fellow citizens from that of a small privileged minority."[59] Here was indicated the major problem of Ceylonese society, the existence of a rich minority of Europeans and Ceylonese and an impoverished mass. The dilemma of the U.N.P. was that it drew from both groups for its leadership, membership, and social base. It drew support from the wealthy and the middle class, who were largely Western educated and English speaking, and it drew support from the peasants, most of them landless and Sinhalese speaking. To solve the problems of the peasants required taxation of the upper and middle classes, the division of some of their land and wealth, and a turning away from the dominance of the English language in the administration of the island and especially in regard to career opportunity. Not to do this would eventually incur the antagonism of the peasants and the alienation of their representatives in the U.N.P. This was the tension between the left wing and the right wing of the party. The solution of the U.N.P., like the "middle path" orientation of its foreign policy, was a compromise. Measures were to be taken to alleviate the condition of the peasant, but with the co-operation, rather than at the expense, of the wealthy. Economic development was to be pursued as a means to raise living standards, but was to be planned on the principle that private property was inviolable and to be implemented through foreign investment and private enterprise. The role of the State was to be kept to a minimum, and no nationalization or sharply graduated taxation was to be imposed. Landlessness was to be solved by colonization of the dry zone. In this way the U.N.P. sought compromise between its various elements, and the result was an inactive government that incurred no direct antagonism by divisive legislation. Its only legislation involved an attempt (described in Chapter 3) to secure the political environment against Marxist political activity.

The second factor holding both the U.N.P. and the coalition together was the dominant personality of the Prime Minister, D. S. Senanayake. He did not so much dictate as he arbitrated between the wings, though in the end he could always impose his will. His career had seen him develop an appeal approaching the charismatic, and his popular support as well as the respect of his colleagues gave him power in the Cabinet. It was largely through his efforts that disputes among ministers were contained in the privacy of the Cabinet and a good measure of cabinet solidarity was maintained. When a cabinet decision had been made, he expected the ministers to present a united front in Parliament. In 1949 he forced the resignation of his Minister of Commerce and Trade because the latter had abstained on a critical vote. In a letter,[60] Senanayake explained that it was a minister's duty to vote with the Government. Differences, he said, could be aired in cabinet meetings, but once a decision was taken every minister had to support it, because the Opposition would exploit any differences that were made public. In any case, if a cabinet minister refused to support a cabinet decision he must resign.[61] The resignation of Suntharalingam, while indicative only of personal dissatisfaction, was the first break in the coalition.

Thus under the leadership of Senanayake the widely disparate elements that composed the U.N.P. coalition remained fairly well united. The first serious break came in July, 1951, when Bandaranaike resigned from the Cabinet and went over to the Opposition. Both personal ambition and dissatisfaction with the Government were involved in his resignation. As Leader of the House, vice president of the U.N.P., and head of an important bloc of supporters, Bandaranaike had reached a position of power from which he might hope to obtain the position of Prime Minister upon the retirement of D. S. Senanayake. For a number of reasons, the most important of which was the growing power of the right wing in the U.N.P., Bandaranaike became convinced that attempts had been made to block his succession. Sir John Kotelawala, as spokesman of the right wing, had emerged as a prime power in the party and was Bandaranaike's chief antagonist. In addition, it appeared that D. S. Senanayake was grooming his son for the succession. Thus, his ambition frustrated, Bandaranaike decided that as leader of a new opposition party he stood a better chance to become Prime Minister.[62]

But there was more than personal ambition involved. Bandaranaike had never been completely content with the U.N.P. When he consented to join the U.N.P., he did so with the provision or expectation that the U.N.P. would manage the political affairs of the nation in what he considered to be a productive and progressive manner.[63] To Bandaranaike this meant a moderate degree of socialism and an emphasis on the interests of the traditionalist cultural group in Ceylon. This brought him into immediate conflict with the U.N.P. right wing led by Sir John Kotelawala, with whom he also had bitter personal conflicts. His ideological inclination and personal prestige made him the natural leader of the U.N.P. left wing. During the election campaign Bandaranaike had not concealed his differences with the central organization, which was under the control of Kotelawala. Contrary to the official stand of the party, Bandaranaike stressed the need for greater independence from Great Britain and argued, along with the Marxists, that economically Ceylon was still a British colony.[64] After the election the *Sinhalese Balaya,* the official newspaper of the S.M.S., edited by Bandaranaike, had blamed the poor showing of the U.N.P. on the reactionary campaign waged by the central organization under the direction of Kotelawala.[65] After this Bandaranaike played a dual role in the U.N.P. As Leader of the House and Minister of Health and Local Government, Bandaranaike became the most articulate spokesman of the U.N.P. in Parliament. In addition he wrote several pamphlets for the U.N.P. in support of its policy and dedication to the cause of building a better society.[66] In this role, also, Bandaranaike contended with Kotelawala for ideological leadership of the U.N.P. At the same time Bandaranaike kept the S.M.S. as a personal base of power and increasingly used it as a forum for the expression of his grievances with the U.N.P. In his address to the S.M.S. in 1948, Bandaranaike protested the inclusion of the Labour party and the Tamil Congress in the Government and suggested that the C.N.C. section of the

77

U.N.P., under Kotelawala, was acting as a separate party. He also suggested that all associates, including the S.M.S., had a duty to criticize the Government if they felt it necessary.[67] By 1949 the central organization of the U.N.P. had come under the control of the right wing, and it began to protest the criticisms of the U.N.P. made by Bandaranaike as leader of the S.M.S.[68] From this point the break was inevitable. At the annual session of the S.M.S. in July, 1951, Bandaranaike said that the fact that the U.N.P. was the only democratic party in Ceylon made it mandatory that the U.N.P. should give full consideration to the policy demands made by the spokesmen of important sections of Ceylonese opinion, such as the S.M.S. He expressed discontent at the policy followed by the U.N.P. and transmitted to the U.N.P. the so-called Madampe Resolutions, outlining policies he desired to see adopted.[69] The refusal of the U.N.P. to accept these resolutions was the pretext for Bandaranaike's resignation from the Government. In explanation of his action, Bandaranaike said that the U.N.P. had failed to provide the leadership necessary for the solution of Ceylon's problems. One month earlier he had said that Ceylon needed parties with clear and precise answers, not policies of "a vague and nebulous nature."[70] The unsatisfactory policies were coupled with what Bandaranaike described as a growing tendency toward dictatorship in the Cabinet. By this he meant the growing power of Kotelawala and the right wing. It was this wing that now controlled the organization of the U.N.P. and was the dominant force in the policy decisions of the party. Bandaranaike thus no longer had reasons of ideology or personal ambition to keep him in the U.N.P.[71]

Bandaranaike's resignation had no immediate repercussions for the U.N.P. Only five other M.P.'s crossed the floor with him into the Opposition. In fact, Sir Ivor Jennings concluded, his defection strengthened the Government by removing a source of conflict in its ranks and pluralizing the leadership of the Opposition.[72] But while his defection may have consolidated the leadership of the U.N.P. and given it a more definite image as a party, it also weakened the party's popular base and challenged its comprehensiveness. Whatever immediate benefit the U.N.P. derived from the defection of Bandaranaike, it would now have to compete with an organization that sought the integration of the same social element on which it itself was based.

CHAPTER 3 The Trend Toward a One-Party System

The operational stability that the new party system attained in its formative period was largely the work of the United National party. Organization of the U.N.P. had prevented extreme party multiplication by uniting prominent men of similar ideological persuasion and by discouraging the formation of personal parties. After the election it was the ability of the U.N.P. to construct a viable coalition that prevented the immediate deterioration of the party system into an inoperative multiparty type. But in the process of inhibiting the tendencies toward multipartism, counter-tendencies toward a one-party system were released. The organization of the U.N.P. and its coalition had combined nearly all the democratic elements in Parliament into one bloc and had left an Opposition consisting of parties that had no confidence in the political system. Thus there existed no party able to provide a democratic alternative to the U.N.P., and the party system, as it was then ideologically and organizationally constructed, depended upon one-party dominance for the very survival of the political structure in which it operated.

Bandaranaike, among others, alluded to this one-party tendency on several occasions. In his address to the Sinhala Maha Sabha just prior to his break from the U.N.P., Bandaranaike said that there was really no democratic opposition to the party in power. There was, he continued, "in fact only one party, as all the important opposition parties are those which, owing to their Marxist beliefs, have no faith in either democracy or the parlia-

mentary system as we understand those terms."[1] The U.N.P.
was not at all hesitant to exploit this situation to its own advantage. As Bandaranaike later remarked, the U.N.P. leadership,
"under the pretext of the need to protect democracy, resorted to
various undemocratic and even anti-democratic methods to keep
themselves in power."[2]

GOVERNMENT AND OPPOSITION, 1947–52

The potential of a revolutionary Opposition was inherent in the
attitude of the various parties toward independence and in their
view of the new political system. Only the U.N.P. expressed
confidence in the political and social implications these changes
had for the development of Ceylon. The Opposition was unanimous in its refusal to support a motion of the Government to
"rejoice" over the coming of independence.[3] The Marxist parties
considered independence to be a sham because of the military
links between Great Britain and Ceylon, and because British
capital monopolized tea production, on which the economy of
Ceylon depends. The Communist party, for example, argued that
independence was merely a transition from direct to indirect
rule by Great Britain.[4] The communal parties felt dissatisfaction
because they interpreted independence to mean only a change
from British to Sinhalese domination.[5]

As for the new political system, the manifestoes and statements
of all the opposition parties in the election of 1947, including
the Tamil Congress, expressed discontent with it and advocated
structural revisions. For the most part, the opposition parties
had no faith either in the ability of the parliamentary system
to operate democratically or in its capacity as a political institution
for solving the social and economic problems facing Ceylon. Both
communal parties foresaw discrimination and minority persecution in U.N.P. legislation, while the Marxist parties anticipated
the imposition of a dictatorship under the guise of the parlia-

mentary system. Colvin R. de Silva, for instance, speaking for the Opposition, said in 1947, "We suffer no illusions about the possibilities of a Parliamentary regime." [6]

In addition to their negative attitude, most of the opposition parties espoused a revolutionary ideology and had international links. One leader of the Lanka Sama Samaja party admitted at the time, "In the Opposition there are three revolutionary parties." [7] A spokesman for the L.S.S.P. proudly confessed that his party "from the very beginning was an internationalist party." It was, he continued, "a Trotskyite Party, a Fourth International Party." [8] Colvin R. de Silva referred to his Bolshevik-Leninist party as "a group with open, clear, definite, international relations." [9] The B.L.P., he continued, was "allied with all revolutionary forces throughout the world and will act in conformity with the principles that govern that movement and also form its foundation." [10] The B.L.P. was to view every domestic political question within the context of the international situation. De Silva argued that the task of the revolutionary was "to apply the internationalism of their approach to every single political question, to the actual fact and reality of the National State." [11] The Communist party, on the other hand, denied that it had links with any foreign power or international organization. In reference to the Soviet Union Pieter Keuneman said, "We have no sinister connections with that country. We are not flirting with Moscow or with any other country." The Communist party, he stressed, viewed political questions from a perspective "dictated by the interests of the people of this country." [12] In spite of this national orientation the Communist party was not committed to the political system as it was then constructed, and repeatedly advocated revolutionary changes.

The only sections of the Opposition that were not revolutionary were the two communal parties. When most of the Tamil Congress crossed the floor to support the Government, the only non-Marxist organization left in the Opposition was the Ceylon Indian Congress, and it had links with the Congress party in

India and contained a large Marxist wing. Thus, for one reason or another, no opposition party had the capacity to serve as a possible democratic alternative to the U.N.P.

The U.N.P. did not hesitate to capitalize politically upon the nonnational character of the Opposition. Though it admitted that an opposition was essential to the operation of a parliamentary system,[13] the U.N.P. refused to consider the parties of the Opposition as loyal and serviceable components of the parliamentary system. This was "not an ordinary Parliamentary Opposition," a cabinet minister said in 1948. "It is an Opposition which plans by revolution to oust this Government and liquidate all Opposition for the future." The parties of the Opposition, he continued, were "tools in the hands of a world-wide movement."[14] The U.N.P. also sought to emphasize the connections between the opposition parties and India, a country that had friendly relations with Ceylon but whose expansionist ambitions had aroused suspicion and fear in Ceylon. In 1948 J. R. Jayewardene accused the three Marxist parties of being under the control of India, partly because the Asian centers of the international movements to which they were attached were located there.[15] This accusation was particularly effective at the time when anti-Indian feeling was strong in Ceylon, especially in the Kandyan areas where Indian residents worked. During the debate on the Indian Residents (Citizenship) Bill, the parliamentary secretary to the Minister of Health and Local Government argued that the Ceylon Indian Congress was the cause of the growing communal problem in Ceylon because it insulated the Indian residents from the mainstream of Ceylonese society. The C.I.C., he contended, wanted "to remain as a communal political organization in order to provide a link for expansionist India to step into this country."[16]

The party system in Ceylon did not lead, therefore, to the compatibility between government and opposition parties so vital to the sound functioning of a parliamentary system. The concept of a loyal opposition failed to materialize, and there was no consensus extending beyond the ranks of the Government in regard to fundamental political beliefs. To an extent the U.N.P.'s characterization of opposition parties as disloyal and revolutionary was justified by their political statements and their ideologies.[17] And yet, opposition parties initiated no action in pursuance of their radical statements or revolutionary ideologies, and their opposition was confined to parliamentary protest. However, the threat of extraparliamentary action was always present. Such a threat was implicit in the contention of a leader of the Opposition that "the struggle of the Opposition in this House is but part of the struggle of the people in this country."[18] And on occasion, especially when anti-Indian or antilabor legislation was being debated, opposition parties would threaten to carry their opposition beyond the floor of the House. But no action was taken. Marxist parties did not make use of the political strike or issue calls for a revolution. In spite of the passage of severe anti-Indian legislation, the C.I.C. organized no extralegal protest. Thus, ideologies and statements to the contrary, opposition parties used Parliament as the main arena of protest.

One reason that no extralegal action was taken by opposition parties may have been the fear of suppression by the Government. An essential part of the U.N.P. legislation during this period was designed to secure the political environment against threats to the "public safety." One of the last acts of the State Council had been the passage of a public security ordinance that empowered the Governor-General to proclaim a state of emergency, to impose censorship and martial law, proscribe organizations "prejudicial to the public safety, the maintenance of public order or the maintenance of essential services," and undertake other measures that might be deemed necessary to control an emergency situation.[19] While no use was made of this ordinance during this period, it nevertheless equipped the Government to cope with any emergency and may have inhibited any thoughts opposition parties entertained in regard to extralegal action. To equip itself further, the U.N.P. raised an army and a navy, and permitted the British to retain bases and troops in Ceylon, the troops to be used in internal disturbances as well as against foreign threats. In addition, a trades union ordinance was passed that restricted strike activity, prohibited union contributions to political parties, and outlawed organizational links between parties and unions. This measure was taken in an attempt to prevent the political use of unions by the C.I.C. and the Marxist parties. But the most severe legislation enacted by the U.N.P. during this period concerned the Indians. A series of acts terminated Indian immigration to Ceylon, provided for the deportation of Indians, and amended the citizenship laws to exclude Indians from Ceylonese citizenship and to deny them the right to vote.[20] While economic and other considerations may have been involved in the Government's decision to enact these bills, one of their main consequences would be the removal from the House of a large bloc of opposition seats, all of which would go to the Government in 1952. The effect was to make the Indians politically impotent. Not only did this legislation remove the entire social base of the C.I.C. from political participation, it also took an important bloc of votes away from the Marxist parties, since the C.I.C. supported Marxist candidates in any constituency in which it was not itself running a candidate. That such a result was at least a partial motivation for introduction of the legislation, was admitted by the Government. One cabinet minister remarked, "the Leftist Parties do stand to lose tremendously by the adoption of the Citizenship Bill and the Emigration Bill."[21]

This is as far as the Government went in repressive legislation. Most of its legislation ostensibly sought to restrain rather than to suppress the activity or careers of opposition parties. Nevertheless, the legislation it enacted in an effort to secure the political environment had an impact on opposition parties at their strongest points—their financial and social bases. The disfranchisement of the Indians shortly resulted in the transformation of the C.I.C. from a political party into a pressure organization, and it greatly weakened the social base of Marxist parties. And the trade union bill removed the most important source of funds for Marxist parties. As a consequence, the potential political impact of opposition parties was severely limited. In Parliament, members of the Opposition were treated fairly and in accordance with normal parliamentary procedure. But here the Opposition was weak, not only numerically but also in its ability to work as a unit. Because of personal feuds and ideological differences there was no leader of the Opposition until 1950, when the Governor-General appointed N. M. Perera to the post.[22] The Marxist Left, all of which had a common personal, organizational, and ideological origin, was split into three parties, each led by personalities who retained memories of bitter personal feuds. In addition, the ideological schisms that separated the three parties were wide, in regard to both tactics and goals, and competition between their trade unions had become a major source of conflict among the parties. The Marxist Left was also isolated from the other, communal groups in the Opposition, who did not share its revolutionary solutions to the social, economic, and political problems of Ceylon. Also, none of the Marxist parties accepted the communal parties' definition of Ceylon's problems as communal in nature, and this, too, prevented the two blocs from co-operating. The two communal parties were themselves at odds with each other, and members of neither community had compassion or offered assistance for the plight of the other. Representatives from the Tamil areas supported anti-Indian legislation and, except for a small faction, backed the Government. Thus the Opposition, that "cosmopolitan group," as Bandaranaike once called it,[23] could not operate as a cohesive unit in opposition to the Government. There was, as Bandaranaike observed, "only one bond and one alone between these various groups—a desire to defeat the present Government."[24] But even in this bond there was no unity. On only a few issues did the opposition parties join in a vote of no confidence. For the most part, no party would support a no-confidence motion of another. Because of this disunity, the Government was greatly strengthened.

THE ELECTION OF 1952

The election of 1952 was more party-oriented than any previous election. Parties had undergone a period of self-definition and organizational development since 1947 that made them better able to compete as organized units. More control was now exercised over the party label, and there were no instances of competition between candidates of the same party, except, of course, in multimember districts where the U.N.P. attempted to capture all the seats. The Marxist parties were better organized by 1952, and their trade union connections were active in organizing the vote for them. Several attempts at Leftist unity had been made. At the Unity Conference of June, 1950, the rift in the Lanka Sama Samajist party was healed when the Bolshevik Samasamajist party, formerly the B.L.P., merged with its parent organization. But the merger gave rise to a new split, for a faction led by Philip Gunawardena walked out of the L.S.S.P. in protest and formed the Viplavakari Lanka Sama Samaja party (V.L.S.S.P.). Looking ahead to the 1952 election, the three Leftist parties issued proposals for a political alliance that would avoid electoral competition between them and thereby prevent the fragmentation of the Leftist vote. A partial success was achieved when in April, 1951, the V.L.S.S.P. and the Communist party formed an alliance (V.L.S.S.P-C.P.) based on a common manifesto. However, conflict and competition between the alliance and the L.S.S.P. were to be intense. The U.N.P. was better organized by 1952, having an efficiently run central office and over two hundred branch associations. It had emerged from the leadership struggle of the preceding year with its organization intact and its personally oriented wings resigned to at least a temporary unity. The communal parties, however, were in hard times by 1952. The C.I.C. was no longer a competitor, since its social base had been disfranchised. On the eve of the election it led a satyagraha campaign in protest. The Tamil communal movement had divided over the decision of the Tamil Congress to enter into a coalition government with the U.N.P. After leading a small group from the T.C. into the Opposition, S. J. V. Chelvanayakam had founded the Federal party, and in 1952 it put seven candidates forward to challenge the domination of the Tamil vote by the T.C.

In 1952 there were fewer candidates contending in the election and proportionately more running under a party label than in 1947. Of the 303 candidates, 85 were independents, 17 were from minor, personality parties, and 201 stood as candidates of the established parties. Thus, major-party candidates comprised two-thirds of all candidates in 1952, whereas in 1947 they were less than half. The ratio of candidates to seats also took an appreciable drop, there being nearly four to every seat in 1947 and slightly less than three per seat in 1952.

The 1952 election, therefore, was primarily a party contest. Strong campaigns were waged by the parties, and their leaders made extensive speaking tours in support of their party's candidates. To some extent, a lack of campaign funds necessitated party reliance on its candidates to operate their own campaigns. But significant progress had been made in the centralization of campaigns in the party headquarters. As in 1947, the U.N.P. was the only party that contested a sufficient number of seats to return a majority. It ran a total of 81 candidates, concentrated primarily in the Sinhalese areas so as not to compete with the Tamil Congress, with which it had a tacit electoral alliance. The L.S.S.P. put forward 39 candidates in a bid to become a major party, and contended in every province except the Eastern. The V.L.S.S.P.-C.P. ran 19 candidates, 6 in the Southern Province and no more than 2 in any of the others. The Tamil Congress and the Federal party, each of which ran 7 candidates, were confined to Tamil areas. Independents ran in every province. The new element in the election was Bandaranaike's Sri Lanka

Freedom party (S.L.F.P.), which sought major-party status by contesting 48 seats.

Despite the loss of D. S. Senanayake, who died in 1952 from injuries received in a fall from a horse, the U.N.P. enjoyed obvious advantages. The Korean war boom had injected vitality into a sagging economy, and in the campaign the U.N.P. was able to refer to what appeared to be a sound and prosperous financial state. A stable domestic situation had been achieved and maintained, and there was as yet no evidence of any general discontent. The U.N.P. also enjoyed definite organizational advantages. In addition to the individual wealth of its candidates, the U.N.P. had a large campaign fund, although there is no proof that it approached Rs. 3 million, as estimated by one member of the Opposition.[25] Also, its root organizations were more mature and more extensive than those of other parties, it had a large staff of paid employees and party workers, a fleet of vehicles at its disposal, a league of local notables either running under its banner or supporting its candidates, and local influence that a network of patronage had helped create. In addition, its members included a number of nationally prominent figures, and it had the total support of the press and the solid backing of almost all the articulate pressure groups on the island except the trade unions. The platform and campaign of the U.N.P. were based essentially on four themes. First, constance reference was made throughout the campaign to the memory of D. S. Senanayake and the role he had played in the attainment of independence. The manifesto of the U.N.P. referred to him as a "seer of visions and a dreamer of dreams with a firm grasp of practical political problems."[26] Stress was placed on the fact that the U.N.P. was the creation of Senanayake, that his son was now leader of the party and its candidate for Prime Minister, and that the party would continue to follow the policy of moderation and dedication that Senanayake had set for it. Second, it claimed a renewed mandate from the people on the basis of the good job it had done in running the country. It alluded to the social welfare measures it had introduced, the land reform schemes it had started, and, in general, pointed to its performance in office as having given Ceylon "inestimable gifts of peace and stability."[27] It defined itself as a private enterprise party, stressed the need for foreign investment, and argued that nationalization was "an undemocratic measure which throws out of gear individual initiative and private enterprise."[28] Third, it pointed out that it was the only party capable of capturing sufficient seats to form a government. As Sir Ivor Jennings observed at the time, "emphasis was laid upon this fact in election propaganda."[29] The choice before the electorate, according to the U.N.P., was between a U.N.P. government or an unstable coalition government formed by several parties that shared no common policy.

But the main theme of the U.N.P. campaign was that the fundamental issue in the election was a choice between democracy and totalitarianism.[30] It claimed that the U.N.P. was the only party that stood for the maintenance of a democratic system of government and the only one that would protect the political, religious, and cultural values of the people. If given the opportunity, the U.N.P. argued, the Marxist parties would suppress individual liberties, persecute religion, initiate a revolution, and establish a dictatorship along the lines, and under the control, of the Soviet Union. In particular, it emphasized what it considered to be the antireligious nature of Marxist parties. In an address before the Ceylon University Buddhist Brotherhood, J. R. Jayewardene compared the teachings of Buddha with those of Marx.[31] He pointed out that Buddha preached a spiritual way of life while Marx advocated a materialistic way of life, and that Marxism is by nature antispiritual and antireligious. Thus, he continued, "subsects of Marxism, such as Stalinists, Trotskyites and other growths from the parent tree . . . all profess the same enmity to the teachings of the Buddha."[32] He concluded by saying that no Buddhist, Christian, Hindu or Muslim could be a Marxist.[33] The Roman Catholic church aided the U.N.P. in its propagation of this argument. Archbishop Thomas Cooray stated that "no Catholic with even an atom of Christian conscience can vote for a candidate who succumbs to a political creed banned by the Church—be it Communism or any other."[34] Thus the condemnation of Marxist parties as antireligious not only helped the U.N.P. gain the votes of Buddhists, but also helped it mobilize the Christian vote, which, as Jennings observed, was "important on the west coast, where communism is strongest."[35]

Organized opposition to the U.N.P. in the Sinhalese areas was provided by the S.L.F.P. and the Marxist parties. Their manifestoes were severely critical of the U.N.P. policy and manner of running the government. All condemned the U.N.P. for its neglect of the traditionalist class, especially the failure to replace English with Sinhalese and Tamil as the official languages of administration. Only the S.L.F.P., however, challenged the U.N.P. within the context of the established economic, social, and political system without advocating revolutionary structural changes. The Marxist parties, while their manifestoes provided alternatives to that of the U.N.P., saw an ultimate solution to Ceylon's problems only in radical changes tantamount to revolution. The S.L.F.P. had several assets. The adherence of local notables in various provinces gave it some areas of strength essential to the growth of a new party. Bandaranaike's national prominence was an asset to the S.L.F.P., and the term he served as Minister of Health and Local Government made him known locally and enabled him to build up a network of local connections. But the S.L.F.P. was newly formed, and it had had little time for organizational development. The central office could do little more than provide candidates with copies of the manifesto. Campaign funds came mainly from Bandaranaike's private fortune, supplemented by whatever S.L.F.P. candidates could provide. For the most part, therefore, the candidates had to run their own campaigns, and there was little co-ordination from central headquarters.

In Tamil areas the election was primarily a struggle between the Tamil Congress and the Federal party. The T.C. ran as an ally of the U.N.P., with the theme of "responsive cooperation." Its view was that Tamil interests were best served by co-operation with the Sinhalese and participation in the Government by continued coalition with the U.N.P. The platform of the Federal party was based on the opinion of S. J. V. Chelvanayakam that the rights of the Tamils could only be ensured by the institution of a federal state. As early as 1947 Chelvanayakam declared that Tamils would have to demand a federal state if they did not get justice under a unitary one.[36] Later, he discerned the beginnings of an anti-Tamil trend in the Government's passage of anti-Indian legislation,[37] and in 1949, during the debate over the Parliamentary Elections (Amendment) Bill, he said that the growing fears of the minorities would eventuate in demands for a federal system of government.[38] By 1951 he was convinced of the anti-Tamil direction of politics in Ceylon and argued that the policy of the Government was "to kill as an entity the Tamil-speaking people of this country."[39] In the campaign of 1952 the theme of the F.P. was that the only solution to Tamil survival was federalism. Chelvanayakam contended that this was a policy designed "to preserve diversity in unity and to obtain unity in spite of diversity."[40]

No one had expected a close election in 1952, but few had anticipated the wide margin of the U.N.P. victory. The party captured 54 seats, enough to give it a majority independent of coalition support from any other party. The Tamil Congress took 4 seats, and the other ally of the U.N.P., the Labour party, returned only its leader to Parliament. The S.L.F.P. won 9 seats and thus did well for a new party; the election confirmed the foundation of Bandaranaike's party and left the way open for its further development. Competition within the Marxist Left fragmented its vote and enabled it to take only 13 seats. The Trotskyite L.S.S.P. remained the stronger of the Marxist parties, taking 9 seats, while the V.L.S.S.P.-C.P. won only 4. The Federal party won 2 seats, although its leader was defeated in a landslide.

Thirteen minor-party and independent candidates were also returned.

Sir Ivor Jennings concludes that the central issue in the election was whether or not the U.N.P. should be returned to power and that its victory was an indication that the people had confidence in it as a government.[41] Neither of these opinions is verifiable, and both are challenged by the configuration of party competition, as well as by electoral statistics. It was not a clear-cut Government versus Opposition election. The opposition vote was not unified, as was the vote of the U.N.P., and the division of the anti-U.N.P. vote among several parties resulted in a U.N.P. victory in many constituencies. In most constituencies there was a triangular contest between the U.N.P., the S.L.F.P., and one or another of the Marxist parties. Then too, in many constituencies more than one Marxist party was in competition, with the result that the anti-U.N.P. vote was still further divided. As it was, the U.N.P. failed to take a majority of the popular vote. Excluding the Northern Province, if the entire non-U.N.P. vote had been combined in each constituency and given to the major opposition party in that constituency, then the U.N.P. and the Opposition each would have won 43 seats. This is clearly unrealistic, because had the electorate merely had a choice between a U.N.P. candidate and one other it may well have given a higher percentage of its vote to the U.N.P. But it does indicate that the U.N.P. was not the overwhelming choice in 1952. Its victory in 1952 was definitely assisted by a fractionalized opposition. In any case, its victory indicated not so much that it had done well in office but that it had not done badly. There was no mass discontent, and the U.N.P. had not alienated either the urban or the peasant vote. There was, however, no general enthusiasm for the U.N.P. The undercurrent that would erupt in 1956 was in motion.

As in 1947, the U.N.P. helped itself by staggering the election to its own advantage. In 1950 a member of the Opposition had introduced a motion to have the next general election limited to one day.[42] The Government defeated the motion, saying that it felt the holding of a general election on one day was still technically impossible, although D. S. Senanayake promised to do it if it were possible.[43] As it happened, the election was held over a six-day period, with four days being allotted to polling. Of the 55 government members, 40 stood for election on the first two days. As Jennings observed, this schedule made it possible for the Government to obtain an early lead and perhaps initiate a strong U.N.P. trend.[44] As it turned out, the Government won 35 seats on the first two days and 25 on the last two. Only 8 of the opposition members stood for election on the first two days, and 29, including its most prominent members, stood for election on the last two days. It appears that the contests were deliberately staggered this way, regardless of whether staggering was necessitated by technical reasons. After the election the Opposition accused the Government of a number of irregularities in its handling of the election and in its campaign. One member of the Opposition accused the U.N.P. of building up a campaign fund of three million rupees on the basis of donations from the United States Embassy and other foreign sources with a stake in the election.[45] Sir John Kotelawala, soon to become Prime Minister, implied admission of this when he said, "If we got money it was to win the elections!"[46] N. M. Perera charged the Government with employing illegal measures in "its utilization of the machinery of government for party political ends."[47] The U.N.P. was accused of using vehicles provided by government servants,[48] employing local headmen to mobilize rural voters,[49] and keeping anti-U.N.P. voters off the register.[50] Just prior to the election a local headmen's conference was held in Colombo under the auspices of the cabinet ministers. According to Perera, at this conference the Government pressured village headmen into supporting government candidates.[51] The Government was also charged with exerting undue pressure on the electorate. Many of its candidates were reputed to have informed their constituents that unless U.N.P. candidates were returned in their areas the Government would do nothing for their constituencies.[52] The election of one M.P. was held void because a commission found him guilty of such a threat.

The U.N.P. had no problem in forming a government, although maintaining its cohesion was to be difficult. It had won a majority in its own right, and with the addition of six appointed members, whom it was allowed to nominate, it had a solid bloc of sixty seats. The four T.C. members joined the Government along with the lone member of the Labour party. Seven independents also supported the Government, bringing its total voting bloc above the two-thirds necessary to pass constitutional amendments. The U.N.P. had, as one member of the Opposition observed, a "dictatorial majority." Because of this, dispensing ministerial portfolios, although they were distributed strategically among the more influential members of the government party, was not necessary to attract support. The composition of the Cabinet was indicative of the U.N.P.'s strength. All the thirteen cabinet posts and the ten positions as parliamentary secretary were filled by members of the U.N.P., except for two portfolios reserved for the T.C., which was, as its critics suggested, merely the extension of the U.N.P. into Tamil areas.

The U.N.P.'s task of governing was facilitated by a numerically weak and divided Opposition. It had only 28 seats and was composed, as before, of ideologically disparate and personally antagonistic members. This was especially true of the Marxist parties, which engaged in polemical warfare throughout the entire period. The L.S.S.P. condemned its splinter offspring as "a dependent satellite group of ex-Trotskyists turned Stalinist." [53] It considered the Communist party to be "a betrayer of the working class and the mass movement." [54] The leadership of the C.P., it argued, was "nothing but a Soviet agency consciously seeking to manipulate the mass movement in Ceylon for the purposes of their Soviet bureaucratic masters." [55] Ideological differences

95

separated the Marxist parties from other members of the Opposition, such as the F.P. and the S.L.F.P. The S.L.F.P., while its members covered a wide ideological range, was primarily centralist in character and opposed to Marxist and revolutionary solutions. But in spite of ideological differences and personal feuds, the Opposition obtained a much greater unity of operation than ever before. Its weakness in confrontation with the Government almost compelled it to do so. Bandaranaike was promptly chosen leader of the Opposition, an obvious choice, since N. M. Perera, who led a party with the same number of seats as Bandaranaike's, was deeply involved in a conflict with the V.L.S.S.P.-C.P. coalition. Operational unity was maintained through the entire period. Motions of no confidence were introduced by Bandaranaike in the name of the Opposition, and on almost every issue the Opposition voted as a cohesive bloc.

Although the Opposition was functioning better than before, no progress was made in the growth of the concept of a loyal opposition. The Government persisted in its negative definition of the Opposition. Again, it was not that the Government failed to recognize the vital place of an opposition in a parliamentary system. The Finance Minister, for instance, remarked in 1953, "The part that an Opposition plays in a democratic Government is as important as that of the Government."[56] It was that the Government did not consider the existing Opposition capable of performing its normal function because of its commitment to "undemocratic" principles and philosophies. "It is the greatest political weakness of Ceylon today," Prime Minister Senanayake remarked shortly before his resignation, "that there is not a party in the Opposition definitely and unswervingly pledged to democratic ideals as such."[57] The C.P. was accused of being financed by the Soviet Union and of being in the employ of the Cominform.[58] The S.L.F.P., which was not Marxist and which had no international connections, was charged with supporting China and the Soviet Union, and "running with the Communists."[59] When by-elections were held, the U.N.P., rather than contend with its opponents on issues of policy, associated the opponents with international and revolutionary conspiracies and falsely portrayed them as subversive to the most cherished interests of the Ceylonese. At Alutnuwara, for instance, Sir John Kotelawala told a rally that "if either the Communists or the Samasamajists get into power you will not only lose the personal liberties you now enjoy, but as a consequence of their policy of opening the door to foreigners, you will be forced to give up your mother tongue of Sinhalese or Tamil and be compelled to adopt the languages of the Indians or the Chinese or the Russians." [60]

While it was true that the Marxist wing of the Opposition retained its revolutionary ideology, it had moved toward acceptance of the democratic and parliamentary structure of Ceylon's political system (a development discussed in Chapter 6). There were fewer statements now about the overthrow of the democratic system, and the Marxists, like other members of the Opposition, were becoming staunch defenders of that system. One observer of Ceylon's politics noted that the Opposition, and especially the Marxist wing, had "consistently in Ceylon displayed a vigilance for democratic principles which the British Liberal Party in its heyday would have envied." [61] N. M. Perera and S. W. R. D. Bandaranaike were vociferous defenders of the parliamentary system, as was Pieter Keuneman, the leader of the Communist party. Repeatedly all three rose to defend democratic principles from what they considered to be encroachments by the Government, and in the process they became the best parliamentarians in the House. Thus, within a decade of independence, the Opposition that had initially indicated no faith in the new political system and structure had come to be its firm supporter. Both the Government and the Opposition were now arguing for the survival of a democratic system, and even the Communist party claimed that it was fighting for "the principle of the Sovereignty of Parliament." [62]

But neither the Government nor the Opposition trusted the commitment of the other to the democratic system. N. M. Perera accused the U.N.P. of creating a political structure that was monolithic and of attempting to institute "single party government." [63] Bandaranaike accused Sir John Kotelawala of taking steps to establish a dictatorship,[64] and during the state of emergency of 1953 the Opposition charged that it had been declared "with a view to suppressing all opposition to the party in power." [65] Relations between the Government and the Opposition had gotten off to a bad start right after the election, and they continued to worsen. In August, 1953, in protest against the Government's lowering of the rice subsidy, the Marxist parties called for a one-day hartal, or work stoppage. The protest got out of hand, and stern Government reprisals led to riots that in turn led to the proclamation of a state of emergency. Soon after the suspension of the emergency Dudley Senanayake resigned, and Sir John Kotelawala became Prime Minister. His succession marked the rise to power of the U.N.P.'s right wing, which was committed to the eradication of Communism in Ceylon. After this it was inevitable that relations between the Government and the Opposition should deteriorate. Marxist parties began to make more frequent use of the strike to oppose actions of the Government, and the Government began to resort to repressive measures. The headquarters of the C.P. were raided on several occasions, the Government banned the importation of literature from Communist countries, passports to Communist countries were difficult, if not impossible, to get, and all demonstrations by the working class were banned save that of May Day. In addition, the U.N.P. began creating quasi-military organizations such as the Naval Volunteer Reserve and the Railroad Engineering Corps as ancillary associations of the party. All these moves were attempts by the Government to contain the growth of Communist influence in Ceylon. The Opposition considered these actions to be part of a Government plot to establish a dictatorship. Several members of the Government who crossed the floor into the Opposition gave as their reason for defection the growing dictatorial nature of the Government under Sir John. There were increasing reports of police and government interference in local elections, and there was speculation that another general election would either not be held or be so arranged as to ensure the U.N.P.'s return to power. Evidence pointed to an attempt on the part of the Government to entrench itself permanently in office. A one-party system appeared to be in the making.

CHAPTER 4 *The Emergence of a Competitive Party System*

Ceylon approached the end of its first decade of independence in a state of growing political restlessness. The prosperous years of the Korean war boom had passed, and the foreign currency reserve built up during World War II had been spent in making life good for the affluent elite who ran the affairs of Ceylon. The resulting higher price of rice and sugar bore heavily on the less affluent, and unrest was spreading in the countryside, for the peasant had lost touch with a government that neither talked his language nor appreciated his problems. The Government had divorced itself from the people, and the protests of the Opposition had now become the real echo of a people in protest. It was time for new politics in Ceylon, and if the party system were to survive, it would have to respond to the call for change.

THE ELECTION OF 1956

Over a year of conjecture was ended when the United National party decided at its conference in February, 1956, to dissolve Parliament and hold a general election two months later. The U.N.P. entered the election campaign confident of winning, although aware that it would probably not be returned with the "dictatorial majority" that it had enjoyed since 1952. It had called the election at what it felt was an appropriate and propitious time, immediately after it had advocated adopting Sinhalese as the official language. Throughout the campaign the U.N.P. alluded to its democratic action in calling an election one year sooner than was legally required and right after it had adopted a language policy contrary to its 1952 manifesto and campaign promises. But even a year earlier the U.N.P. had anticipated the election and had begun to reactivate its extensive organization. As early as March, 1955, the Prime Minister had instructed the Cabinet to give special attention to the needs of constituencies that had returned U.N.P. members in 1952.[1] In addition, the Chief Government Whip had distributed a circular to every U.N.P. member of Parliament saying, "The Rt. Hon. Prime Minister has directed me to request you to be good enough to send in a list of three main items of work which you desire to be carried out in your constituency and included in the Budget Estimation for the financial year 1954–55."[2]

There was a great deal of speculation that the U.N.P. was pre-arranging the election to suit itself and employing illegal or unethical tactics in an effort to gain majority support from the people. The normally pro-Government *Ceylon Observer* charged that the U.N.P. was threatening to disfranchise voters who dared vote for opposition parties and to withdraw government aid from any constituencies not returning a U.N.P. member to Parliament.[3] In another instance the Prime Minister was reported to have said that the amount of aid going to a constituency would be in proportion to the size of the vote that it gave to the U.N.P.[4] Also, the U.N.P. was accused of having local headmen distribute pamphlets warning the peasants that if a U.N.P. member was not returned in their area, their land allotments and rice ration books would be taken from them.[5] The patronage connections that the U.N.P. had established over its years in office were also being manipulated to acquire support. Claims were made that land revenue officers, district revenue officers, headmen, and government agents were all working for the U.N.P.[6] There were charges that the police intervened in elections[7] and that the U.N.P. was allowing foreign agents, mainly United States Embassy personnel, to print and distribute anti-Communist pamphlets.[8] The U.N.P. again staggered the election to its own advantage. Technical difficulties were made the excuse for scheduling a three-day election period, but the pro-Government *Ceylon Daily News* (March 12, 1956) and N. M. Perera, among others, saw deliberate manipulation in the scheduling of the contests. Sir John Kotelawala, for instance, stood for election on the first day, while S. W. R. D. Bandaranaike, leader of the anti-U.N.P. alliance, ran on the last day.

There was a significant reduction in the number of candidates seeking election. For the 95 seats, 241 candidates came forward, 62 less than in 1952, and 120 less than in 1947. A major reason for the decline in the number of candidates was the biparty character of the election. Except for the independents it was a two-party contest in almost every constituency in the Sinhalese provinces. Opposition parties had either combined in, or they were supporting, the Mahajana Eksath Peramuna (M.E.P.—"People's United Front"), a coalition formed on the eve of the election for the explicit purpose of organizing the anti-U.N.P. vote and defeating the Government. As a result, opposition parties competed against each other in only twelve constituencies, and it was almost a straight U.N.P. versus anti-U.N.P. election. Both the U.N.P. and the M.E.P. sought majority status. The U.N.P. ran 76 candidates and the M.E.P. 60. The Lanka Sama Samaja party ran 21 candidates in a bid to obtain a strong third-party position for entry into a possible government coalition with the M.E.P. The Communist party ran 9 candidates, and the Labour party 4. Sixty-four independents ran, two-thirds of them in the Tamil provinces of the north and east. In these provinces, also, the Federal party had 14 candidates and the Tamil Congress 1, and 2 ran under the label of the Tamil Resistance party. Only the parties of the Marxist Left ran on an island-wide and inter-communal basis, since the eruption of the language issue and the espousal of "Sinhala only" by both the U.N.P. and the M.E.P. had introduced communal cleavage into the party system.

But while the communalism now prevented a national alignment of political forces, there was for the first time, if only in
the Sinhalese areas, a choice between alternative governments.
This was the major issue of the election, and all the other issues
converged on it. The U.N.P. pointed to its past record to justify
its claim to another mandate and argued that it was the only
party that could ensure stability in the foreseeable future.[9] It
recalled the stable government that Ceylon had enjoyed under
its rule, the development schemes it had introduced, and the pre-
eminent place it had afforded to Buddhism in Ceylon. But the
major emphasis of the U.N.P.'s campaign was on its language
policy. At its Eighth Annual Session the party had decided to
advocate replacing English with Sinhalese as the official language,
and Sir John Kotelawala had said that the U.N.P. would seek
its mandate primarily on the basis of this policy change.[10] During the campaign Sir John asked for a two-thirds majority in
order to enable passage of the constitutional amendment necessary to enact "Sinhala only" legislation.[11] Sir John argued that
although the M.E.P. also stood for a policy of "Sinhala only," it
would not be able to implement the policy if it came to power
because it would be dependent upon the votes of the L.S.S.P.
and the C.P., both of which advocated "parity of status" between
Tamil and Sinhalese, rather than Sinhala only.[12] He also argued
that the M.E.P. could not form a stable government because it
incorporated a wide range of divergent views and ideologies that
inevitably would erupt in divisions once the M.E.P. assumed
power. The U.N.P. also sought to associate the M.E.P. with Communism, one party member referring to it as the "Marx Engels
Party."[13] Sir John argued that an M.E.P. government would be
so dependent upon the votes of the L.S.S.P. and the C.P. that
eventually it would come under their control, especially since the
M.E.P. already had Communist elements in it.[14] The Marxist
parties were condemned by the U.N.P. as being antireligious and
anti-Buddhist and as desiring to "sell" the country to India and

the Soviet Union.[15] In short, Sir John described all the opponents of the U.N.P. as "the declared enemies of democracy."[16]

The pulpit again came to the support of the U.N.P.—the Methodist church endorsed the party,[17] and Roman Catholic priests exhorted their parishioners not to vote for Marxist candidates. The Vicar-General, the Very Rev. Father A. Serru, said, "No Catholic can abstain from voting and no Catholic can vote for any candidate who is an adherent of doctrines opposed to the doctrines of the Church." He continued, "No Catholic can support or vote for a candidate with a materialistic doctrine like Communism which is against the doctrine of spiritualism which is the goal of the Church."[18] The U.N.P. bent its efforts to keeping the Buddhist clergy out of the campaign. There had been a Buddhist reaction against the Westernization of the U.N.P. and against what many considered to be its pro-Christian attitude. As a result, many Buddhist priests, or bhikkus, had come out in support of the traditionalist-oriented M.E.P. Sir John denounced what he termed "political bhikkus,"[19] and the coleaders of one sect of Buddhists that supported the U.N.P. issued a statement directing bhikkus not to take an active part in politics.[20]

The common theme in the campaigns of the opposition parties was the defeat of the U.N.P. Bandaranaike, whose Sri Lanka Freedom party was the major unit of the M.E.P., told the people that if for any reason they could not vote for the M.E.P., they should vote for the L.S.S.P. or any candidate opposed to the U.N.P.[21] Bandaranaike spoke in every constituency in which an M.E.P. candidate ran, as well as in several non-M.E.P. constituencies in support of the L.S.S.P., the C.P., or independent candidates. The L.S.S.P. argued that the growing tendency in the U.N.P. toward the establishment of a fascist state necessitated that it be ousted from office and an alternative government installed. It recognized that by itself it could not form a government, so it called for the return of an M.E.P. government, to be formed with the assistance of the L.S.S.P.[22] It asked for the return of at least twelve seats so that it could aid the M.E.P. in Parliament, and asserted, "The L.S.S.P. also stands firm on the principle of the freedom of political parties rival to itself to function when a Sama Samaja Government is in power."[23] The C.P. also stood for the defeat of the U.N.P. and the return of a new government. Pieter Keuneman exhorted the people to vote for the M.E.P. if no candidate of the C.P. was running in their constituency.[24]

While the opposition parties shared other policies in addition to their anti-U.N.P. front, they came into serious though muted conflict in regard to the language issue. Both the L.S.S.P. and the C.P. stood for "parity of status" between Tamil and Sinhalese, while the M.E.P. advocated the adoption of Sinhalese as the only official language. Like the U.N.P., the M.E.P. made this one of the major issues of its campaign. Bandaranaike charged that the U.N.P. had a secret pact with the Tamil members of its government party not to implement a "Sinhalese only" policy once it was returned to power.[25] If the U.N.P. were returned, Bandaranaike continued, English would remain the state language.[26] For his part, Bandaranaike said, he would make Sinhalese the official language within forty-eight hours if the M.E.P. formed the next government.

The Tamil areas were separated from the mainstream of politics by the coming of the language issue. No Tamil individuals or organizations other than Marxists now advocated co-operation with the Sinhalese, and there was an attempt by the Tamil elite to form a Tamil united front to demand a separate Tamil state. Their hope was to confront the Sinhalese with a united Tamil organization. However, the Tamil United Front failed because of its inability to agree on a common list of candidates.[27] The failure of this attempt at unity left the Federal party as the dominant political force in the Tamil areas. It felt that events had proved the validity of its argument over the years that only in a federal state could Tamil interests be guaranteed. In its campaign it referred to its history of opposition to a Sinhalese-dominated government and demanded the institution of a federal state based on the Swiss model.[28] Its main competition was provided by independents, as the disgrace of association with the U.N.P. had all but ended the career of the Tamil Congress, and only its leader contested for election in 1956. The Federal party accused independents of being political opportunists, whose return would weaken organized Tamil resistance to the Sinhalese government. It argued that only a disciplined and organized party could effectively defend Tamil interests, saying that "the party counts much more than the individuals—the Federal Party is the bulwark of the Tamil-speaking people and of all minorities." [29] Its main organized opponent was the C.P., which it accused of being irreligious and Sinhalese dominated. In the main, the independents argued against the feasibility of a federal state. They contended that the Tamil areas were not economically self-sufficient, that Tamil employment was largely in Sinhalese areas, and that federalism was not a solution to the language problem.[30] S. Nadesan, a former member of the government party, maintained that strong demands for federalism would eventuate in a civil war with the Sinhalese.[31]

The results of the election surprised everyone. The electorate cast an overwhelming vote of no confidence in the U.N.P.: of the 76 candidates who ran under its label, only 8 were returned. The M.E.P. won an impressive mandate from the people to form an alternative government, for it won 51 seats, and the L.S.S.P. and C.P., which had backed it, took 14 and 3 seats, respectively. Eight independents were returned. The Federal party emerged as the dominant organization in the Tamil areas, winning 10 of the 14 seats it contested. The T.C. returned the one member who ran under its label.

The results of the election both reflected and gave further realization to a new turn in Ceylonese politics. The one-party trend was arrested, as an entrenched and self-assured party was displaced in a "silent revolution." The transfer of power to new political forces came about as quietly as had the revolution that had demanded it. The U.N.P. made no attempt to negate the popular will, and the control of government passed to the M.E.P. In these events a competitive party system found beginnings.

The M.E.P. was, as one observer described it, "a coalition of resentment against the U.N.P." [32] The resentment had been a long time growing, and the M.E.P. provided the organization through which it could be articulated and mobilized. The U.N.P. had gradually alienated the social elements from which it drew its strength, and in the process many of its notables became disaffected and left the party. Thus, as the U.N.P. became progressively disorganized, the erosion of its social base produced an electorate receptive to a new party. Both social and organizational factors, therefore, were involved in the displacement of the U.N.P.

The Organizational Factor

The disorganization of the U.N.P. relates to the nature of its origin. It had been founded primarily on the political opportunity that its organization provided for elite elements, and its power base was constructed on the association of local and national notables who were included in its organization and who collectively had mass influence. But its source of strength was also a source of weakness. There were divisive tendencies in an organization of so many notables and of so wide an ideological spectrum. Ideological conflict and competition for personal power were inherent from the beginning. It was thus inevitable that "wings" and "tendencies" should form about personalities within the party, especially as the demands of government necessitated definite policy commitments by the party. The U.N.P. included heavily weighted right and left wings from the start. The left wing, which was traditionalist and socialist, formed about Bandaranaike, while the Westernized and conservative right formed about Sir John Kotelawala. There was tension between the wings, and for a while they were held in balance by the dominant personality of D. S. Senanayake and his policy of the "middle way."

Bandaranaike's defection in 1951 was the first serious break in the unity of the U.N.P. Only a small group crossed the floor with him into the Opposition, but their defection was the beginning of the erosion of the U.N.P.'s base in the Kandyan areas and among the traditionalist element. The death of D. S. Senanayake, within a year of Bandaranaike's defection, deprived the party of its main cohesive force and exposed it to internecine conflict over the succession. Sir John Kotelawala, as Leader of the House, was in line for the succession, but a bloc in the Cabinet gave notice of its intention to resign if he were summoned. In addition, it was reported that D. S. Senanayake had requested the Governor-General to appoint his son in the event of his death.[33] In any case, Sir John accepted the Governor-General's decision to do so, and Dudley Senanayake became Prime Minister without a rupture in the U.N.P. Dudley Senanayake's assumption of leadership concealed and tempered for a time the serious conflict between the left and right tendencies in the U.N.P. that was at the root of the succession crisis. He was a centralist like his father, a liberal who had the respect of the people as well as of the ideological and personal-power wings of the party. But he was not a politician, in spite of his long political career, and under him the U.N.P. right wing moved into a decisive position in regard to policy formulation. This became evident when the subsidy on rice and sugar was reduced in 1953. With the right wing now manifestly the dominant power center in the party, the left wing began its movement out of the party.

Maithripala Senanayake was the first to leave. Disgruntled at the U.N.P.'s repudiation of its campaign pledge to maintain the subsidy on rice and sugar, and bitter over his failure to obtain a portfolio, Senanayake resigned from the Government.[34] While his defection was numerically unimportant to the U.N.P., his loss challenged the U.N.P. base in the North Central Province, where his popularity had led the U.N.P. to a near sweep of the province in 1952. The reduction in the subsidy also led to the hartal of August, 1953, which eventuated in a state of emergency and the consequent resignation of Dudley Senanayake. The strain of his father's death, his apparent aversion to leadership, and the eruption of the hartal crisis, believed by some to have been engineered by the right wing in order to drain his energy, were the reasons for Senanayake's resignation. Sir John Kotelawala became Prime Minister, and the final step was taken in the climb to power of the right wing. The cohesion provided by the Senanayakes was gone, and the breakup of the U.N.P. was accelerated. When Sir John became Prime Minister, Sir Lalita Rajapakse, a national figure and head of an influential family in the Southern Province, was dropped from the Cabinet and resigned from the party. G. G. Ponnambalam, leader of the U.N.P.'s extension in the Tamil areas, gave in to pressure from Sir John and resigned his post after a long absence from the House. In explanation of his resignation, Ponnambalam cited "the emergence of unmistakable signs of undemocratic and Fascist rule."[35] In addition, he charged that during Sir John's administration the Government had followed an anti-Tamil policy revealing "a desire for the establishment of racial hegemony under the guise of majority rule."[36] While none of the other T.C. members of the government party crossed the floor with him, Ponnambalam's defection cost the U.N.P. it most valuable asset in the Tamil areas and marked the beginning of the erosion of its Tamil base. In 1956, after the U.N.P.'s adoption of "Sinhala only," all the Tamil supporters of the U.N.P. coalition resigned. In 1954 the Kandyan base of the U.N.P., shaken by the defection of Bandaranaike and others who formed the S.L.F.P., was further weakened when T. B. Pannabokke Dissawe resigned from the party for "reasons of self-respect."[37] The most serious defection was that of R. G. Senanayake, Minister of Commerce and leader of the U.N.P. in the North Western Province, where he was immensely popular.[38] He was leader of the U.N.P.'s left wing and had repeatedly come into collision on economic and foreign policy matters with J. R. Jayewardene, Minister of Finance and ally of Sir John. A year after resigning his cabinet post Senanayake also resigned his post as Chief Government Whip,[39] although he remained in the U.N.P. in order to lead what was becoming a rear-guard action of the left wing. In the 1956 election Senanayake opposed Jayewardene in the latter's home constituency and defeated him.[40]

But it was the actions of Dudley Senanayake that hurt the U.N.P. the most. After his resignation he retired to solitude for a time to regain his health and to think over his future. He became increasingly disenchanted with the actions of the U.N.P. and Sir John, and in 1955 he refused to speak at U.N.P. rallies.[41] Just prior to the 1956 elections Senanayake announced his decision to retire permanently from politics and to resign from the U.N.P.[42] The U.N.P. suffered not only the loss of Senanayake as an active campaigner but also the discredit cast on the party by his actions. Implied in his retirement was a condemnation of the U.N.P. that the Opposition would highlight during the campaign. In addition, Senanayake's resignation from the party led to the defection of a number of party members. One village committee chairman, for instance, said that if Senanayake could not see fit to stay in the U.N.P. then neither could he.[43]

Thus, by 1956 the U.N.P. was no longer an inclusive party. As the right wing assumed power and the party ideology became more specifically conservative, the party's base of notables gradually drifted away. Since its strength in various areas derived mainly from the influence of member notables from those areas, the U.N.P. lost popular support with every notable who left the party. Its organization suffered also, as each person's defection brought with it a separation from the party of a number of officials and influential members of its local organizations. The U.N.P.'s attempt to achieve a rigid centralization of party nominations also led to disaffection at the local level.[44] To a significant degree it was the arrogance and dictatorial nature of Sir John Kotelawala that was responsible for many of the defections from the party. He did not possess the finesse or the patience to provide effective party leadership at a time when compromise and consensus were necessary. He imposed his views and those of the right wing on an organization that was built and could only survive on compromise. In any case, the disorganization of the U.N.P. provided material for the Opposition. The defections resulted in a reservoir of notables, together with their supporters, from whom a potential opposition could draw valuable assistance.

The U.N.P. had never been as popular as the number of seats it won would seem to indicate. It had not won a majority of the vote in either 1947 or 1952. It was a plurality party that won a majority of the seats because opposition to it in the electorate was dispersed among a number of parties and independents. The electoral rewards of an anti-U.N.P. coalition were always apparent to opposition parties, but the organization of an anti-U.N.P. front repeatedly failed because of ideological and personal antagonisms. Prior to the 1952 election a special session of the L.S.S.P. passed a resolution suggesting a united front with the C.P., the C.I.C., and the V.L.S.S.P., and calling for "united action" with the S.L.F.P. and the F.P.[45] Later, Pieter Keuneman recommended that all anti-U.N.P. forces combine in an effort to defeat the U.N.P.[46] However, N. M. Perera said that the L.S.S.P. would not sacrifice principle to form a united front against the U.N.P.[47] and that the L.S.S.P. would not consider a merger with the C.P., because it was a foreign-ruled party.[48] The V.L.S.S.P. and the C.P., however, came to a working agreement in 1952, which for a time seemed to promise the beginnings of Left unity. At a conference of the L.S.S.P. in 1953 a number of the younger generation of party members revolted against the leadership, and 210 of them walked out of the conference because of its refusal to consider a resolution calling for "closer association" with Leftist parties.[49] They subsequently called themselves "Section II" and formed an alliance with the V.L.S.S.P.-C.P.[50] As a result, Pieter Keuneman contended that the L.S.S.P. "could no longer be called a political party."[51] But whatever Leftist unity was achieved soon crumbled because of personal and tactical conflict among the leadership. In 1955 the V.L.S.S.P.-C.P. alliance broke up,[52] and all hopes of a C.P.-L.S.S.P. merger seemed permanently ended when an L.S.S.P. leader stated that his party was "not concerned with any comprehensive political agreement with the Communist Party."[53]

Other attempts at unity or co-operation also had failed. In 1953 Bandaranaike tried to negotiate a merger of his S.L.F.P. with the L.S.S.P., but N. M. Perera refused even to consider it.[54] Bandaranaike's attempt to merge with the V.L.S.S.P.-C.P. also came to nothing.[55] In 1953 an organization called the People's Front was created by Somaweera Chandrasiri for the purpose of forging Leftist unity. His objective was to provide a "neutral organization" that could serve as a center for co-operation among the leaders of Leftist parties.[56] However, it got nowhere. In 1955 an attempt to form a comprehensive organization of the parliamentary opposition also failed, as the Opposition Unity Group, which was formed by S. D. Banda, W. Dahanayake, C. Suntharalingam, and S. Chandrasiri, was stillborn.[57]

From 1952 to 1956 the parliamentary opposition did at least work together more harmoniously than before, and the numerous attempts at unity were a definite indication of a growing common interest among opposition parties in some kind of organized action against the U.N.P. The major obstacle in the way of unity was the fear of losing personal power that haunted the leaders of the opposition parties. This was a factor not only in the top echelons of each party but also among the entire elite cadre, whose power depended on the posts they held in the party organizations at various levels. It was clear that if unity were to be realized, it would have to be based on some kind of association that would permit each party to retain intact its organizational identity and individual power structure.

The main impulse to the formation of an opposition coalition in 1956 was the fear that were the U.N.P. returned to power in that year, it would continue its movement toward becoming a one-party dictatorship. This fear motivated the discussions that took place between the opposition parties in late 1955 and into the first months of 1956. The objective of the discussions was to form a front organization capable of opposing the U.N.P. in the coming elections and to conclude an electoral pact that would prevent fragmentation of the anti-U.N.P. vote. The S.L.F.P. of Bandaranaike was the natural pivot of a front organization. He was nationally prominent and the most respected of the opposition leaders, and both he and his organization had remained neutral in the many conflicts that had plagued the Marxist Left. He was the person most acceptable to others in the Opposition. In addition, his party was the most ideologically neutral, and its spectrum was broad enough to include all shades of opinion. At the same time it was sufficiently weighted in the center to balance the extreme ideologists whom it also incorporated. Then too, the S.L.F.P. had developed an impressive organization, although it contained conflicting elements that later would make its operation difficult. It had a youth league called the Tri Sinhale Jatika Peramuna, which in 1952 claimed seventy branch associations.[58] In January, 1956, the S.L.F.P. organized a trade union connection, the Independent Industrial and Mercantile Employees Trade Union.[59] In addition, the S.L.F.P. organization contained a number of notables who had local influence and on whom the organizational branches of the party ultimately depended. While its organizational structure was thus feudal, it was one that could exert mass influence. Because of all this, the S.L.F.P. was the strongest opposition party by 1956.

Bandaranaike was the main force in the discussions that took place among the leaders of the opposition groups. After long negotiations, agreement on a common manifesto and a single slate of candidates was reached. On February 22, 1956, two months before the elections, the Mahajana Eksath Peramuna (People's United Front) came into being. It was composed of Bandaranaike's S.L.F.P., the V.L.S.S.P of Philip Gunawardena, and the Bhasa Peramuna, a communal organization advocating "Sinhala only" and led by W. Dahanayake and S. Chandrasiri. In addition, a group of independents under the titular leadership of I. M. R. A. Iriyagolle also joined the M.E.P.[60] The most arduous task during the negotiations was to reach agreement on a single slate of candidates. The final agreement was that of the 61 candidates whom the M.E.P. would run, 41 were to come from the S.L.F.P., 6 from the V.L.S.S.P., and 7 from the B.P., and 7 were to be independents.[61] Each of the parties that formed the coalition retained its separate organization. The M.E.P. was not organizationally consolidated, and its executive committee, composed of the leaders of its various organizations, merely served as a center for the co-ordination of the M.E.P. campaign.

The next object of Bandaranaike's negotiations was the conclusion of no-contest pacts with those opposition groups that did not join the M.E.P. Right after the formation of the M.E.P. he announced that it would be his purpose not to clash with opposition candidates.[62] By the end of February he had succeeded in reaching no-contest pacts with both the C.P. and the L.S.S.P.[63] Largely because of his efforts the L.S.S.P. and the C.P. also came to an agreement not to oppose each other. The agreements not to run candidates against each other in the election worked out extremely well. The M.E.P. came into competition with the C.P. or the L.S.S.P. in only twelve constituencies,[64] and the L.S.S.P. and the C.P. clashed in only one.

The coalition and the no-contest arrangements were the primary organizational factors involved in the defeat of the U.N.P. In nearly all constituencies the anti-U.N.P. vote was unified, and the result was a landslide victory for the M.E.P. and its electoral allies. Although the Opposition significantly increased its popular vote, while that of the U.N.P. declined by nearly 300,000, it was primarily the organization of the vote that led to the landslide (see Table 1).

TABLE 1. Popular Vote, 1947–56

	1947[a]	1952[a]	1956[b]
U.N.P.	727,685	1,019,854	740,845
Opposition[c]	1,010,931	1,127,400	1,579,537

SOURCE: Data obtained at Office of Commissioner of Elections, Colombo.
[a] Excludes vote in Northern Province.
[b] Excludes vote in Northern and Eastern provinces.
[c] Consists of all non-U.N.P. candidates in included provinces.

The Social Factor

The period from 1947 to 1956, and especially that between 1952 and 1956, witnessed the progressive alienation of the social base of the U.N.P. and the gradual erosion of its electoral strength. In all sectors of Ceylonese society, among all economic, social, and cultural groups, discontent with the ruling elite grew until, by 1956, it was a mass phenomenon. It was from this reservoir of discontent that the M.E.P. was to draw its electoral majority.

The most serious neglect by the U.N.P. was its failure to articulate the awakening Buddhist revival that began in earnest after 1950. In 1953 a book[65] was written in commemoration of the twenty-five hundred years of Buddhism. It analyzed the history of Buddhism in Ceylon and sought to discern its role, as well as the function of the clergy, in modern political and intellectual life. It called for a Buddhist renaissance and prescribed a greater role for the bhikku and the Sangha (the ancient, loose-knit association of the Buddhist clergy) in the political, social, and cultural affairs of Ceylon. In both 1947 and 1952 there had been evidence of bhikku participation in politics, but it had been sporadic and unorganized. After 1952 political participation by bhikkus increased, and Bandaranaike, who saw political opportunity in the emergent Buddhist revival and political orientation, encouraged bhikkus to take an active part in politics.[66] The Buddhist revival movement was at the forefront of the traditionalist revolt that protested the prominence of Western values in Ceylon and the political dominance of Christians. The Buddhists wanted a government commission appointed to investigate their grievances and the status of Buddhism, but the U.N.P. refused to appoint one. Consequently, in 1954, following a resolution adopted by the All-Ceylon Buddhist Congress at Kegalle on December 27, 1953, a nongovernmental committee of prominent Buddhists was appointed "to inquire into the present state of Buddhism in Ceylon and to report on the conditions necessary to improve and strengthen the position of Buddhism and the means whereby these conditions may be fulfilled." [67] Its report was published just prior to the 1956 elections. It listed a host of grievances and related how Buddhism had declined under the British occupation.[68] It also charged that there had been continuous legislative favoritism for certain religious bodies, presumably the Catholics and other Christian religions. In its conclusion, it demanded the appointment of a commission to investigate "the economic, political and social activities of religious bodies" and called for a wide program of government assistance in raising Buddhism to its rightful place in Ceylon. The U.N.P. promised to give its "most earnest attention to the Committee's recommendations at the earliest opportunity." [69] The manifesto of the M.E.P., on the other hand, stated, "We generally approve the recommendations of the Buddhist Committee of Inquiry."

It seems certain that under the U.N.P. Christians had received special advantage, although this was partly because Christians as a group were more highly educated and more career oriented than Buddhists. But there was government aid to parochial schools, and Christians did occupy the majority of elite positions in Ceylonese society, especially in government and civil service occupations. This had begun under the British and was continued under the U.N.P. In addition, the U.N.P symbolized the Westernized value system, and under its rule the values and customs of

Western society predominated in political and social circles. In the past the U.N.P had maintained its Buddhist base partly because the Buddhists were unorganized and politically inarticulate, and partly because there was no other political force to which the Buddhists could turn. U.N.P. propaganda to the effect that the Marxist parties were antireligious and materialistic had found Buddhist circles receptive, especially the more articulate, wealthy sects. The formation of the S.L.F.P. changed this, because it provided a non-Marxist party receptive to Buddhist protests and interests. Thus, by 1956 the Buddhists were sufficiently antagonized to revolt from the U.N.P. and organizationally capable of revolt.

The common interest shared by the Buddhists submerged for a time the parochial differences between sects. As early as 1953, Sangha Sabhas, or Bhikku Associations, were formed throughout the island, dedicated to the spiritual revival of Buddhism. A number of these associations combined into the Sri Lanka Maha Sangha Sabha, while other Buddhist societies formed the All-Ceylon Congress of Bhikku Societies. Just before the 1956 election these two organizations combined to form the Eksath Bhikku Peramuna for the explicit purpose of aiding the M.E.P. in each constituency and defeating the U.N.P.[70]

Several of the same grievances had alienated much of the Kandyan element from the U.N.P. Neither Christianity nor Western values had penetrated the Kandyan areas to any great extent. The area and its people had remained culturally and socially apart from the Western invasion, and as a result, a cultural distinction developed between the Kandyan Sinhalese and the low-country Sinhalese, who were far more Christianized and Westernized. The Kandyans considered themselves the heirs of the traditional culture. The U.N.P. had originally gained the Kandyan vote by integrating Kandyan notables into its organization and by enacting anti-Indian legislation beneficial to the Kandyans. Its conservative policy was also appealing, and national prosperity helped to conceal the worsening economic condition of the Kandyan peasant. But the Kandyan base began to erode as a number of notables broke from the U.N.P. and as the S.L.F.P. began to develop pockets of strength in the area. Peasant poverty was on the increase, and mass alienation developed as the U.N.P. pursued policies not geared to Kandyan interests.

In response to representations made by the Kandyans, the U.N.P. government appointed a commission in 1949 to investigate the social and economic problems of the Kandyan peasantry in Central and Uva provinces and to make recommendations regarding measures to be taken to ameliorate their condition. The voluminous report issued by the commission in 1951 was an indictment of the long years of official neglect.[71] Some of the problems of the Kandyan area that the report dealt with were the intense pressure of population on the land, the monopoly of arable land by tea companies, the fragmentation of peasant holdings into uneconomic units, the high rate of adult illiteracy, the lack of adequate educational and health facilities, the poor condition of the road system and consequent problems of marketing goods, the lack of a secure system of land tenure, and the problem of landlessness.[72] The Cabinet accepted the recommendations of the report "in principle," although it stated that it "was opposed at that time to regional development." [73] Lack of funds and the deterioration of the island's economic condition prevented the Government from taking any action, although on the eve of the election it announced plans for a program of regional development.[74] But the Kandyan peasantry was troubled, and relief was too slow in coming. The Government appeared unresponsive to the needs of the peasants, who by 1956 were open to appeals from more responsive political forces.

The Kandyan protest expressed only a part of the discontent being felt throughout the entire swabasha-educated class (those educated in the "mother tongue," either Sinhalese or Tamil). As a group these people, brought up in the indigenous tradition, felt that their interests were subordinated to those of the Westernized elite. Members of the swabasha-educated elite were especially antagonized, because they had no prestige and no access to circles of the social elite. In the schools, those who taught in English were more highly paid and worked in better conditions than those who taught in Sinhalese. Fluency in English was a requisite to entry into the civil service, and all official business, including telephone, telegraph, and postal service, was conducted in English. Higher education was in English. English was the language of the courts and the government administration, as well as the official language of the House of Representatives. Not until 1948 was an M.P. permitted to speak in the House of Representatives in Sinhalese, and even then the length of speeches in Sinhalese was restricted because of problems of transcription and translation. These realities led I. M. R. A. Iriyagolle to remark in 1950, "Our people are slaves because they are being governed through a foreign language." [75] Colvin R. de Silva argued that there could be no democracy in Ceylon unless the people could communicate with its government and administration, and that they could not do so if the government did not speak their language. [76]

In spite of the long years of British occupation only a small percentage of Ceylonese spoke English, and these were mainly Burghers, Tamils, and low-country Sinhalese. In 1921 1.3 per cent of the Kandyans were literate in English, while 5.9 per cent of the low-country Sinhalese and 8.5 per cent of the Tamils were literate in English. In 1953 nearly 62 per cent of the population spoke only Sinhalese, and English was spoken by only 6.5 per cent. The bulk of the English-speaking population was in urban areas. Of the 402,276 people who spoke English, 186,406 were in Colombo, 35,344 were in Jaffna, and 33,322 were in Kandy, the one up-country area of Western penetration. [77]

Proposals to replace English with the indigenous languages were not new. [78] In 1944 J. R. Jayewardene, soon to become Finance Minister in an independent Ceylon, introduced a motion to replace English with Sinhalese as the official language within a reasonable time. [79] The U.N.P. government, while approving the eventual change, felt that it could be implemented only over a long period.[80] But in spite of its apparent recognition of the need to elevate the status and increase the use of native languages, the U.N.P. made little effort to do so. Because of this neglect, a mass social group became increasingly alienated from the U.N.P.

The movement to replace English as the official language became more militant and more of a Sinhalese nationalist movement. After 1952 especially, less was heard of replacing English with Sinhalese and Tamil, and the demand for "Sinhala only" became more vocal; this demand was of particular importance to the Sinhalese intelligentsia who had to compete with the more energetic Tamils for government jobs. At a rally of the All-Ceylon Congress of the Sama Samajist Youth League in January, 1955, Philip Gunawardena opened the appeal for the institution of Sinhalese as the only official language and the use of Tamil as a regional language in Tamil areas.[81] Right after this, Bhasa Peramunas formed to agitate for the adoption of Sinhalese as the official language. These groups combined into the All-Ceylon Bhasa Peramuna, while in the up-country area the Kandyan National Assembly organized the Tri Sinhale Jatika Peramuna.[82] So popular had the "Sinhala only" policy become by 1956 that both the U.N.P. and M.E.P. had to adopt it as a main campaign issue.

The demand for "Sinhalese only" was the main unifying element in the campaign of the traditionalists for greater recognition and higher status. The idea appealed to both the Sinhalese elite and the Sinhalese masses—to the former because of the career opportunity its adoption would provide, and to the latter because Sinhalese was their idiom and its use would facilitate their relations with the public services, among other things. It united the Kandyan and the low-country Sinhalese and came to symbolize the traditionalist revolt against the impositions of the West. It was the unifying issue of the whole militant protest of this group, which by 1956 had become the majority social element.

The U.N.P. had alienated other groups, as well. Unemployment was mounting, and in 1956 over 100,000 persons were registered as unemployed, only 8,485 of whom were eventually placed in jobs.[83] The end of the Korean war had depressed the rubber industry, the prosperity that the war had brought was over, and the cost of living had risen for everyone. A depression began to settle in. The situation was made worse by the shortage of public facilities, mass poverty, and the tremendous population increase that occurred in Ceylon as malaria was eradicated.[84] The U.N.P. appeared almost apathetic about these problems and was unwilling to introduce any relief measures that might increase taxation of its wealthy supporters. The Westernized population also was becoming disenchanted with the U.N.P., and the usually pro-U.N.P. press was more and more apprehensive about what it saw as the dictatorial tendencies of its rule.[85] There was discontent among government employees, especially after Sir John restricted their union activity and informed them that they could not strike against the Government.[86] It was becoming evident to all that the time had come for a change.

To all these discontented citizens, the M.E.P. made an appeal. Its ideology and program was as wide as the majority social base that it hoped to attain. To an extent, its attempt at mass appeal was organizational. Its organization included three parties that together represented the main ideological streams in Ceylonese society. The V.L.S.S.P. provided a Marxist base that appealed to the Leftist intelligentsia and working class. In addition, it had extensive trade union connections that would help organize the labor vote behind the M.E.P. And it had been at the forefront of the "Sinhala only" movement, and the indigenous brand of socialism that its ideology expressed was based on, and articulated, the traditional values that the emergent Sinhalese and Buddhist nationalism incorporated. The Bhasa Peramuna confirmed the M.E.P.'s dedication to "Sinhala only," for it was a coalition of associations that had emerged to agitate for the language change. The S.L.F.P. of Bandaranaike was itself an inclusive party. Its members ranged from Marxists to conservative representatives of the peasants and private capital. It also attracted middle-class intelligentsia and Westernized social elements disenchanted with the U.N.P. The S.L.F.P., like the U.N.P., expressed Western values and was dedicated to the maintenance of Western-style political structures and traditions, so that people felt they could trust the S.L.F.P., and especially Bandaranaike, to set things straight in Ceylon without a revolution. But the S.L.F.P. also appealed to Buddhists and traditionalists. After all, it had been Bandaranaike who had formed the S.M.S. in the 1930's to articulate the interests of this group, and the S.M.S. was the founding organization out of which the S.L.F.P. had come. Bandaranaike had a long history of association with the Kandyan and traditionalist element. In short, his adherence augmented or substantiated the M.E.P.'s credentials as the organization most dedicated to a traditionalist-oriented nationalism. And other notables, like Iriyagolle, also helped to confirm this. Thus the M.E.P. was organizationally well equipped to mobilize the support of the masses.

Its manifesto had a programmatic appeal that was as attractive to the masses as was its organization. While it promised the fullest freedom of worship and conscience to all and accepted the position that there should be no discrimination on religious grounds, the manifesto stated that it "generally approved" the recommendations of the Report of the Buddhist Commission of Enquiry. On the language issue, the manifesto of the M.E.P. said, "Immediate provision must be made . . . declaring Sinhalese to be the only official language of the country and immediately thereafter the necessary steps taken for the implementation of this provision." Later, during the campaign, Bandaranaike promised to make Sinhala the official language within forty-eight hours, while the U.N.P. stated that it would require from two to three years.[87] In regard to Kandyans, the M.E.P. pledged itself to an extensive program of development to ameliorate the poor conditions in which the peasants had to live. The manifesto included planks designed especially to appeal to all discontented groups. It promised a neutralist foreign policy divorcing Ceylon from any association with power blocs, the removal of British bases, preparation of a plan for economic development, adjustment of the tax structure to relieve the poor, reductions in the price of rice and sugar, support for the indigenous medical profession, a reorganization of "the system of education to meet to the fullest the spiritual, cultural, social and economic needs of the country," public health and housing schemes, old-age pensions and unemployment insurance, the intensification of land cultivation and the opening up of uncultivated lands, village expansion schemes for the landless, the progressive nationalization of "all essential industries including foreign-owned plantations, transport, banking and insurance," the repeal of repressive legislation, and the granting of full trade union rights to public servants. There were as many contradictory elements here as in the wide-based organization of the M.E.P. and its association with its Marxist allies. To an extent its manifesto was irresponsible because of this, and also because some of its promises seem hardly capable of realization, at least in a short period. But it gained popular support, and this was its purpose.

These are the reasons behind the "silent revolution" of 1956.[88] The disorganization of the U.N.P. was accompanied by the organization of the opposition forces. The social base that the U.N.P. alienated looked elsewhere for leadership, and the M.E.P provided it. As a result, a competitive party system was realized.

GOVERNMENT AND OPPOSITION, 1956–60

The M.E.P. was returned with a numerical majority conducive to the establishment of a stable government. However, as in the case of the U.N.P. from 1952 to 1956, while the formation of a government was easy, the maintenance of its cohesion was not. The M.E.P. had a majority in its own right. It had won 51 seats, and the 6 appointed members raised its total to 57. In addition, several independents joined the government parliamentary party, and both the L.S.S.P. and the C.P. promised to support the Government in the enactment of "progressive legislation." It thus enjoyed a stable parliamentary position. Careful dispensation of cabinet posts was dictated by the coalition character of the M.E.P. Men and organizations of power and influence had to be satisfied, and recognition had to be given to the various shades of opinion and ideology that the coalition incorporated. Bandaranaike assumed the posts of Prime Minister and Minister of Defense and External Affairs. W. Dahanayake, leader of the Bhasa Peramuna, took the post of Minister of Education, and the leader of the V.L.S.S.P., Philip Gunawardena, was made Minister of Agriculture. Another member of the V.L.S.S.P., P. H. William de Silva, became Minister of Industries and Fisheries, thus giving the more radical socialist section of the M.E.P. a powerful voice in directing the economic policy of the Government. R. G. Senanayake, who had become an independent associate of the M.E.P., was made Minister of Commerce and Trade, a post he had held in the former U.N.P. government. The other portfolios went to the S.L.F.P. Thus, of the 14 cabinet posts, 2 went to the V.L.S.S.P., 1 to the B.P., 1 to an Independent-M.E.P., and 10 to the S.L.F.P., which in its own dispensation of portfolios had to recognize its various wings and powers. Of the 13 posts as parliamentary secretary, 2 were given to independent associates of the M.E.P., 1 to the B.P., and 10 to the S.L.F.P. The Cabinet thus united the leadership of the M.E.P., and all of the various ideological streams represented by the M.E.P. were joined there.

The Opposition was numerically and operationally impotent. The size of its bloc of 38 seats was deceptive, as a large section of it had pledged itself to co-operation with the Government. Originally, both the C.P. and the L.S.S.P. had aspired to positions in the Cabinet, as they had not expected the M.E.P. to be returned with a majority. When this ambition was frustrated, they decided to support the Government. The C.P. adopted a resolution to "extend its support to the new Government in all measures designed to strengthen independence, extend democracy and better the conditions of the people."[89] However, it differed with the M.E.P. over language policy and announced that in spite of its support it would continue to fight for the protection of minority rights. The L.S.S.P passed a resolution stating that it would sit in the Opposition, from where it would "follow a policy of responsive cooperation aimed at ensuring the effective and complete implementation of the M.E.P.'s announced program of amelioration measures."[90] The L.S.S.P. then presented the M.E.P. with an eleven-point program, which it hoped the Government would introduce.[91] One week after this, N. M. Perera, the head of the L.S.S.P., was elected Leader of the Opposition and head of a "shadow cabinet" consisting entirely of L.S.S.P. members.[92] Thus, of the 38 members of the Opposition, 17, including the Leader of the Opposition, gave notice of co-operation with the Government.

The eight U.N.P. members in the Opposition were reduced to six when two of them crossed the floor to the Government within a year of the election.[93] The U.N.P. was isolated within the Opposition, for the communal discord that had arisen prevented its co-operation with the F.P., and the anti-U.N.P. attitude of the Marxist parties had become extreme. At the first meeting of the Opposition the U.N.P. walked out because of criticisms of it made by the C.P. After that there was an attempt to prevent U.N.P. members from attending future meetings of the Opposition, but N. M. Perera held that all members of the Opposition had a right to attend its meetings.[94] One week later one independent and three C.P. members walked out of an opposition meeting because U.N.P. members were present.[95] In fact, there was more division within the Opposition than between the Government and the Opposition. The Opposition could muster only seventeen votes on a "regret motion" to the first speech from the throne, and in answer to the budget speech N. M. Perera said that, while great differences divided the two sides of the House, there was also a great feeling of goodwill toward the Government. He promised that any criticisms by the L.S.S.P. would be constructive and would be made with the intent of urging the Government to move on with the enactment of its program.[96]

Gradually, however, co-operation between the Government and the Marxist parties broke down, and members of the Opposition began to work together. The L.S.S.P. was the first to withdraw support from the Government. In May, 1957, the party adopted a resolution announcing a major revision in strategy: it had decided to oppose the M.E.P. and act as an alternative Government.[97] Many members of the L.S.S.P. had never fully accepted the decision of their leaders to follow a policy of "responsive co-operation" with the M.E.P. The radical wing, led by Edmund Samarakkody, had strongly opposed that policy and had refused to follow the party line. Within a year of the election several things occurred that strengthened this view in the party and ultimately led to a change in the strategy of the L.S.S.P. First, the M.E.P. enacted the portion of its manifesto with which the L.S.S.P. agreed and that had been an essential factor in L.S.S.P. support of the Government. Second, the right wing of the M.E.P. emerged as the main power center of the coalition, and there was a consequent modification of the M.E.P.'s original plans for extensive nationalization of industries and services. Both of these events severely limited the common-policy basis for co-operation between the L.S.S.P. and the Government. In addition, conflict between the trade unions of the M.E.P. and those of the L.S.S.P. had broken out, and the increase of communal tension throughout the island had confirmed the view held by the L.S.S.P.'s radical wing that support for the M.E.P. would hamper the development of the class struggle by submerging it beneath communal hatred. In June, 1957, the L.S.S.P. introduced a motion of regret in answer to the throne speech and confirmed its policy of total opposition to the Government.[98]

The C.P. continued its policy of support and expressed confidence in the "progressive orientation" of the Government, although its regretted the slowing down of its nationalization program and its failure to end communal discord.[99] This statement reflected the decision that the C.P. had made to come out in full support of the Government by leaving the opposition benches and forming an independent group in the House.[100] In a pamphlet, *Defend and Carry Forward the Gains of April 1956,*[101] the C.P. explained its decision as due to fear that "reactionary forces" were working themselves back into power. There was a resurgence of U.N.P. strength as evidenced by the comeback it had made in local elections. In addition, a split between the right and left wings had developed in the M.E.P., and the enactment of its progressive policy had been retarded. The C.P. condemned the "sterile opposition" of the L.S.S.P. and sought to strengthen the Leftist elements in the M.E.P. by offering its full support to the effort to implement the M.E.P. program. The C.P. continued its support of the Government until June, 1959. By then the M.E.P. had ousted its Marxist wing, and power had passed to the more conservative elements. At this point the C.P. ended what it then called its policy of "critical support" and went back into the Opposition.[102]

The weakness of the Opposition was to some extent compensated for by the fact that the power of the M.E.P. was limited by antagonisms and conflicts within its own ranks. For a short time these were contained, and the M.E.P. worked well as a government. In its first year it suffered only four defections. In the main, they were due to personal disaffection or disappointment, and none reflected any serious schism in the M.E.P. Two of the defectors were language extremists who resigned from the Government because of what they considered to be unwarranted concessions to the Tamils.[103] In December, 1956, the lone member of the Labour party resigned, condemning the Government as "inconsistent and unenlightened."[104] The fourth defector was I. M. R. A. Iriyagolle, who was disgruntled from the beginning, when he was made a parliamentary secretary rather than given a portfolio.[105] When Bandaranaike would not consent to a cabinet appointment, he resigned and went into the Opposition.[106]

The initial ability of the M.E.P. to work as a cohesive unit was due to its emphasis on common objectives. The first year and a half of its rule was its most productive period. The Port (Cargo) Corporation Bill was passed, putting the port facilities under state ownership, and the buses were nationalized as a result of the passage of the Motor Transport Bill. The State Industrial Corporation was created to set up state enterprises, and the National Planning Council was established to work out a systematic scheme for the economic development of Ceylon. The working class benefited from legislation giving more rights to trade unions, a workmen's compensation bill that extended insurance benefits to more workers, and the Wages Board Ordinance, which permitted unions to file suit for wages due their members. A policy of "dynamic neutralism" replaced the pro-Western foreign policy of the U.N.P., relations with the Soviet Union and China were established, and restrictions on the importation of Communist literature were lifted. The Department of Indigenous Medicine was set up, and the Official Languages Bill was passed, making Sinhala the official language. Most important, the Paddy Lands Bill of Philip Gunawardena was passed, establishing credit facilities for peasants and providing security of tenure for tenant cultivators.

But after this, tension began to appear, and by late 1957 the M.E.P. had become, as one M.P. put it, "a Government composed of people who are pulling in different directions." [107] Bandaranaike had never intended his Government to be a radical one that would introduce extensive, revolutionary changes. He also had no intention of making any fundamental changes overnight. He admitted after the election that the M.E.P. victory signaled a peaceful revolution, but he recognized that he had to work within a parliamentary structure and that the machinery of democracy inevitably slows things up.[108] Because of this, he said, the Government would have to go slowly in the implementation of its social and industrial plans.[109] The Minister of Finance, Stanley de Zoysa, said that the M.E.P. had not come into office "by any kind of revolutionary upheavals such as they [the Marxist opposition] contemplate." The M.E.P. come into power through the free votes of the people, he continued, "and our purpose is to adapt the opportunities that now present themselves to us within the existing framework and ultimately to alter the framework by democratic methods."[110] There was in Ceylon, he went on, a large middle class that also must live.[111] Later he defined the ideology of the Government as "democratic socialism,"[112] which he saw as meaning a great deal of private enterprise, a limited entrepreneurial role for the state as a main, but not the exclusive, agency for development,[113] a limited program of nationalization that never involved "expropriation without compensation,"[114] and a "sympathetic response to the legitimate aspirations of the working class," as long as its wage demands were realistic and its strikes not politically inspired.[115] Bandaranaike described the economic policy of the M.E.P. as being similar to that of the U.N.P.—with the vital difference, he said, that the M.E.P. would implement it.[116] There was to be no revolution. The Government had gone as far as it was going to go and there would be no further concessions to the radical wing that wanted a rapid transition to a socialist state in which all major services and industry, including plantations, were state owned.

By 1958 the ideological differences in the M.E.P. and the personal antagonisms that were to an extent based on these differences began to appear openly. Conflict between Marxists and conservatives took place within both the Cabinet and the organization of the S.L.F.P. At the Sixth Annual Conference of the S.L.F.P. in February, 1958, a group led by three cabinet ministers, C. A. S. Marikkar, Stanley de Zoysa, and C. P. de Silva, was formed to purge the party of its Communist element and to save "this country from the Marxists."[117] A joint secretary of the S.L.F.P. resigned his post because of the Communist element in the party,[118] and the Minister of Health walked out of a meeting of the Executive Committee because S. D. Bandaranayake, a Marxist, was elected president of the Youth League.[119] Later, C. A. S. Marikkar publicly stated that Philip Gunawardena,

Minister of Agriculture and the leading Marxist in the Cabinet, should resign.[120] In his turn, Gunawardena admitted that a clash had occurred in the Cabinet between "the forces of progress and the forces of reaction." [121] This conflict was the most serious that had developed so far, and a rupture was prevented by Bandaranaike's efforts to maintain unity and the Cabinet's acceptance of a "code of conduct." [122]

But a break was inevitable. The Marxist element suffered its first casualty when S. D. Bandaranayake was expelled from the Government in July, 1958, because of his anti-Government actions and speeches.[123] One month later, C. R. Beligammana was expelled because of his refusal to support the Reasonable Use of Tamil Bill.[124] The Government was crumbling, as social and communal extremists became discontented with the moderate policy that the Government was now pursuing in all areas. In April, 1959, conflict had reached such a point that Prime Minister Bandaranaike warned the Cabinet that the Government would collapse if ministers continued to attack each other publicly.[125] But the right wing knew it was the power center of both the S.L.F.P. and the M.E.P., and it had become convinced that Gunawardena was attempting to establish a dictatorship pivoting about his own ministry. In May, ten ministers led by Dahanayake and De Zoysa demanded the resignation of Gunawardena and informed Bandaranaike that they would not attend any more cabinet meetings if Gunawardena were present.[126] To avoid a crisis, Bundaranaike shifted some departments under the authority of the Minister of Agriculture, most importantly, the Co-operatives Department, to ministries controlled by more conservative ministers.[127] One day later, at the Seventh Annual Conference of the S.L.F.P., Bandaranaike announced his own disassociation from the Marxist element in both the M.E.P. and the S.L.F.P.[128] As a result, Gunawardena and the V.L.S.S.P. bloc resigned from the coalition the next day.[129] Gunawardena explained his decision as caused by the transfer of his authority to other ministries and the basic ideological cleavage that existed in the Cabinet and that would impair his ability to work in it.[130] P. H. William de Silva mentioned departmental relocation as the immediate issue and ideological differences as the basic one.[131]

The fracture ended the Government's majority and resulted in a greater unity within the Opposition. The loss of the V.L.S.S.P. bloc transferred 6 votes from the Government to the Opposition.[132] One day later, 6 members of the S.L.F.P. "Forward Bloc" crossed the floor into the Opposition.[133] This gave the Government a total of 46 members, including the 6 appointed members. The Opposition had a potential of 54. Negotiations and a cabinet re-shuffle caused a shift of some members back to the S.L.F.P., and by the end of the month the division stood at 49 to 49, not counting 3 members absent from the House for a prolonged period.[134] One day later Hugh Fernando left the Opposition and rejoined the Government, and the Government had a majority of 2. The fact that the Government had to depend on the appointed bloc for its majority led to an opposition demand for it to resign, on the grounds that it had no "moral authority" to rule. N. M. Perera argued that appointed members were not meant to prop up a minority government, or to be, in his words, "the six pillars on which the rotten edifice of a government . . . should be sustained."[135]

But the Government carried on. Its first test came on the "vote of thanks" in response to the throne speech in July. N. M. Perera, as Leader of the Opposition, presented a comprehensive motion of regret that was intended to topple the Government. The motion was defeated by a vote of 50 to 41, with 3 abstentions. The motion of thanks carried by a vote of 50 to 42.[136] The Government had survived, and its survival had not depended upon the votes of the appointed bloc. After this, Bandaranaike became adamantly anti-Communist, maintaining that "Marxist parties have no place in this country," as they could only come to power by revolutionary means.[137]

The assassination of Bandaranaike in September, 1959, removed the dominant personality and main cohesive force of the government party. For a long time it had been his efforts and his alone that had held the Government together. He had been the balance, like D. S. Senanayake in the U.N.P. government, the central force whose moderation had kept the extreme left and right wings of the M.E.P. from destroying its unity. His death saw the passage of power to W. Dahanayake, whose efforts on behalf of the right wing had ousted the Leftist forces from the M.E.P. He entered his office with the intention of governing. Parliament was suspended until October 27 because of the assassination. When it met again, N. M. Perera argued that a government dependent upon appointed members had no moral right to rule and lacked the confidence of the House.[138] Dahanayake admitted that he had no moral right to rule but argued that his was a caretaker government that was in office to help the country pass through the difficult period caused by the assassination. Publicly he announced his intention of carrying on the Government until its term expired in April, 1961. But his majority now depended upon the appointed bloc, since Perera's motion of no confidence had been defeated by a vote of 48 to 43. The Opposition now pressed for dissolution and a general election. Dahanayake suspended Parliament from October 30 to November 24 in an effort to rearrange his forces and rebuild the strength of the Government. However, there was dissension within its ranks, and a large section of the S.L.F.P. demanded dismissal of the Minister of Health and the Minister of Finance on suspicion of their implication in the assassination. On October 21 the Minister of Health resigned,[139] and on November 2 Dahanayake was informed that a bloc would resign if the Minister of Finance did not.[140] When the House met again, the Opposition introduced a motion of censure of the Minister of Justice because of his handling of the assassination investigation.[141] The Government survived by a vote of 46 to 45. Dahanayake now considered several courses of action, including prorogation, in an attempt to stay in office.

Aware of the growing popular unrest and the militant organization of opposition forces because of his attempt to maintain office, he finally decided on dissolution on December 5, 1959. Elections were to be held on the following March 19, and Parliament was to open again on March 30. The period of M.E.P. rule had come to an end.

The M.E.P. had come to power dedicated to the security and extension of democracy. In its campaign it had pledged the repeal of "repressive legislation" and the termination of the "dictatorial trend" that had set in during the latter years of the U.N.P. rule. The speech from the throne repeated these pledges, and in particular it referred to the repeal of the Public Security Ordinance.[1] But within a year the needs of government forced a reconsideration, and Bandaranaike began talking of amendment rather than repeal of the ordinance.[2] Yet the early period of M.E.P. rule did bring a welcome change. More time was alloted to Opposition debate in Parliament, the ban on the importation of Communist literature was lifted, and the Marxist parties felt more secure from police surveillance and interference. The mere fact of an alternative force being in power was a relief, and Bandaranaike's announcement that his approach would be reformist gave some assurance to those who feared a revolution.[3] Much more than before, the Government was composed of villagers and other persons close to the common people—men who, like the majority of Sinhalese, wore the indigenous costume and followed customs common to the traditionalist social group. It was a government with which the majority of the people could easily identify.

The Tamils, however, saw no hope, and had no faith, in the new government, in view of its language policy. This was no "people's government," one Tamil M.P. observed at the outset of its rule; it was a "Sinhalese people's government."[4] In May, 1956, the Federal party decided to launch a satyagraha, or passive resistance, campaign when the pending Official Languages Bill was introduced in the House of Representatives, in June.[5] On the day after the bill's presentation the leader of the F.P., S. J. V. Chelvanayakam, and other Tamils demonstrated in front of the House, and communal rioting broke out in Colombo, Batticaloa, and Gal Oya. The Government responded by calling out the volunteer forces of the army and banning meetings and processions. In July, under the inspiration of the F.P., the United Tamils Action Committee was set up to co-ordinate Tamil resistance and to agitate for an independent Tamil state. In the same month the F.P. led a peaceful protest march of four thousand people to its annual conference in Trincomalee,[6] at which meeting several civil disobedience campaigns were planned for the following months. As the provisions of the "Sinhala only" legislation began to be implemented, protests increased, and as the crisis deepened, the Government took repressive measures that stirred anger and alarm.

THE ANTIDEMOCRATIC TREND

Whatever might have been the case otherwise, the rise of communal discord led the M.E.P. to adopt measures that were not compatible with democratic procedure and tradition. The first indication of a trend in this direction was the announcement by the S.L.F.P. on May 26, 1957, that it intended to build a 100,000-man force attached to its organization to counter the disobedience campaign that the F.P. was planning for August, and to help keep the peace between Tamils and Sinhalese.[7] This led to a wave of fear and criticism. Dudley Senanayake condemned it as being the formation of a "political army" and a "threat to democracy."[8] In the House a motion was introduced condemning the recruitment of a private volunteer force by the S.L.F.P. and other "undemocratic and unconstitutional activities of the Government."[9] The press was very apprehensive. "We opposed proposals for private armies when the United National Party was in power," the *Morning Times* commented, "because private armies are the beginning of fascism." The *Ceylon Observer* asked, "What assurance is there that this volunteer force will be disbanded when peace is restored?" The *Ceylon Daily News* noted that "to preserve law and order in a democratic country is the responsibility of the State, not of any political party—even the party in power. For a party to attempt to usurp this function even on the plea of assistance is an action whose consequences may well be destructive of law and order itself." And in London, the *Times* cited the inevitable dangers implicit in the rise of a "political army." [10]

The U.N.P. argued that this was one of several signs that the M.E.P. was moving toward the establishment of a totalitarian regime. Dudley Senanayake pointed to the Government's use of Radio Ceylon for "party propaganda" [11] and its banning of a U.N.P. protest march to Kandy as further evidence. [12] In the House, N. M. Perera introduced a motion of no confidence because the Government dissolved the Colombo Municipal Council after an election had returned a U.N.P. majority. The people, he said, voted for the U.N.P., and their verdict should be allowed to stand. [13] There were other disturbing signs. Colvin R. de Silva complained that the Government did not provide a quorum in the House on private member days, [14] and Pieter Keuneman was troubled by the fact that the Government refused to support any bill introduced by a member of the Opposition. [15]

Bandaranaike realized the seriousness of the growing communal discord and the need for some kind of an arrangement to satisfy the Tamils. In July, 1957, after long and interrupted negotiations, he reached agreement with Chelvanayakam in what became known as the Bandaranaike-Chelvanayakam Pact. [16] Among other things, the pact promised that Tamil was to be recognized as the language of the national minority, and while the rights of the Sinhalese were not to be impinged upon, Tamil was to become the language of administration in the Northern and Eastern provinces. This concession led to the organization and agitation of Sinhalese extremist groups, such as Mettananda's Sinhala Jatika Sangamaya, the Sinhala Basha Peramuna of K. M. P. Rajaratna and F. R. Jayasuriya, and the Sinhala Jatika Bala Mandalaya, all of which opposed concessions and called for hartals in protest. The Working Committee of the United National party demanded abrogation of the pact,[17] and Dudley Senanayake referred to it as "an act of treachery."[18]

Bandaranaike bent under this extremist pressure, and on April 10, 1958, he announced the abrogation of the pact.[19] Some communal fighting broke out, and the F.P. announced its adoption of the "method of non-violent civil disobedience."[20] Fights quickly turned to rioting, and in a short time Tamil and Sinhalese mobs were killing each other in Colombo and other areas. On May 27, 1958, the Governor-General proclaimed a state of emergency.[21] Bandaranaike had not consulted the Opposition before having the state of emergency proclaimed, and N. M. Perera criticized him for this as well as for his handling of the whole language question.[22] Bandaranaike explained that there had been no time for consultation, that the actions of the F.P. were responsible for the rioting, and that any government coming to power in 1956 "would inevitably have been faced with these gathering storm clouds."[23] Under the state of emergency a number of regulations were issued by the Governor-General without parliamentary sanctions. A Competent Authority was established to censor the press, strikes and meetings of trade unions were prohibited, all public meetings were prohibited, martial law was proclaimed, and the F.P. and the Jatika Vimukthi Peramuna (J.V.P.), a Sinhalese extremist party, were proscribed. Arrests were made, and the F.P. members of the House and other leaders were taken into custody. In addition, power passed into the hands of the Governor-General, not only formally but also actually. Bandaranaike seemed incapable of running the affairs of state, and Sir Oliver Goonetilleke took over the task of leadership in the crisis. This led one M.P. to observe that the rule of Parliament was being "seriously infringed."[24] The measures that had been taken, he argued, had "enthroned a Governor-General's government." [25] The criticism by the Opposition of Bandaranaike's actions led him to challenge its loyalty. While he admitted that in a parliamentary system it is the role of the Opposition to criticize, he argued that in party systems "party interest often outweighs national interest." [26]

At this time the Tamil Language Bill, providing for the "reasonable" use of Tamil, was introduced in the House. The L.S.S.P. members refused to attend because the F.P. members were not present and the Tamils were not represented. [27] The U.N.P., the T.C., and some independent members joined the walkout, and the bill passed with hardly any opposition.

After the rioting had been quelled, the efforts of the Opposition were bent toward repeal of the state of emergency. It appeared that the Government was unnecessarily prolonging the emergency and was perhaps continuing it to conceal an attempt to consolidate a one-party regime. N. M. Perera alluded to this in several no-confidence motions that he introduced. [28] He asked for the repeal of all regulations issued under the Public Security Act and cited the failure of the Government to end the emergency and restore democratic rights as evidence of a totalitarian trend. Pieter Keuneman accused the Government of using its emergency powers unfairly and of continuing the emergency when there was no longer a need for it. The Government rejected all proposals. [29]

The Government did, however, repeal some of the emergency regulations shortly after their issuance. In September, 1958, the ban on political meetings was lifted except for those of proscribed parties. [30] On September 5 the Tamil M.P.'s were released from detention, although their parties were still proscribed. [31] And finally, on October 27, the ban on the two parties was lifted. [32] Other regulations, however, were continued, and it was not until March 14, 1959, that the emergency was declared over. There is no doubt that the nearly ten-month state of emergency was useful to the Government. The M.E.P. was torn asunder by conflict within itself and was finding the conduct of government increasingly difficult. An emergency situation encouraged cohesion and enabled the M.E.P. to avoid confrontations over the policies and personal differences that divided it. Then too, Bandaranaike may genuinely have feared the uniting of his left wing and the Marxist opposition in an attempt to take over political power. The Trotskyist parties had issued a call for a one-day hartal in February, 1959, in protest against the Public Security Ordinance, and the Indian trade unions threatened to come out in support of the hartal. This provided an excuse for extending the emergency for another month, during which time the army was alerted for possible action. Because of a fear of revolution, Bandaranaike had the police stationed in the House of Representatives, and on one occasion they cleared the galleries and forcibly removed the Leader of the Opposition.[33]

Either because Bandaranaike had decided that both the communal and the Marxist danger had passed, or because dissension in his own government compelled him, he lifted the emergency in March. Then came the breakup of the M.E.P. and the prorogation of Parliament from May 8 to May 26 and again from the end of May to the end of June, as Bandaranaike sought to reorganize a majority, and finally the assassination of Bandaranaike in September. The assumption of leadership by Dahanayake and his effort to stay in office led to further tensions and crises. The Opposition accused him of unduly extending the state of emergency proclaimed after Bandaranaike's assassination. Pressure from the Opposition and dissension in the Cabinet turned Dahanayake from his original course of action, and in December the emergency was lifted and Parliament was dissolved.

But the crisis had not passed: few people were convinced that the election would be held as promised, and many feared an imminent revolution. On January 20, 1960, Dahanayake established a Ministry of Internal Security. It was set up, he said, because he had intercepted a letter directed to the youth league of the L.S.S.P. instructing it to prepare for "direct action."[34] The Opposition felt that this was the first step in Dahanayake's attempt to set up a dictatorial rule, and on January 21, 1960, the opposition parties called an all-party conference to consider the implications of the internal security establishment.[35] At the conference the parties warned the Government not to postpone the elections and issued an appeal to the armed forces, police, and civil service not to carry out any illegal orders.[36] Dahanayake accused the Marxist parties of taking action to prevent the election, and both the Opposition and the press saw this as a possible excuse for undemocratic action planned by Dahanayake.[37] He refused to permit strikes and warned the unions that if they did strike, he would use the army to do their jobs. "Strikes," he argued, "were justified under the British occupation but now that the Government has passed into our own hands strikes are tantamount to rebellions against the Government."[38] Later he promised that he would "drive out the Communist plague from Ceylon"[39] and that in a year's time he would wipe out the L.S.S.P., the C.P., and the M.E.P.[40] As the election approached, Dahanayake alerted the army and threatened to station it throughout Ceylon during polling. There was relief when he subsequently changed his mind. On March 19 the elections went off as scheduled, and another challenge to the survival of the party system was overcome.

THE ELECTIONS OF 1960

There had been several constitutional changes since the last election. The voting age had been lowered from 21 to 18. It was expected that this would increase the number of votes for radical parties. In addition, the Ceylon Constitution (Amendment) Bill of 1959 had increased the number of electoral districts to 145, returning 151 members because of the retention of multimember districts. These changes, in combination with the confusion of events prior to the election, resulted in a large number of candidates running for election in March. The lack of no-contest pacts was also a factor. The attempt at unity between the C.P. and

L.S.S.P. had broken down,[41] and although the C.P. promised to support any strong leftist government,[42] it was not prepared to enter an electoral alliance. There was talk of a coalition between the S.L.F.P. and the U.N.P., but this ended when Dudley Senanayake announced his refusal to associate with a "murderous party."[43] Thus there were 899 candidates for the 151 seats, an average of nearly 6 per seat. Of these, 167 were independents, the rest belonging to the 23 political parties recognized by the Commissioner of Elections.

The mushroom growth of parties was related to the organizational breakup of the M.E.P. and the consequent fragmentation of its social and predispositional base into units formed about personalities who articulated distinctive group-oriented policies. Most parties, therefore, were pressure-group parties, and most were formed under the leadership of personalities who had at one time broken from the M.E.P. The Jatika Vimukthi Peramuna of K. M. P. Rajaratna and F. R. Jayasuriya ran several candidates. Both leaders were language extremists who had left the M.E.P. in 1957 because it was contemplating concessions to the Tamils. Iriyagolle, after his resignation from the Government, had formed the Samajavadi Mahajana Peramuna (S.M.P. —"People's Socialist Front") and was running a number of candidates in an attempt to obtain a personal bloc of power in the House.[44] In July, 1958, after his expulsion from the S.L.F.P., S. D. Bandaranayake formed the Sri Lanka Janatha Socialist party,[45] which by 1959 had become the Bosath Bandaranayake party (B.B.P.).[46] C. R. Beligammana, who was expelled from the M.E.P. in 1958 for failing to support the Reasonable Use of Tamil Bill, formed the Sinhala Jatika Sangamaya (S.J.S.) in September, 1959. In August, 1959, the Udarata Peramuna (U.P.) emerged to contest all the seats in the Kandyan areas in an attempt to form a solid Kandyan bloc in the House of Representatives.[47] On the eve of the election, Mettananda, a Sinhalese extremist who previously had been engaged in the formation of communalist groups, organized the Dharma Samaja party

(D.S.P.).[48] And there were other less important parties, based only on personalities, that ran one or two candidates.

The large number of candidates was primarily due to the fact that five parties were contesting a majority of the seats and two others were contesting in the neighborhood of one-third. Only in 1956 had more than one party sought majority status. The U.N.P. hoped for a resurgence and ran 127 candidates, contesting seats in every province except the Northern. The S.L.F.P. competed in all provinces except the Northern and ran 109 candidates in expectation of gaining a majority. The L.S.S.P., which also had the support of 8 independents, made its first bid to become a major party, running 101 candidates. After the breakup of the M.E.P., Philip Gunawardena retained its name in the hope of developing it into a majority party. On the eve of the election he entered into a no-contest pact with Mettananda's D.S.P., and the two parties issued a joint manifesto.[49] They ran 89 candidates under the M.E.P. label. The Lanka Prajathantrawadi Pakshaya (L.P.P.) was formed by Prime Minister Dahanayake shortly before nomination day on January 4, 1960. He had resigned, and then had been expelled, from the S.L.F.P. in the preceding month. In the election, 101 candidates ran under the L.P.P. label. The C.P. for the first time made a considerable effort, running 53 candidates. Forty candidates ran under the label of Iriyagolle's S.M.P. Thus, of the 899 candidates vying for election, 527 were attached to potential majority parties and 93 others belonged to parties that aspired to major-party status.

There was no unifying theme or central issue in the election. As before, it was not a national election, for communal cleavage and antagonism resulted in the running of different parties in the Sinhalese and Tamil areas. In the Sinhalese areas each of the parties sought to convince the electorate of its legitimate claim to office, and much more than before, there was unity and cohesion in the campaigns of at least the major parties. Ceylon had come to the time of real party struggle. The U.N.P. was helped considerably by the fact that Dudley Senanayake had returned from retirement in February, 1957, to assume the presidency of the U.N.P. and assist in its reconstruction.[50] He would be the Prime Minister if the U.N.P. were returned to power. In the U.N.P. manifesto Senanayake stressed that he had assumed the leadership of what he considered to be the party "which offers the most favorable prospects of re-establishing the stability and unity of the nation." The U.N.P. made its claim to votes on the basis of the dedication and integrity of its leaders, and referred to its past record of government as proof of its ability to give stable and harmonious rule to Ceylon. It charged that the language policy of the M.E.P. government had unleashed "forces of disruption" and that the Government had become so preoccupied with the communal tension that ensued that "the problem of increasing the productive capacity of our nation became relegated to the background." The objective of the U.N.P., it continued, would be to solve this problem and "restore law, order and the stability which will make it possible to pay due attention to the development of the economy." The party was for the first time running under the ideology of "democratic socialism," which it had adopted at its conference in 1958.[51] It consisted of a pragmatic approach to the solution of social and economic problems. The U.N.P., Senanayake stated during the campaign, rejected the thesis that "the road to socialism is through state ownership." [52] In its approach there was room for private enterprise, state ownership and entrepreneurial initiative, and co-operative enterprise, whichever was most feasible and productive in a particular instance. The manifesto listed a number of measures the U.N.P. would introduce if it were returned. In the campaign the party warned that the S.L.F.P. was incapable of providing peaceful, stable government and that the M.E.P. would destroy religion if it came to power.[53] It informed the electorate that their choice was between Marxism and democracy.[54]

The S.L.F.P. attempted to profit from the popularity of its late leader. Bandaranaike had achieved a certain charisma, and while it had faded somewhat during his last years in office, it had been somewhat revived in the mass sympathy for his death. The manifesto of the S.L.F.P. stressed his virtues: that he opposed extremism and "lived for and worked for the political emancipation of the common man with economic and social justice to all." Under his administration, it continued, "the people of this country regained their self-respect, and the people should never forfeit this hard-won privilege, at the instance of either Rightwing or Leftwing parties." It then listed all the gains Ceylon had achieved, and promised the continuation of the socialist policy initiated by Bandaranaike. The program it promised to implement was not unlike that in the M.E.P. manifesto of 1956.[55] C. P. de Silva led the S.L.F.P. While he was known in the Kandyan area, he shared none of the national appeal that Bandaranaike had possessed. For this reason, and also because the S.L.F.P. had to convince the electorate that it, and not Gunawardena's M.E.P., was the heir of Bandaranaike, the party attempted to persuade Mrs. Bandaranaike to take part in the campaign. She refused to contest a seat, but she became patron of the S.L.F.P. and made speeches on its behalf. She identified herself with the party, and on more than one occasion exhorted the people to vote for the S.L.F.P. "in the name of my dead husband." [56]

The M.E.P. of Philip Gunawardena claimed responsibility for the progressive legislation that had been passed between 1956 and 1960, especially the Paddy Lands Act, which had been devised by Gunawardena. It argued that its program was designed "to establish by non-violent means a People's Government" oriented to the traditionalist values and the economic problems of the people. It stressed its commitment to a Sinhalese and Buddhist cultural revival and promised to take over the land and redistribute it among the people. In short, it argued that it was the only party that could provide a stable government that was truly nationalist and socialist.[57]

The L.S.S.P. manifesto asserted that it was generally accepted that the L.S.S.P. had "an incorruptible leadership of capacity and courage" and that all that remained was "to test out the

L.S.S.P. as a party in charge of the government of the country."
It claimed that L.S.S.P. leadership possessed the "best brains" of
any party leaders and argued that because the L.S.S.P. was organized on an intercommunal basis it was the only party that
could unite the nation. It criticized the scandal, communal discord, social unrest, "seeping corruption," unemployment, and
falling living standards that it said had come about as a result
of the M.E.P. government. The manifesto also promised to reduce
the price of rice, devise a definite program of development, and
solve other problems of Ceylonese society.[58] In the campaign,
however, the L.S.S.P. argued mainly against the reinstatement
of U.N.P. rule.

The L.P.P. of Dahanayake issued a hastily drawn manifesto
of twenty-two points dealing with various social and economic
problems. It espoused an ideology of "democratic socialism" not
unlike that of the U.N.P. and the S.L.F.P. It offered no radical
solutions, but the whole emphasis of Dahanayake's campaign was
on his promise to eradicate Communism if he were returned to
power. The S.M.P. of Iriyagolle ran on a platform that promised
to implement the report of the Kandyan Peasantry Commission
and localize the control of police, health, housing, and education
departments.[59] The C.P. ran on a socialist program, and in its
campaign it emphasized the fact that it now advocated "Sinhala
only."

The Tamil parties, the L.S.S.P., and the C.P. contested seats
in the Northern Province, and the Tamil parties, the L.S.S.P.,
the L.P.P., and the M.E.P. ran candidates in the Eastern. The
T.C. attempted a comeback, and eight candidates ran under its
label in the Northern Province. Its main theme was that the
F.P. was an extremist party that had weakened and divided the
Tamil people. It argued that "if the problems facing the Tamil
people cannot be solved under a unitary constitution, they can
much less be solved under a Federal constitution." It called for
a constitution based on equality of status for all communities on
"the principle of non-domination of minorities."[60] But the F.P.

was the main force in Tamil politics, especially after having led the Tamil reaction to the events of 1958. Its manifesto did not advance an economic or social policy, but stated that the F.P. would support any "progressive measures" introduced by any government. It said that the main objective of the F.P. was to strive "by non-violent methods of Satyagraha to achieve the conversion of the present Constitution of Ceylon from a unitary one to a federal one." It went on to list a number of other communally oriented measures it favored and concluded that it was "the only party working for the unity of the Tamil-speaking people without distinction of caste, creed or geography." A number of independents also ran in the Tamil areas, some of them under the label of minor personality parties.

The results of the election were indecisive, but they nevertheless produced and reflected several important trends and developments. The U.N.P., under the energetic leadership of the popular Dudley Senanayake, made a comeback. From 1956 to 1960 the U.N.P. had survived as a party because of its successes at the local level of politics, but 1960 brought it back as a vital political force nationally. The gloom of the 1956 disaster, which had led at least one member to leave a party that he considered "virtually dead and which did not enjoy the confidence of the people,"[61] had been dispelled. The U.N.P. had recovered, and its resurgence augured well for the stabilization of a competitive party system. The 50 seats that it won were not a majority, but the plurality they represented gave the U.N.P. a pivotal position in the construction of a government party. Its 908,996 votes also were a plurality. The S.L.F.P. suffered a setback, but the 46 seats and 648,094 votes that it won confirmed its position as a major party. Thus the results of the election sustained the growth of the party system into a bipolarized multiparty system capable, at least organizationally, of providing alternative governments. The electorate also rejected the attempts of new and third parties to reach major-party status. The L.P.P. of Dahanayake was routed. It received only 125,344 votes and won 4 seats. For the first time in his political career, Dahanayake lost his seat. The M.E.P. suffered a similar fate. It won 10 seats and captured 325,832 votes and thus lost its claim to major status. So did the L.S.S.P. It won only 10 seats and 322,352 votes. The S.M.P. was not even able to return its leader, and the hopes of the C.P. were crushed when only 3 of its 53 candidates won seats. All the other Sinhalese parties together won only 5 seats, and their total vote was slightly over 100,000. The F.P. received its expected confirmation as the major Tamil force, winning 10 of the 12 seats it had contested in the Northern Province and 5 of the 6 in the Eastern. The Tamil Congress returned one member, and seven independents were successful. The results of the election thus were a resounding vote of confidence in the party system. Of the 151 members elected, 134 belonged to long-established parties.[62]

The construction of a government proved impossible. The task of forming one fell first to the U.N.P. because of its plurality. Dahanayake advised the L.P.P. members to support the U.N.P.,[63] and together with the appointed members they gave the U.N.P. a potential bloc of 60 seats, 19 short of a majority. During the campaign Senanayake had announced that he would not even consider entering a coalition government, especially with the S.L.F.P. After the election he reiterated this stand.[64] In spite of this, discussions took place, and it was reported that Sir John Kotelawala was trying to rally S.L.F.P. support for an anti-Marxist government.[65] This report was squelched the next day when the S.L.F.P. announced its refusal to consider any alliance.[66] Public negotiations were then carried on between the U.N.P. and the F.P. The F.P. had 15 members of its own and exercised a controlling influence over 5 others. An F.P.-U.N.P. coalition could therefore count on an 80-seat bloc. The demands that the F.P. made in return for its support went beyond what the U.N.P. could accept. Among other things, it wanted a federal constitution that provided for regional autonomy on a provincial basis, parity of status for the Tamil language, and the use of Tamil as the language of administration in the Northern and Eastern provinces.[67] It would have been political suicide for the U.N.P. to accept these demands, and as a consequence, negotiations broke down. Chelvanayakam said that he would not support the U.N.P. because of its previously anti-Tamil policy.[68]

It was evident from its failure to gain support that the U.N.P. government would fall at the end of the debate on the throne speech. The U.N.P. candidate for Speaker had been defeated, and a member of the Opposition was elected to the post by a vote of 93 to 60, with 1 abstention. Before the vote on the throne speech a leading U.N.P. member, J. R. Jayewardene, appealed for support on the grounds that the people were not ready for another election. He also asked the House if it could prefer an S.L.F.P. government supported by the Marxist parties when so many of the language and social policies of the two parties conflicted with each other.[69] But this was to no avail, and the motion of regret carried by a vote of 86 to 61, with 8 abstentions.[70] Two S.L.F.P. members voted with the U.N.P., one because the S.L.F.P. was "drifting" into an alliance with the Marxists.[71] Philip Gunawardena and six of his party members abstained. Three voted with the Opposition. On the recommendation of Dudley Senanayake, the Governor-General dissolved Parliament on April 23 and called for a new election.

A constitutional debate ensued because of the Governor-General's action in granting a dissolution on the basis of advice from a minority government. Dudley Senanayake had used the threat of dissolution to attract support to his government. He announced publicly that he would advise dissolution if the throne speech failed.[72] In the meantime, support to form an alternative government had rallied behind the S.L.F.P. The Opposition announced publicly that should the U.N.P. fail to carry a vote of thanks, then the Governor-General should call on the S.L.F.P. to form a government.[73] The M.E.P., which refused to support either an S.L.F.P. or a U.N.P. government, advocated an all-party "national government." [74] But the L.S.S.P., in spite of the opposition of its radical wing,[75] offered its support in the formation of an S.L.F.P. government.[76] Both the C.P.[77] and the F.P. also pledged support.[78]

The constitutional controversy turned on the question of whether the Governor-General should have accepted the advice of the Prime Minister to dissolve. Dudley Senanayake quoted Harold Laski to the effect that the Crown must accept the advice of the Prime Minister.[79] A member of the S.L.F.P. answered that according to Sir Ivor Jennings, the sovereign does not have to accept the advice of the Prime Minister if the Opposition is willing and able to form a government.[80] Senanayake retorted that there was no alternative government as the Opposition had no basis for unity.[81] The U.N.P. view was sustained by Lord Soulbury, a former Governor-General. He argued that if the Prime Minister advised dissolution the sovereign was "bound to accept his advice." [82]

It was true, however, that after the Governor-General received the advice of the Prime Minister, he consulted with opposition leaders on the possibility of the formation of an alternative government. It was after this that he dissolved Parliament. Except for the M.E.P., the entire Opposition signed a protest because it had been willing and able to form a government.[83] Many thought the Governor-General had involved his office in party politics and breached its impartial character; A. J. Wilson felt that he had involved himself in "an unconstitutional act." [84] But the verdict held, and a new election was set for July 20, 1960.

The central campaign issue and the arrangement of political forces was different in July. The major Sinhalese parties of the Opposition had come to another understanding with each other and had concluded a no-contest pact. The motivation behind the arrangement was the general anger at the U.N.P. for forcing dissolution and a common fear among opposition forces of a resurgent U.N.P. The conclusion of a no-contest pact was anticipated as early as May, when the C.P., the L.S.S.P., and the S.L.F.P. independently announced their intention of conducting their campaigns on a platform denouncing the U.N.P.[85] The C.P., which had the most fear of the U.N.P.'s return to power, was the driving force in the multiparty negotiations, although the S.L.F.P., because of its strength, would again be the pivot. At the initiative of the C.P., the S.L.F.P. appointed a committee to discuss a no-contest arrangement with both the C.P. and the L.S.S.P.[86] The M.E.P., because of Gunawardena's anger at his former associates in the S.L.F.P., refused even to consider a pact. There were also groups within the S.L.F.P., the L.S.S.P., and the C.P. who opposed any kind of interparty arrangement. The radical wing of the L.S.S.P. was adamant in this regard, as it considered any association with a bourgeois party an obstacle in the class struggle and a betrayal of working-class interests. The conservative wing of the S.L.F.P. was also adamant, and even before the conclusion of the pact ten of its youth league branches, together with the joint secretary of the Youth League, resigned from the party.[87] After the conclusion of the pact, C. A. S. Marikkar, a conservative minister in the former M.E.P. government, who had been active in the ejection of the left wing, resigned from the party.[88] And R. G. Senanayake, who had been so helpful to the M.E.P. in 1956, said he would limit his participation in the anti-U.N.P. campaign because he did not want to help the Marxists.[89]

Nevertheless, agreement was reached in less than a month. On May 5 it was announced that the S.L.F.P. would contest 103 seats, the L.S.S.P. between 18 and 20, and the C.P. 6.[90] A week later the S.L.F.P. and L.S.S.P. totals were changed to 108 and 17.[91] By election time this count had again been altered, and the S.L.F.P. wound up contesting 98 seats, the L.S.S.P. 21, and the C.P. 7. It had been difficulty in reaching a precise agreement on which seats each party would contest that had held up conclusion of the pact. But on May 14 the S.L.F.P. and the L.S.S.P. announced their agreement,[92] and three days later the C.P. announced its.[93]

But while agreement was reached in regard to the arrangement of constituencies in the anti-U.N.P. alliance, each party interpreted the implications of the agreement differently. N. M. Perera had announced prior to the agreement that he expected the next government to be formed by the S.L.F.P. on the basis of the L.S.S.P.'s support.[94] After the conclusion of the pact, Colvin R. de Silva said that both the L.S.S.P. and the C.P. would help the S.L.F.P. form a government.[95] In spite of pressure from its radical wing, the L.S.S.P. endorsed the pact with the expectation of actually participating in the next government. At the conference of the district representatives of the L.S.S.P. summoned in July to ratify the pact, it was resolved that the L.S.S.P. would accept office in an S.L.F.P. government if it met the minimum program of the L.S.S.P. This included nationalization of the export-import trade and insurance, and the take-over of "assisted schools," that is, the Catholic parochial schools.[96] The S.L.F.P., on the other hand, understood the agreement to be an electoral alliance only, designed to defeat the U.N.P.[97] The text of the pact substantiated this position. It stated explicitly that the S.L.F.P. entered into an electoral pact "in order to form an independent and stable government with an absolute majority in Parliament." Once the S.L.F.P. had elected a parliamentary majority, it had no intention of entering a coalition, and the purpose of the pact, as the S.L.F.P. understood it, was to provide for a no-contest arrangement and for mutual support against the U.N.P. in the election.[98]

The difference in interpretations of the agreement was obviously related to considerations of strategy and the particular needs of each party to the agreement. The S.L.F.P. was anxious to convince the electorate of its ability and intention to form a government without entering a coalition with the Marxist parties. Such a coalition would have antagonized large blocs of the social base of the S.L.F.P. and would have alienated the anti-Marxist wing of the S.L.F.P. to such an extent that a rupture might have occurred. The L.S.S.P. and the C.P., on the other hand, had an interest in convincing their social bases that they both stood a good chance of participation in the next government. Both parties had been in the opposition too long, and their members' ambitions for power had been frustrated. Not only were large blocs of the social base of these parties moving toward the S.L.F.P. because of its better chance for power acquisition and policy implementation, but some of their members as well were gravitating to the S.L.F.P. because of the greater opportunity for power that it offered. Thus it was to the advantage of these parties to portray themselves as possible coalition parties, in spite of the fact that such a move might alienate portions of their radical wings. Then too, both the C.P. and the L.S.S.P. anticipated an indecisive election. The no-contest arrangement, they expected, would not give the S.L.F.P. a majority but would return it as a plurality party dependent upon them to form a government. Many expected N. M. Perera to become Minister of Finance in such a government, and the U.N.P. went so far as to expect him to be made Prime Minister.[99]

The no-contest arrangement helped to limit the number of candidates who would contest the election in July. In addition, the March disaster of the parties that had mushroomed in anticipation of the first election of 1960 caused most of them to dissolve soon after the election. Those that survived contented themselves with their status as minor personality parties, and in July they contested only a limited number of seats. The electoral experience of March had shown that there was only room in Ceylonese politics for two major parties, and the bipolarized multiparty system that had evolved was confirmed. For the 151 seats, 393 candidates came forward, a reduction of 500 from the preceding election. Only two parties sought majority status. The U.N.P. contested 128 seats, and the S.L.F.P. competed for 98. The M.E.P. had learned little from its defeat in March and put forward a slate of 55 candidates, although this might be explained as an attempt to split the vote of the S.L.F.P. and its Marxist allies. The L.P.P. of Dahanayake, responding to its experience in March, ran only 6 candidates. The L.S.S.P. and the C.P., respectively, ran 21 and 7, and the J.V.P. ran 2. The F.P. had 21 candidates, and the T.C. attempted a comeback by running 8 candidates. In addition, there were 39 independents and 6 candidates of personality parties. The U.N.P. was the only party that contested seats in every province, although in the Northern Province it competed for only one seat. The communal cleavage that the events of 1956 had introduced into the party system was thus continued.

In the Sinhalese areas the parties ran on essentially the same platforms as they had in March, although the no-contest arrangement turned the election into a two-party contest that canalized all the issues into a choice between alternative governments. The U.N.P. again claimed that it was the only party that could form a stable government. It argued that the S.L.F.P. could not form a government without alliance with Marxist parties and that not only did such alliance exhibit fundamental policy conflicts, but it would eventuate in a Marxist take-over of the government.[100] Dudley Senanayake claimed that the S.L.F.P. was controlled by Marxists and that forty-five of its candidates were Marxists.[101] Because of this and the fact that an S.L.F.P. government would be backed by Marxist parties, Senanayake concluded that the country would be run by Marxists. The U.N.P. argument that the election was a choice between democracy and Marxism was echoed by the press.[102] The U.N.P. also tried to associate the S.L.F.P. with the F.P., a campaign issue it said it would stress from the beginning.[103] The U.N.P. charged that the S.L.F.P. had sold out to the F.P. by promising not to implement the "Sinhala only" policy. This charge stemmed from the secret negotiations that transpired between the S.L.F.P. and the F.P. after the March elections, and the consequent pledge of support that the F.P. gave to the S.L.F.P. in the formation of a government. The U.N.P. also challenged the ability of Madame Bandaranaike, who was now leading the S.L.F.P., to succeed as Prime Minister. It charged that she lacked political experience and was not competent to be the leader of the nation.[104] It also asked how she intended to carry out the policy of her late husband, a main campaign theme of the S.L.F.P., when even he himself had been unable to do so.[105] Finally, the U.N.P. expressed doubt as to whether she really intended to be Prime Minister, as, for one thing, she was not contesting a seat. It suggested that her candidacy was an electoral trick to influence votes and that if the S.L.F.P. won, then somebody else, most probably N. M. Perera, would be made Prime Minister.[106] On the positive side, the U.N.P. stressed that during its brief tenure in office it had lowered living costs and had reduced the price of rice.

The main change in the campaign of the S.L.F.P. was related to its leadership by Madame Bandaranaike. In May she became president of the S.L.F.P.,[107] and shortly thereafter the S.L.F.P. announced that if it formed the next government, Mrs. Bandaranaike would become Prime Minister. This time she took a more active part in the campaign and spoke in every constituency in which an S.L.F.P. candidate ran. Her appeal was mainly that she knew the thoughts of her husband better than anyone and that in office she would pursue the policy direction set by her husband. Sympathy for her was evident, and the S.L.F.P. hoped that she would attract the mass of female voters. In a press release issued by her nephew Felix Bandaranaike the S.L.F.P. clarified its previous manifesto. It stated that its main objective was the defeat of the U.N.P. It also announced revision of its educational policy. It promised to set up a nonsectarian educational system, establish a central authority to operate it, and "bring the entire system of education under a Central Authority." In tune with Buddhist demands, the S.L.F.P. said it would take over the assisted schools.[108]

The L.S.S.P. conducted its campaign on the basis of its expected participation in a coalition government. In a statement released as a supplement to its March manifesto, the L.S.S.P. explained its reasons for entering a no-contest pact. It defined the U.N.P. as the instrument of the capitalist classes and imperialism, and said, "The broad aim the party sets itself in this election is the defeat of the U.N.P. Government." This could best be done, it continued, through the "instrument of the S.L.F.P." Thus it concluded that "the replacement of the U.N.P. Government by an S.L.F.P. Government would constitute a step forward, and that accordingly the party would support such a Government." [109]

The C.P. ran under the same manifesto as before, although it now stressed the election of an S.L.F.P. government. The M.E.P., which no longer had the support of the D.S.P.,[110] claimed that it could form a government if it won 40 seats. The L.P.P., which now ran only 6 candidates, ideologically clarified itself as a party of the center.[111] There was hardly a contest in the Tamil areas. The F.P. ran 21 candidates in the Northern and Eastern provinces and was opposed by 10 candidates of the T.C., 2 of the C.P., 3 of the M.E.P., 2 of the L.S.S.P., 3 of the U.N.P., and 3 of the S.L.F.P. In the Northern Province 2 independents ran, and in the Eastern, 6. In the latter province, 2 ran under the label of the All-Ceylon Islam United Front.

The results of the election confirmed some patterns and characteristics of the gradually maturing party system. The F.P. further consolidated its command of the Tamil vote. In the Northern Province it took 10 of the 13 seats. Two independents and one member of the T.C. were also returned. The most important casualty was G. G. Ponnambalam, who was displaced from his traditional Jaffna seat by one of the independents. In the Eastern Province the F.P. won 6 of the 7 seats it contested, thus making a virtual sweep of the dominantly Tamil constituencies there. Two independents and two members of the S.L.F.P. also won. Thus the F.P. returned a bloc of 16 members and enjoyed a mandate from the Tamils sufficient to enable it to exercise a degree of leadership and control over the whole Tamil bloc in the House.

In the Sinhalese areas the no-contest arrangement turned the election into a choice between a U.N.P. and a non-U.N.P. government, ideologically a choice between conservative and progressive socialism. The no-contest pact worked extremely well, since only in the multimember Colombo Central constituency did the parties of the alliance clash. It was expected that competition from the M.E.P. would divide the leftist vote and help the U.N.P. The M.E.P. opposed candidates of the alliance for 55 seats, thus turning the election in their constituencies into a three-way contest between the U.N.P., the M.E.P., and a party of the alliance. The M.E.P. clashed with the S.L.F.P. in 41 constituencies, the L.S.S.P. in 10, and the C.P. in 2. However, its impact was minimal. Outside of the constituencies in which it won three seats for itself, the M.E.P. vote, had it gone to candidates of the S.L.F.P., the L.S.S.P., or the C.P., would have altered the results in only two constituencies. In Kolonna the M.E.P. vote helped defeat the L.S.S.P. candidate, and in Wattala it helped defeat the S.L.F.P. candidate. Both seats went to the U.N.P.

The results of the election indicated a clear two-party tendency among the electorate (a development discussed in Chapter 7). The S.L.F.P. was returned with an independent majority of 75 seats. Although the U.N.P. obtained a popular plurality, it won only 30 seats, a distortion that clearly indicated the significant electoral impact of the no-contest arrangements between the S.L.F.P. and the parties of the Left. The U.N.P. received 1,143,290 votes, while the S.L.F.P. obtained only 1,022,154. The Leftist parties returned a numerically powerful bloc, but internecine differences again prevented united bloc action. The L.S.S.P. returned 12 members, and the C.P. increased its seats to 4. Only 3 of the 55 M.E.P. candidates were returned, and again its ambition to reach major-party status was frustrated. The L.P.P. returned 2 members, the J.V.P. 2, and other minor parties none. Two independents won seats in the Sinhalese areas. One was an ex-member of the M.E.P. who had campaigned on a pro-S.L.F.P. platform and who won in the constituency of Horana, in the Western Province. The other won in the constituency of Katugampola, in the North Western Province. He had not been given the endorsement of the S.L.F.P. because he was opposing the Speaker of the House; after his election he rejoined the party. The rout of the independents was one sign of the trend toward party voting in Ceylon. Another was the large number of candidates who had to forfeit their deposits because they obtained less than one-eighth of the vote in their constituencies. Seventy-nine of the 393 candidates lost their deposits. Of these, 42 were members of the M.E.P., 4 of the L.P.P., and 2 of the T.C., and 26 were independents or minor-party candidates. The S.L.F.P., U.N.P., F.P., L.S.S.P., and C.P. each had only one candidate who lost his deposit. The established party pattern had been confirmed.

GOVERNMENT AND OPPOSITION, 1960–65

The election had returned an apparently strong S.L.F.P. government, although in time it would be weakened by inner conflicts. With the addition of the six appointed members, the S.L.F.P. had 81 seats. It also had the support of six independents[112] and the commitment of the C.P. and the L.S.S.P. to co-operate in implementing its progressive policies. The vote on the throne speech was an indication of the almost dictatorial majority that it initially enjoyed. On the vote of thanks the Government carried by a vote of 98 to 31, with 19 abstentions. The F.P. abstained, the C.P. and L.S.S.P. voted with the Government, and only the U.N.P. opposed it. The vote on the appropriations bill was similar. It carried by a vote of 94 to 32, with 16 abstentions. The contents of the throne speech and the appropriations bill, and the facility with which both passed, indicated that the Government was prepared to carry out its campaign promises. Prime Minister Bandaranaike, however, who had assumed an appointed seat in the Senate, was prompt to announce that her Government and its orientation were not to be Marxist. She explained that she was not a Marxist and that her intention was to carry out the policy of her late husband.[113] She interpreted the victory of the S.L.F.P. as a popular vote of confidence in the policy of her husband and an expression of the people's appreciation of his dedication to their interest.[114] In the throne speech she promised to follow a foreign policy of neutralism and nonalignment, to revise the Constitution to make Ceylon a republic, to take over the assisted schools, to take over newspapers published by the Times and by the Associated Newspapers of Ceylon, and to nationalize important areas of the economy. She announced that the Government would not nationalize estates and plantations, at least not at the moment.[115] In pursuance of this program the Government passed the Assisted Schools and Training Colleges (Special Provision) Bill; the Insurance Cooperation Bill, which set up a state insurance corporation; the Ceylon Petroleum Corporation Bill, which was followed shortly by the complete take-over of the petroleum industry; the Peoples Bank Bill, setting up a state bank; and other bills of interest to the voting bloc that had supported the S.L.F.P. The take-over of the press was postponed pending the report of a commission of inquiry. The Government had a mandate, and it intended to carry it out.

The Opposition was numerically strong but functionally weak. Again it was composed of antagonistic parties that found cooperation difficult, and in addition, a group that had been counted among the Opposition was supporting the Government. After the election the L.S.S.P. issued a press release announcing that it would "cooperate with the S.L.F.P. Government as an independent party in every activity which carries the country along progressive lines."[116] Its hopes for a coalition frustrated by the S.L.F.P. majority, the L.S.S.P. stated that it would not join the Opposition but instead would function as an independent group in Parliament. The aspirations of the C.P. to coalition had also been frustrated, and it adopted the same strategy as the L.S.S.P. Its leader informed the Government that it would have the full support of the C.P. as it moved toward the goal of socialism.[117] The U.N.P. was again an isolated group in the Opposition, since the other parties refused to co-operate with it. The F.P. refused to place itself under the Opposition Whip,[118] and the L.P.P. said that it would not recognize the U.N.P. as the official Opposition and would work with the Government in some ways in order to create political stability.[119] The M.E.P. was at first indecisive.[120] Finally it decided to support the Government in regard to progressive measures.[121] Thus the Opposition, as before, was fluid and unstable. As a leading member of the U.N.P. remarked, his party was the only opposition party in the House.[122]

But ruptures in the Government developed, accompanied by a growing unity in the Opposition, causing a shift in political forces that would precipitate the fall of the Government. Within a year of the elections the S.L.F.P. government was severely criticized at the Ninth Annual Sessions of the L.S.S.P. Youth League.[123] And in Parliament both the C.P. and the L.S.S.P. had become more critical of the Government, although they still refused to oppose it. Fear of the U.N.P. was the main reason. In November, 1961, for instance, N. M. Perera said that the main enemy of the L.S.S.P. was the U.N.P. and that his party would do everything in its power to prevent the U.N.P.'s resurgence.[124] At a conference of the Ceylon Trade Union Federation, the main trade union organization of the C.P., M. G. Mendis said that the C.P. was supporting the S.L.F.P. in order to prevent the U.N.P. from returning to power. Admitting that the S.L.F.P. government was not socialist, Mendis stated that "so long as it carried out progressive measures to which it was pledged" the C.P. would support it.[125]

It was inevitable that there should be a slowdown in the policy implementation of the Government. The S.L.F.P. still had its heavily weighted wings to balance, and the policy it enacted had to be the product of consensus and compromise among its elite and power centers. During its first year in office it implemented most of the program on which there was common agreement in its ranks, and even then fissures had appeared and defections had taken place. The time had ended when the S.L.F.P. could pursue a radical course. Then too, economic realities had to be faced. Ceylon did not have the capacity to finance many of the enterprises and schemes that the Government may have wanted to initiate, at least not immediately and certainly not on a broad scale. Development had to be slow and piecemeal, geared to the economic ability and potential of Ceylon. The Left could talk as it wished, but it was the S.L.F.P. that had to govern. Thus, in time the Left became disenchanted. Toward the end of 1961 Pieter Keuneman was saying that the peasants and workers must unite to push the Government along progressive lines,[126] and Colvin R. de Silva noted that the S.L.F.P. was following the same capitalistic path as the U.N.P.[127] The Government's left wing echoed this disenchantment, and Leftist-controlled unions again began strike activity. Conflict in the alliance became serious, and there was increasing talk of Leftist unity. Philip Guna-wardena issued a call to the C.P. and the L.S.S.P. "to align themselves with the progressive forces to set up a stable government."[128] Within a week talks toward this end began between the M.E.P. and the L.S.S.P.[129]

The Government had been faced with serious problems almost from the beginning of its rule. Its passage of the Language of the Courts Bill, which provided for Sinhalese to be the language used in court cases, aroused communal tensions to the point of crisis. On January 2, 1961, the F.P. held a one-day hartal protesting the bill, and in February it launched a satyagraha campaign in Jaffna. The Government sent troops into the Northern and Eastern provinces, and when negotiations with the F.P. broke down and communal tension increased, the Government proclaimed a state of emergency on April 18, 1961. The F.P. and the J.V.P. were again proscribed, and again several of the F.P. members of Parliament were detained. Except for the M.E.P., all the parties condemned the F.P. and blamed it for the disturbances.[130] As the tension subsided, the F.P. leaders were released. Some were freed in August, 1961, and by October all the M.P.'s had been released.[131] The F.P. threatened to take further action during the whole period of S.L.F.P. rule, but only token actions were taken.

During the emergency period the S.L.F.P. used its powers not only to contain communal conflict but also to restrict strikes. This

angered the Marxist leadership and helped accelerate its alienation from the Government. It also occasioned attempts at Leftist
unity. However, in January, 1962, a coup was attempted against
the Government by leaders in the armed forces. The attempt was
abortive, and the leaders were arrested. The result of the attempt
was to retard the movement of the Left away from its support
of the Government, because many regarded the coup as a rightist
plot to seize political power. In a press release the C.P. promised
full support to the Government in anticoup actions.[132] Later it
suspended its strike in the port areas so as not to weaken the
Government.[133] The conservative and radical wings of the L.S.S.P.
had opposing views on the situation. The radical group, led by
Edmund Samarakkody, accused the U.N.P. of being involved in
the coup.[134] The main body of the L.S.S.P. expressed fear that
the Government might use the coup as an excuse to establish a
military dictatorship.[135] N. M. Perera went so far as to charge
Felix Bandaranaike, the Finance Minister, with being implicated
in the plot.[136] However, the L.S.S.P. supported the treason bill
introduced to try the coup plotters, although it did so with the
understanding that the bill would apply to the current coup
only.[137]

The halt in the drift of the L.S.S.P. away from its support of
the Government was only temporary. In April, 1962, N. M. Perera admitted that it was the function of the Opposition to criticize
the Government.[138] In July the L.S.S.P. gave notice of its intention
to oppose the throne speech,[139] and for the first time since the
election the entire Opposition, except for the C.P., confronted
the Government with a vote of regret.[140] At its annual conference
a few weeks later, the L.S.S.P. resolved to oppose the "S.L.F.P.
Government's entire policies." It criticized it for extending the
emergency and discerned in its actions signs of "creeping totalitarianism."[141] The U.N.P. had much earlier accused the Government of the same tendency. Dudley Senanayake had charged
the Government with moving toward totalitarianism[142] and had
pointed to the take-over of the assisted schools and the intended

take-over of the press as unmistakable signs.[143] In answer to these charges, Felix Bandaranaike said that if it solved problems, he didn't mind a "little measure of totalitarianism."[144]

The C.P. was slower to move from its position of support. In the spring of 1962 Pieter Keuneman called for unity between the progressive wing of the S.L.F.P. and the Left.[145] Toward the end of the year the C.P. agreed to the request of the S.L.F.P. for a no-contest pact in local elections.[146] But a strategy change by the C.P. was indicated a month later when it issued a joint manifesto with the L.S.S.P. in the Colombo municipal elections.[147] It was around this time that Philip Gunawardena was trying to forge Leftist unity. In February, 1963, the C.P. agreed to work toward the realization of unity,[148] and one month later the central committee of the L.S.S.P. voted to engage in discussions with the other Marxist parties.[149] The movement for Leftist unity was not without its casualties. Several defections occurred in the M.E.P., and a section of the L.S.S.P. was incensed to the point of separating from the party. The so-called China wing of the C.P. split because of the negotiations and the parliamentary orientation that was one of the points of agreement. P. Kumarasiri, an extremist on the Politburo of the C.P., argued that "the only road to socialism is the revolutionary overthrow of the capitalist system and the establishment of the working class state."[150] However, negotiations proceeded, a joint secretariat was established, and on August 12, 1963, the United Left Front (U.L.F.) agreement was signed at a joint rally.[151] It appeared that after long years the unity of the Marxist Left had been re-established.[152]

The conclusion of the U.L.F. agreement came at about the same time that the left wing of the S.L.F.P. moved into a position of power in the party. The government had been able to remain remarkably cohesive throughout its early years in office, but there was growing dissension in its ranks caused by antagonisms between ideological wings and personal conflicts for power. On several occasions the Cabinet had to change or withdraw policy proposals because of cabinet disunity or fear of a backbench revolt. It had to proceed on consensus, and it had to compromise often with power units in its ranks. Several ministers of finance had to resign because of their inability to find majority support in the Government for their proposals. But only a few defections occurred, and these were compensated by defections in the Opposition. By the spring of 1963 a rift in the Government had become so serious that the Prime Minister prorogued Parliament from April 9 to July 17 in order to make adjustments and mobilize her majority. In the growing dispute between the left and right forces in her government, the Prime Minister tried to maintain a balance and stressed that her objective was to forge a "middle path" to socialism and democracy.[153] But the power of the left wing in the Government was dominant, and if a fissure was to be avoided it was this wing that had to be placated. On May 29, 1963, a cabinet reshuffle and departmental relocation took place, and the left wing was given control of the Ministry of Finance. There was fear that this maneuver would so alienate the right wing that a split would be inevitable. There was speculation that the Government would not survive the vote on the throne speech. But after long round-table discussions conducted by the Prime Minister, the Government held firm, and its motion of thanks was passed by a vote of 81 to 61.

But the ascendency of the left wing in the S.L.F.P. government challenged the loyalty and commitment of the right wing to the legislative program of the Government. So much compromise was needed to maintain cohesion that legislative sterility and inaction became the dominant aspect of the Government. It survived, but was no longer productive as a government. It was also faced with Leftist strikes. All this, together with the initiative of the S.L.F.P.'s left wing, led to talks in the spring of 1964 with the L.S.S.P. concerning a possible coalition. The choice of the L.S.S.P. was dictated by the Prime Minister's refusal to consider the participation of the C.P. because of its international ties and antireligious attitude,[154] and by the inability of the cabinet ministers to work with Gunawardena and his M.E.P. The L.S.S.P.

was also stronger than the other parties, and its ideology was closer to socialist reformism than it was to Communist revolution. An L.S.S.P. conference authorized N. M. Perera to engage in negotiations, and agreement on coalition with the S.L.F.P. was quickly made. This led to a split in the L.S.S.P., and the radical wing, led by Samarakkody, walked out of the party and formed the L.S.S.P. (Revolutionary Section). The action of the "reformist majority" in entering a coalition, Samarakkody argued, was "a complete violation of the basic principles of Trotskyism on which the revolutionary program of the party is based."[155] The basis of the coalition was a fourteen-point program, one objective of which was "to suppress the power of reactionaries and colonial elements according to the constitutional and parliamentary system and to establish more securely democracy and socialism in this country."[156] Members of the L.S.S.P. were given three cabinet posts, with N. M. Perera obtaining his long-sought post as Minister of Finance. The leftist tendency in the S.L.F.P. had triumphed, as its aspiration for coalition with the L.S.S.P. had been realized.

The right wing had become completely alienated, and its defection was inevitable. It could no longer support what it considered to be the totalitarian tendency of the Government. The break came on an opposition motion of regret in December, 1964. At the end of the debate, C. P. de Silva, leader of the conservative wing of the S.L.F.P., resigned his cabinet post and crossed over to the Opposition. He took the conservative bloc with him, and the opposition vote carried by 74 to 73, one appointed member, R. Singleton-Salmon, voting with the Opposition. Despite the advice of R. G. Senanayake and others not to dissolve, the Prime Minister advised dissolution. A general election was set for March 24, 1965.

AFTERMATH: THE RESURGENCE OF THE U.N.P.

It had been nearly five years since the last general election. The Prime Minister had been reluctant to dissolve earlier because it

appeared that the Government was losing its popularity and because many observers discerned in the results of local elections a
definite national trend favorable to the U.N.P. Ever since the
election in the summer of 1960, the U.N.P. had bent every effort
to build its political machine in preparation for the next general
election. It had made something of a comeback in July, 1960,
and a sense of optimism had replaced the gloom that pervaded
the party after its disaster in 1956. The electorate had confirmed
the survival of the U.N.P. as a party, and prospects were good
that with more effort the U.N.P. might again obtain the confidence of the people. To a large extent, the comeback of the
U.N.P. in 1960 was due to its adoption of an ideology (described
in Chapter 6) that attempted to articulate the aspirations of the
people. What was now needed was a greater organizational effort
that would bring the party into direct contact with the people
and make its new identity known to the masses. This was the
task that the party set for itself after 1960, an endeavor that was
facilitated by the accumulation of a sizeable campaign fund
through the contributions of many who were now more hopeful
of the U.N.P.'s return to power.

The main organizational effort of the U.N.P. after 1960 was
oriented toward the youth of Ceylon. I. M. R. A. Iriyagolle was
given command of the Youth League of the U.N.P., and under
his direction a youth training program was inaugurated for the
purpose of disseminating U.N.P. propaganda among people between the ages of 15 and 25. A political program was formulated,
and provincial and national conferences were held at various
times throughout the year. At the conferences, which usually
lasted for about a week, youths would attend lectures given by
leading members of the U.N.P., such as Dudley Senanayake and
J. R. Jayewardene, and literature would be distributed describing
the ideology and program of the U.N.P. and challenging the
Marxist and radical socialist analysis and solution of social and
economic problems. One of the main objectives of the program
was to train young leaders who, inculcated with the political
philosophy of the U.N.P., would return to their areas and or-

ganize branch associations of the Youth League. By 1964, twenty thousand youths had attended these conferences, and the U.N.P. claimed that it had recruited between twenty and three hundred youth leaders in each Sinhalese constituency.[157] In the next election their task would be to help organize the vote for the U.N.P., raise campaign funds, and distribute U.N.P. literature. The U.N.P. fully expected that its Youth League would be the most important and useful section of its political machine in future elections.

While none approached the size and efficiency of the U.N.P., all the major parties had developed powerful organizations by 1965. All had their youth leagues, women's societies, trade unions, and branch associations. The S.L.F.P. had the most amorphous and personality-oriented organization of the established parties, and it had been hurt organizationally by the defection of its conservative wing. The organizations of the Marxist parties were highly developed, but were restricted to constituencies and areas of Marxist strength, and the M.E.P. and the J.V.P. lacked efficient and disciplined political machines. For the most part, however, the election of 1965 was the most co-ordinated and organized election under party direction in Ceylon's history. As the *Times of Ceylon* noted after the election, in every constituency most parties had "well-organized district campaigns which involved house-to-house visiting."[158]

In the Sinhalese areas the election reflected a bipolarized division of political forces between coalitions pivoting about the U.N.P. and the S.L.F.P. The S.L.F.P., the L.S.S.P., and the C.P. again concluded a no-contest pact and ran a co-ordinated anti-U.N.P. campaign designed to prevent the return to power of "reactionary forces" which would "deprive the people of the real freedom conferred on the poor peasant and workers by the late S. W. R. D. Bandaranaike in 1956."[159] The S.L.F.P. described the election as one fought between the "progressive parties" of its coalition and "reactionary, imperialist, opportunist parties like the U.N.P., F.P., M.E.P., J.V.P. along with the treacherous group [the conservatives led by C. P. de Silva] that broke away from the S.L.F.P."[160] Its manifesto went on to list the popular legislation that the S.L.F.P. had introduced during its period of government and the policies it intended to implement if it were returned to power. It was a manifesto of mass appeal, whose orientation was primarily, if not exclusively, to the interests of lower-income groups—the workers and peasants. While it hoped to obtain a majority of its own, the S.L.F.P. announced its willingness to form a coalition government with the L.S.S.P. The S.L.F.P. ran 101 candidates, the L.S.S.P. 25, and the C.P. 9. Each party ran candidates in areas of its strength, and each avoided competition with candidates of other parties in the coalition so as not to split the "progressive" vote.

The major organizational novelty of the election was that for the first time since 1952 the U.N.P. entered the election with the support of other parties. Its electoral and parliamentary isolation had considerably hurt the party politically, and it had been defeated in the second election of 1960 partly because of the no-contest arrangement that had been organized against it by the S.L.F.P. and the parties of the Left. But now it, too, had a coalition, which would help unite the U.N.P. vote at the same time it would help split the vote of the S.L.F.P. and its allies. The common factor that united the components of the U.N.P. coalition was the same kind of antipathy toward the party in power that had led to the organization of an anti-U.N.P. coalition in 1956. The U.N.P. was the dominant organization in the coalition, and it ran 116 candidates in an attempt to obtain a majority of seats in the House of Representatives. The main theme of its campaign was that the incumbent government was following a "road to the establishment of a dictatorship."[161] It pointed to the failure of the S.L.F.P. to solve Ceylon's problems and promised that if the U.N.P. were returned to power it would solve Ceylon's ills in a democratic and efficient manner. It, too, had a manifesto of wide appeal designed to win the votes of the peasant and lower-income groups as well as the minorities and the affluent. Another element in the coalition was the conservatives who had defected from the S.L.F.P. Under the leadership of C. P. de Silva this group organized the Sri Lanka Freedom Socialist party (S.L.F.S.P.) and ran 32 candidates. The leaders of the U.N.P. and the S.L.F.S.P. worked out a carefully planned strategy to maximize the political effect of both parties. In those constituencies where leading notables of the S.L.F.S.P. ran, the U.N.P. did not compete and instead put its local organization at the disposal of the S.L.F.S.P.; local notables of the U.N.P. came out in support of the S.L.F.S.P. candidate and helped finance his campaign. In the inland constituencies of Ceylon where a close contest between the U.N.P. and the S.L.F.P. was expected, the S.L.F.S.P. ran candidates in an attempt to drain some of the vote from the S.L.F.P. candidates. The U.N.P. worked out a similar arrangement with the M.E.P.-J.V.P., led by Philip Gunawardena and K. M. P. Rajaratna, which was a recently formed alliance designed to pool the two parties' meager campaign resources. The J.V.P. ran candidates in Uva Province, where the Rajaratnas have personal influence. In three constituencies, where the J.V.P. appeared to be strong, the U.N.P. did not run candidates. In others the J.V.P. ran candidates in order to cut into areas of S.L.F.P. strength and help U.N.P. candidates. In areas of leftist strength the M.E.P. ran candidates in order to split the leftist vote and help the U.N.P. Where it appeared likely that an M.E.P. candidate might win, as in Philip Gunawardena's constituency, the U.N.P. did not compete. In all, 71 candidates ran under the label of the M.E.P.-J.V.P., over three-fourths of whom lost their deposits because of failure to obtain one-eighth of the vote. As it was organized, therefore, the election in the Sinhalese areas was primarily a contest between the coalitions of the S.L.F.P. and the U.N.P.

There were 98 candidates running as independents, and the revolutionary sections of the L.S.S.P. and the C.P. ran 4 candidates each. The T.C. decided to attempt a political comeback, and in the Northern Province 12 candidates ran under its label. In the Northern Province the F.P. ran 14 candidates, and in the Eastern

Province it ran 7. The campaign of the F.P. again stressed the need for a federal state, and the party made repeated reference to itself as the primary political spokesman of the Tamil people. The T.C., on the other hand, denied the feasibility of a federal state and proposed as a solution to Tamil problems a co-operative attitude toward the Sinhalese and a greater degree of regional autonomy for the Tamil areas.

The vote in the Sinhalese areas was almost equally divided between the two coalitions. The U.N.P. and its allies together took 1,836,608 votes, while the S.L.F.P. coalition obtained 1,643,-207. The U.N.P. won a plurality with 1,591,936 votes, over 350,000 more votes than the S.L.F.P. received. The 66 seats that the U.N.P. won were also a plurality. The S.L.F.S.P. won 5 seats, and the M.E.P.-J.V.P. 2. The S.L.F.P. was returned with 41 seats, while the L.S.S.P. and the C.P. won, respectively, 10 and 4. The 3 seats won by the T.C. helped its return as a party, though the 14 seats won by the F.P. confirmed its position as the dominant political organization of the Tamils. Six independents won seats, 2 in the Eastern Province, 1 in the Southern, 2 in the North Western, and 1 in Uva Province. Over 81 per cent of those eligible to vote did go to the polls, and their vote indicated overwhelming confidence in the established parties. Deposits were forfeited by 106 candidates, of whom only 8 were members of established parties. Among those losing their deposits were 77 independents and minor-party candidates, 63 candidates of the M.E.P.-J.V.P., and 22 who ran under the label of the S.L.F.S.P.

The plurality obtained by the U.N.P., together with pledges of support from other parties, enabled it to form a national government under Dudley Senanayake. The U.N.P. had 66 seats, and the addition of 6 appointed members brought the party close to a majority. In addition it had the support of the 5 members of the S.L.F.S.P. and the 2 members of the M.E.P.-J.V.P. After negotiations the F.P. and the T.C. decided to join in the coalition, and the national government of Dudley Senanayake had a bloc of 96 seats. Cabinet posts were distributed in an effort to cement the coalition that formed the Government. The S.L.F.S.P. was given two cabinet posts, with C. P. de Silva being made Minister of Lands, Irrigation, and Power, and W. Dahanayake being made Minister of Home Affairs. Philip Gunawardena was appointed Minister of Industries and Fisheries, and M. Tiruchelvam, of the F.P., was made Minister of Local Government. There were divisive tendencies in the Cabinet as there were in the coalition led by the U.N.P. The legislative program that the Government would introduce would have to be a product of compromise between the Tamils and the Sinhalese and between advocates of various shades of socialism. Whether or not the consensus necessary for action could be achieved would largely depend upon the leadership ability of Dudley Senanayake and the willingness of other leaders in the coalition to co-operate.

The election of 1965 was important in the political development of Ceylon. The U.N.P. reaped the reward of its hard work and its willingness to change its ideology to conform to the aspirations of the people. Its return to power in 1965 confirmed the ability of the party system in Ceylon to produce stable and alternative government. The election also marked the return of the Tamils to effective political participation at the parliamentary level, as both the T.C. and the F.P. found it possible to co-operate with Sinhalese parties. In addition, the Opposition was united when both the C.P. and the L.S.S.P. willingly placed themselves under the S.L.F.P.-appointed leader of the Opposition. That all of this was possible by 1965 was a definite result of the changes undergone by parties since 1947.

CHAPTER 6 *Parties as Identifiable Units*

The growth of parties can be measured by the extent to which they are able to mobilize voters on the basis of party label rather than on the basis of the personal influence of their candidates. In established democracies, parties usually possess more or less stable funds of votes that are committed to them because they have developed popular images as distinct and meaningful political units. Such stabilized blocs of votes are a form of good will that parties build up over the years by serving the interests of various groups in society and by maintaining a relatively clear ideological orientation. It is by developing such images that parties become identifiable to the electorate. An electorate cannot define a party if its personality is schizophrenic, if its ideology and policy commitments are vague and contradictory, and if its elite is composed of leaders who pull in opposite directions. When a party system is composed of parties of this nature, voters tend to vote for personalities because party label is not by itself a meaningful basis upon which to judge the policy orientation of candidates. The development of a party-conscious or party-responsive electorate, therefore, depends as much upon parties as it does upon the electorate.

The persistence of a personality-oriented electorate and the inability of parties to mobilize voters impersonally—that is, by building and exploiting a fund of good will—are characteristics of party systems in which parties are immature. A mature party can be considered one that is able to stand on its own feet; one that can operate as a distinct political entity and mobilize votes on the basis of its image and through the use of its own organization. In this sense, party maturation depends upon the development of a viable organization and the possession of an ideological image meaningful to voters. The growth of parties, therefore, is a twofold process. In the first place, a party must strive to adopt an ideology that reflects a consensus among its members and that can be made visible to the public. In the second place, a party must construct an organization capable of transmitting its message and image to the people, mobilizing their votes and support, and galvanizing its members into a cohesive and operative combination. It is the realization of all this that makes a party a unit identifiable both to itself and to the people. In Ceylon, the biographies of the established parties reveal their search for such identity and their gradual growth into more distinct and identifiable units.

THE UNITED NATIONAL PARTY

The U.N.P. has evolved over the years from a loosely knit association of politically ambitious men into the most extensively organized party in Ceylon. Its defeat in 1956 was a major event in the history of the party, and it provides a convenient dividing line for a discussion of the development of the U.N.P. Both ideologically and organizationally, the party that restored itself after the disaster in 1956 bears little resemblance to the one that ran Ceylon from 1947 to 1956. Of all the parties in Ceylon, the U.N.P. provides the prime example of a party that was compelled by the pressures of political life to adapt itself to the social environment in which it operated.

From 1947 to 1956

The U.N.P. was formed for the explicit purpose of obtaining the powers of government for the notables who had joined in its foundation. While its leaders shared a common belief in the

values of Western political democracy and supported the trans-
plantation of these values to Ceylon, they were not linked by a
common social, cultural, or economic program. But together they
gave the U.N.P. the inclusive character it needed to win mass
support. At its beginning the U.N.P. obtained the support of
peasants, workers, and business interests; Catholics and Buddhists;
the Westernized population and traditionalists; low-country and
Kandyan Sinhalese; and all the minority groups. They gave their
support not because the party articulated an ideology or a program
suited to their interests, but because it included the notables who
had their confidence. The only commitment made by the U.N.P.
other than to the new political system was to a pragmatic approach to the solution of problems.

The political image that the U.N.P. acquired during this period
did not derive primarily from a conscious effort on the part of
its leading members to define the party publicly. It is true that
the party issued manifestoes, campaign literature, and press re-
leases, and that its national leaders made headlines and public
speeches from time to time. All these played some part in building an image of the U.N.P. But the real links between the voter
and the U.N.P. were the M.P.'s and candidates of the party, and
they did little to communicate an image of the U.N.P. as an
entity to the people. During election campaigns the candidates of
the U.N.P. were prone to take credit themselves for any benefits
that their constituents may have gained from the government,
and for the most part they presented themselves to the voter for
election on the basis of their personal merit. Few did much to
popularize the program or the name of the U.N.P., although
the party did gain indirectly from having so many locally influential people run under its label. The political image of the U.N.P.
during this time was mainly the natural and automatic by-product
of the U.N.P.'s role as the government party. The management
of the country's affairs required the party to make decision after
decision, and in its response to the issues of the day the true
character of the U.N.P. was revealed to itself and to the people.

From instances of its action or inaction in office, and from defections of leading notables from its ranks, an image of the U.N.P. developed that, unfortunately for the party, divorced it spiritually and programmatically from the people. The extent of its defeat in 1956 in spite of the fact that its candidates were locally prominent and influential is definite proof that the name of the U.N.P. had become electorally meaningful. The unfavorable image it evoked could not be overcome by the personal influence of the party notables.

The defeat of the U.N.P. in 1956 led many observers to assume that it was a "thoroughly finished party." [1] Two of the eight M.P.'s whom the party had managed to elect crossed over to the Government shortly after the new Parliament convened. Dudley Senanayake had resigned from the party and, as he said in an interview many years later, had "resolved to gradually fade out from politics and devote more of my time to religious work." [2] Within a year after the election Sir John Kotelawala decided to retire to his country estate in Kent, and throughout the island many of the local notables of the U.N.P. left a party that they considered more of a liability than an asset to their own political careers. With its reputation apparently ruined and with the defection or retirement of its national and local leaders, there seemed little hope for the resurrection of the U.N.P. Its survival appeared especially unlikely because it had no organizational framework to sustain a defeated party or upon which to construct a more energetic one. Organizational development had proceeded slowly since the founding of the party in 1947, and by 1956 the U.N.P. was little more than a "party of notables" structurally linked at the apex by the parliamentary caucus and extended organizationally among the voters by means of local electoral associations composed largely of friends and relatives of the notables who ran under the U.N.P. label.

The plan for a formal organization that the U.N.P. adopted at its inception was mass oriented and was devised to conform to the organizations of mass parties in the United States and

Great Britain that the party sought to emulate. Membership in the party was open to all who subscribed to its policy of maintaining "the present economic system with an ample measure of progressive social reform."[3] It meant little more than sending a request for membership along with twenty-five cents to the central office. The election of 1947 came before the party had had time to build its organization, and it had to rely almost entirely upon those who ran under its label for contact with the masses. Branch associations were formed in the name of the party on an *ad hoc* basis by candidates who consented to run under the party label. These associations, composed of the friends and relatives of the respective candidates, were entirely under the candidates' control. The candidates themselves ran almost entirely on the basis of their own merit and local influence, and the informal organizations that they hastily put together dissolved after the election. The only organization that the party itself had in 1947 was its central office. This was located in Colombo, and it was here and in other areas of the Western Province that the propaganda section of the office was most active. It had a few trucks, loudspeakers, and assistants who helped in the campaign of U.N.P. candidates in and around Colombo, and the reported $40,000 the party had in its campaign chest went mainly for advertising, pamphlets, and posters, almost all of them distributed or posted in the Western Province. The party provided no financial assistance for its candidates, most of whom were wealthy or financially comfortable in their own right. The funds that the central office had at its disposal came primarily from the wealthier members, although some money was contributed by major business firms on the island.

It was not until after the election that the U.N.P. made efforts to build an organization. In 1951 the U.N.P. claimed that it had established ninety-six branch associations in forty-nine electoral districts.[4] These had increased to over two hundred by the time of the election of 1952, and many of them were able to supply U.N.P. candidates with vehicles so that pro-U.N.P. voters could be conveyed to polling stations. The formation of branch associations continued, and by the election of 1956, according to I. D. S. Weerawardana, wherever "a constituency was represented by an active U.N.P. member or by a prospective U.N.P. candidate there were one or more U.N.P. branches."[5] In January, 1949, the U.N.P. organized a youth league that the party claims had three thousand members at its inception.[6] Within three years the league had formed fifty-five branches in thirty electoral districts,[7] and by 1956, according to Weerawardana, "the youth leagues appeared to be considerable in their membership."[8] However, the party does not seem to have made as full use of its Youth League as it might have during the 1956 election campaign. W. Howard Wriggins claims that the league "confined its activities to enlisting young men to appear at public celebrations and to cheering at political meetings."[9] The Women's Union, which the party formed in 1949, was another ancillary organization that promised more than it fulfilled. At the beginning of 1952 it had established only five branches in four electoral districts,[10] and only a few more branches had formed by the election of that year.[11] The Women's Union had been formed to engage in social and welfare enterprises with the objective of spreading the influence of the U.N.P. It was relatively inactive in this regard, however, and it became little more than a social club for the wives of U.N.P. members.

The central organization of the U.N.P. developed significantly after 1947. The propaganda office under Sir John Kotelawala was active in printing pamphlets, leaflets, and booklets to popularize the U.N.P. and to attack its Marxist and other opponents. Two party newspapers, the *U.N.P. Journal,* in English, and the *Siyarata,* in Sinhalese, were published weekly and were available to subscribers at Rs. 4 per annum, including postage. A party fund was established, and in 1952 a U.N.P. "Protect the Country Fund" was initiated under the direction of Sir John Kotelawala to raise three million rupees for the election of that year.[12] This sum was reputed to have been raised by means of subscriptions to, and advertisements in, the party journals, from membership fees, direct contributions to the Protect the Country Fund that ranged from fifty cents upwards, and contributions from wealthy individuals and firms with a stake in the return of the U.N.P. By the time of the 1956 election the central organization was able to provide valuable assistance to its own candidates, including the provision of funds and campaign literature, and the use of vehicles and speakers. Other parties were also providing greater assistance to their candidates in 1956. Weerawardana, while he notes that in 1956 "the preponderant majority of party candidates were financially self-supporting in their election expenses," was nevertheless impressed by "the increasing degree of the dependence of the candidate on his party for electoral and financial assistance." [13]

While the organizational growth of the U.N.P. between 1947 and 1956 seems impressive, it was in many ways more apparent than real. In essence the formal organization of the U.N.P. lacked vitality, purpose, and function. In the first place, the formal party apparatus suffered from undue centralization of power in the hands of a few individuals at the apex of the party, the effect of which was to give the party members almost no role at all in decision making. In the second place, the electoral associations of the party were either controlled completely by the party M.P.'s who represented the constituencies in which they were formed or they were functionally displaced by the personal organizations of these leaders. Thus, while the party operated under rigid centralization at the top, it suffered from a personalized decentralization at the bottom, both of which had the effect of devitalizing the formal party organization. But most important, the influence of the U.N.P. on the voter did not derive from, or depend upon, its formal organization. Some of its influence came from the prominence of its national leaders, and some came also from the party image itself. For the most part, however, the influence exercised by the U.N.P. on the voter depended upon an elaborate personal-influence structure that functioned alongside the formal party organization, making the latter impotent from top to bottom and severely inhibiting its growth.

The personal-influence structure that served as the essential link between the U.N.P. and the voter was in fact composed of two mutually supportive networks: that built on the influence wielded by its candidates for office in their home districts and that springing from its control of appointments to the government service. The former was the more important network and was formed by the clusters of locally influential contacts which were linked informally to the party through the notables whom the U.N.P. nominated as its candidates for office. Right from the beginning, the U.N.P. was receptive to the nomination of any candidate who appeared to have sufficient local influence to win a seat in Parliament. Such notables welcomed U.N.P. nomination because it offered them the opportunity of serving in a government, and the U.N.P. had no difficulty in recruiting candidates. In 1947 the central office was deluged by the applications of over two hundred individuals who wanted to contest the election under the party label. The Executive Committee of the party was responsible for choosing the nominees. Since those to whom it refused nomination would run as independents, the committee had to evaluate carefully the local influence of the many applicants in the effort to nominate the ones most likely to succeed. This proved an impossible burden, and the committee became so free in conferring the party label that in the election of 1947 U.N.P. candidates competed against each other in many constituencies.

The U.N.P. could afford to be more economical with its label in 1952, because its ability to win office and influence in the government for its candidates had been confirmed. The burden of nomination had also become easier because the election of 1947 had served as a filter that showed clearly which men had substantial local influence and which were merely pretenders. In addition, many of those who were elected in 1947 as independents had subsequently joined the U.N.P., and the party was therefore able to approach the election of 1952 confident of the vote-getting power of most of its candidates. None of this had changed by 1956. In spite of the defections from its ranks and growing popular discontent with the government of the U.N.P., the party was still able to attract influential men. Sir John Kotelawala reported that even before the dissolution of Parliament he had received over 170 applications for U.N.P. nomination.[14] The party used the same procedure as before in the selection of candidates. Weerawardana noted at the time that it "was obvious that one of the chief considerations in the choice of U.N.P. nominees was their chance of electoral success."[15] The process of selection was somewhat more difficult, however, because the growth of the Sri Lanka Freedom party had provided an alternative organization to which candidates could turn if the U.N.P. refused them nomination. Because of this the U.N.P. did not content itself with voluntary applications, and it used some of its most influential members to scout and recruit locally influential men to run under its label. Often this meant enticing prospective S.L.F.P. candidates to accept U.N.P. nomination.[16] While the party had a nominations board in 1956 to screen candidates, neither it nor the branch associations had much influence on party nominations. The Prime Minister interviewed most of the applicants, and his personal opinion was decisive in the choice of candidates. Weerawardana reported that Sir John assumed that "the personal standing of the individual candidate was of great importance to his electoral success," and that "wherever possible preference was given to the local applicant."[17]

The network of notables that the U.N.P. established by nominating locally influential men gave the party influence with the voters and provided it with organizational extensions throughout the island. The candidate himself provided the link between the voter and the party, and both the influence and the organization of the U.N.P. were products of the multiplication of these links. The whole arrangement was clearly one of mutual exploitation that worked to the advantage of both party and notable. In return for the electoral influence and organization that a notable gave the party, he was given office and influence in the Government. This, as well as "pork barreling," helped sustain the influence of the notables in their areas. The price that the U.N.P. had to pay for this was the decentralization of its organization. The candidates themselves formed election committees, which operated only during the campaign and were composed of "relations, supporters and sympathisers" who were personally loyal to the candidate.[18] These were the lieutenants and party hacks whom the M.P. rewarded as he could with patronage and favors, and these were the workers who would move out of the party with their leader if for any reason he saw fit to leave it. Each of the M.P.'s returned by the U.N.P., therefore, acted as leader of his own self-contained party. For the most part he provided his own campaign funds, put a personal electoral association into action, and conducted a campaign that stressed his personal qualities. The personal influence of each M.P. gave him a relatively stable voting bloc. Many of his constituents were employed by him on his estate or in other enterprises, his family name and influence counted with the voter, and he was allied through personal contact with pressure groups and other men of local influence. All these efforts the M.P. put forth to obtain his own election; at the same time, whether the M.P. knew it or not, he was helping the U.N.P. to become known as a unit distinct from himself.

The other aspect of the personal-influence structure that the U.N.P. brought into service was the highly centralized government service. The party's control of ministerial posts provided it with the means to exert pressure on government officials who were influential locally throughout the island. Government agents, district revenue officers, and especially village headmen who were heads of locally influential families were employed by the U.N.P. to generate popular support for its candidates. In addition to this, government-owned vehicles and public facilities were used to help U.N.P. candidates secure election. This personal-influence structure was controlled by the Cabinet, to whose pressure civil service personnel and local government personnel were especially sensitive. Control of this structure amplified the power of those who controlled the central organization of the U.N.P., since the top organ of the party consisted primarily of cabinet ministers.

Thus the U.N.P.'s influence among voters derived primarily from the dual personal-influence structure that the party had at its disposal. Voters were mobilized on behalf of the U.N.P. by local organizations under the control of notables and by government servants under the control of the Cabinet. The structure provided a highly efficient election machine, and it both inhibited and made unnecessary the growth of a formal party organization. The notables in particular resisted the development of a formal party organization, as it was in their interest to keep the party dependent upon their own personal organizations. W. Howard Wriggins observed that "the party's members of parliament resisted efforts of the central party staff to organize active local branches."[19] Thus not only did an efficient personal-influence structure make the development of a formal party organization unnecessary, but it also actively discouraged and worked against its growth.

Besides being faced with these obstacles, the formal organization that the U.N.P. had developed lacked incentive within itself to grow. It was never sufficiently employed in campaigns or consulted in decision making to generate that kind of enthusiasm among the rank and file so vital to the growth of organizations. The branch associations generally had very little to say in regard to nominations, although Weerawardana contended that in respect to the nominations of 1956, "it seems reasonable to assume that party branches were consulted where it suited the party high command to do so."[20] More than one party branch complained about its lack of participation in the nominating process, and many obviously became dispirited for the same reason. In 1956 both the Matara and the Bandarawela branches of the party complained because they had not been consulted concerning candidates who were nominated in their areas.[21] One official of a U.N.P. branch association argued that "it is not democratic to make decisions according to the wishes of individuals and to order the branch associations to work for candidates nominated by the high command without the consent of branch associations." [22] Such treatment as this discouraged the operation and growth of branch associations and aroused dissatisfaction among the ranks of the formal party organizations. Party loyalty and effort was not rewarded either by nomination or by influence on nominations. Thus the formal organization of the party at the local level, already subverted and bypassed by the high command through its utilization of other informal structures and channels, had no incentive to develop.

Power in the formal organization of the U.N.P. had become so concentrated at the top that the lower echelons had very little if anything to say about the government of the party. According to the constitution of the U.N.P.,[23] the annual party conference was to be the decision-making center of the party. It was attended by the parliamentary members of the party, party officials, and representatives of the youth leagues, branch associations, and women's unions, and the thousand or so delegates were empowered to decide questions of party policy and to elect party officers. The delegates elected the Executive Committee, which consisted of about fifty members and which was responsible for running the party between the sessions of the annual conference. The Executive Committee in turn elected the Working Committee, consisting of about twenty of the most influential members of the party, including its office bearers and ministers. It was the Working Committee that was the real power center of the party, and the conference became a rubber stamp that adopted proposals submitted to it by the Working Committee, as Wriggins comments, "with virtual unanimity." [24] Thus, prior to 1956 whatever formal organization the U.N.P. had developed was disregarded by the leadership of the party and was functionally replaced by the personal-influence structures on which the success of the U.N.P. so much depended.

The organization of the party was such that the parliamentary caucus and the Working Committee were the dominant power centers of the party. All the leaders who together controlled the entire power apparatus of the party were members of at least one of these bodies, and within this group the greatest power went naturally to those individuals who linked caucus and Working Committee by means of membership in both. Each member of the caucus had his own power base that consisted of his personal influence in his constituency, his own local organization, and his personal link to local pressure groups and social elements in his area. Collectively the caucus represented almost the entire organizational network upon whose influence the U.N.P. depended to mobilize voters. The power of the cabinet ministers derived from the same sort of personal power base as that of the backbenchers, but was greatly augmented by the ministers' greater prominence nationally, their control over the administrative influence structure of the party, and their ability to dispense patronage and perform other personal services. The Working Committee of the U.N.P. acted as the cabinet of the party, and most of the cabinet ministers in the Government had a seat on it. In addition to whatever other posts they had, members of the Working Committee had control of the party fund, the propaganda organs of the party, and any other facilities to which the party had access. The main problem that developed within the party, and one that led to a number of defections, was that power at the top of the party became progressively concentrated in fewer and fewer hands. By 1956 Sir John Kotelawala and a few others around him virtually dictated to the whole party. Sir John was leader of the party, Prime Minister, and a one-man nominations board for party candidates. In addition to this, he controlled the party fund, personally obtained contributions from firms and other sources, ran the propaganda organs of the party, including its newspapers, exerted personal pressure on government officials, transformed the U.N.P. Youth League, the most active ancillary organization of the party, into almost a private army, and just about dictated policy. There is little doubt that many of the defections that weakened the U.N.P. from 1952 to 1956 were due to this situation. In spite of a good deal of party regularity in voting in Parliament, the party had become dispirited, and only a common interest in holding office held it all together.

Thus the organization of the U.N.P. prior to 1956 was characterized by centralization of power in a clique at the top and a network of local electoral associations controlled by notables associated with the party at the lower levels. The organization of the party consisted almost entirely of an elaborate personal-influence structure that sufficiently served the interests of the party and its notables. Linkage to pressure groups was also highly personalized and in effect provided the U.N.P. with a third personal-influence structure supportive of the other two. Leaders of the All-Ceylon Muslim League and the Moors' Association occupied top positions in the party hierarchy as well as posts in the Cabinet. This put these two important communal organizations at the disposal of the U.N.P., and at election time their local branches could be activated to mobilize the Muslim and Moor votes on behalf of U.N.P. candidates. In many constituencies Muslim and Moor leaders of branches of the association and the league ran as U.N.P. candidates. Other communal leaders and organizations also were linked to the U.N.P. by appointment to posts either in the Cabinet or in the higher organs of the U.N.P. Positions in the Senate and seats as appointed members were similarly used. Through the appointment of pressure-group leaders to these posts the U.N.P. was able to obtain the services of highly influential organizations. Personal contact was also maintained between the top members of the U.N.P. and affluent pressure groups who served the party more through the provision of funds than through the mobilization of votes.

But the whole structure of the U.N.P. was tenuous and liable to disintegration once the party lost its control of government. It was this control that served the ambition of the notables who had placed their personal-influence structures at the disposal of the party, and it was this control that gave the party access to an administrative influence structure so valuable to its mobilization of voter support. The defeat of the U.N.P. in 1956 removed both structures of influence from the party and left it with a formal party organization that had never functioned. But the organizational dichotomy of the U.N.P., with its centralization at the top and decentralization below, began to pull the party apart even before its defeat in 1956. Defections from the party were facilitated by the personal nature of its local organizations and were encouraged when centralization of power at the top led to the adoption of policies that injured the interests of groups to whom M.P.'s were electorally bound and committed. The influence that M.P.'s had with their constituents ultimately depended upon their ability to satisfy their constituents' aspirations or, at the minimum, upon their disassociation from and opposition to a government and party that was pursuing policies detrimental to these aspirations. Association with the party had been motivated by the personal profit to be gained from such association, and defections came when that association no longer appeared profitable. Most of those who failed to leave the party suffered defeat in 1956. And with this defeat the whole structure of the U.N.P. crumbled. Thus, by 1956 the U.N.P. found itself not only ideologically divorced from the people but organizationally apart as well.

From 1956 to 1965

The years from 1956 to 1965 comprise the second generation of the U.N.P. They were years of change and growth for the U.N.P., when it reached maturity as a party. Under the direction of a core of hard-working leaders, the U.N.P. made a persistent effort during this time to overcome the mistakes, deficiencies, and especially, the fatal aloofness that in the preceding decade had alienated both the people generally and its own ranks. It was quite evident that rehabilitation would require an almost complete ideological and organizational renovation. It was also manifest that this could not be accomplished in a short time. The restoration of the party image required more than mere ideological revision. Time would be needed to regain the confidence of the people and to convince them that in its change the U.N.P. had truly adopted an ideology and policy oriented to the interests of the people. In addition, the organization of the U.N.P. was in such disarray that a construction program would have to be launched to rebuild the party from top to bottom. Much work would be needed to develop organizational extensions capable of linking the party to the people, and the inner apparatus of the party had to be repaired to allow for wider participation in the decision-making process within the organization. Only in this way could a spirited and energetic party be built that would efficiently convey its image and its message to the people.

The immediate problem that the U.N.P. faced in 1956 was not so much the monumental task of reconstruction as it was the generation of confidence among its members that such reconstruction was possible. The party was not only dispirited— many of its own members, as well as the public, considered it to be dead. The discreet retirement of Sir John Kotelawala from the leadership of the party shortly after the election considerably helped matters. His command had alienated many of the subordinate leaders of the U.N.P., and his retirement was important in fostering a spirit of co-operation among these leaders for the task of rebuilding the party. The return of Dudley Senanayake to leadership of the party in 1957 was extremely valuable to the U.N.P. He resumed his post for the explicit purpose of rebuilding the U.N.P. into a party that would effectively express the best interests of the nation. He was well liked by the rank and file of the party as well as by its leaders, and he had a popular image as an honest, dedicated, and devout leader. His disassociation from the party before the ruination of its image sustained his own image with the public, and his return to the party gave the U.N.P. a leader who had suffered none of the disparagement attached to the party during its last few years in office. Thus the return of Dudley Senanayake not only helped give the party an improved public image, but it also brought it greater life and co-operation. The many local offices held by notables of the U.N.P. also helped sustain it in the initial period of its restoration. The national defeat suffered by the party in 1956 was not repeated as extensively in local elections, and many U.N.P. members retained or shortly regained control of local offices. With Senanayake again at the helm, these leaders, with their networks of local influence, found association with the U.N.P. more comfortable than it had been and were more willing to co-operate in rebuilding the party. In addition, the U.N.P. had the support of the more affluent pressure groups, which had a stake in the survival of the party and would help provide it with funds for its development.

The first step taken by the U.N.P. toward its reconstruction into a major political force was the appointment of a special committee to investigate the reasons for the defeat of the party in 1956 and to recommend measures for its rehabilitation. The committee blamed the defeat of the U.N.P. on, among other things, its lack of a defined goal adapted to the aspirations of the people and on a party organization insufficiently linked to the people and one in which the membership had no contact with the Cabinet. It recommended the formulation of a mass-oriented ideology and the development of organizational links to the masses and to pressure groups. In particular, it advised the formation of trade unions, the establishment of an advisory board to connect the U.N.P. to Buddhist societies, the multiplication of branch associations, and revitalization of the youth leagues and women's societies of the party.[25] The recommendations of the committee provided a program for the rehabilitation of the U.N.P., and the development of the party between 1957 and 1965 was largely due to the implementation of this program.

The first significant change made by the U.N.P. in its effort to improve its image for the voter was the adoption at its annual conference in 1958 of the ideology of "democratic socialism." [26] To the U.N.P. this meant an economic order that combined private enterprise, state entrepreneurial initiative and ownership, and co-operative enterprise, using whichever was most feasible and productive in a particular sector of the economy. Thus, while the new ideology of the U.N.P. accepted measures of socialism and aimed at a more equalitarian social order, it also announced its commitment to personal initiative and private enterprise. As Dudley Senanayake said later, the U.N.P. rejected the idea that the only "road to socialism is through state ownership." [27] In the manifesto it issued for the 1960 election, the U.N.P. described its ideology as envisaging "a society dynamic in its propensities for the creation of wealth, ensuring a greater dispersal and de-centralization of political and economic power by giving the community a greater stake in the ownership and management of its institutions." [28] The manifesto then listed a number of measures the party intended to implement if it were returned to power.[29]

By the adoption of "democratic socialism" the U.N.P. sought a more centralist ideology that would place it in an optimum position to gain mass support through response to the demands of the social environment in which the party had to operate. It sought to make a direct appeal to the people by articulating their interests and aspirations. The adoption of such an ideology and platform helped substantially to improve the image and ap-peal of the U.N.P. To some extent, the strength shown by the U.N.P. in the elections of 1960 was a result of its ideological change. But a party image is not only a product of ideological commitment, and the U.N.P. had a reputation to outlive before it could fully regain the confidence of the voter. Nevertheless, the ideological renovation of the U.N.P. was important. It marked the first stage in the rehabilitation of the party; a rehabilitation whose fruition had to await the construction of an efficient organization to disseminate and popularize the new image of the party, and to draw its membership into a cohesive unit committed to the realization of the promises conveyed by the party ideology.

The organizational reconstruction of the U.N.P. after 1956 transformed it into the most effectively organized party in Ceylon. H. L. D. Mahindapala, an editor of the *Ceylon Observer,* noted in 1963 that "the U.N.P. today has built a closely-knit, well-disciplined Party organization with links in the major part of the country—a thing which no other can boast of."[30] Its youth leagues, women's societies, and branch associations have been multiplied and strengthened, and the party has developed extensions to the working class through the formation of two unions, the National Employees Union and the Lanka Jatika Estate Workers Union. The reorganization undertaken by the U.N.P., particularly after 1960, had the dual objective of extending the party into an effective political force and transforming it internally into a more democratically functioning organization. In line with the latter aim, the party adopted a revised constitution at its Twelfth Annual Conference, held in 1961.[31] Alert to the observation made by its special committee that its defeat in 1956 was partly due to the Cabinet's aloofness from the party organization,[32] the party sought, in the new constitution, to make the formal party organization a more vital center for policy decisions. The document stipulated that the work of the party should be carried out under "the direction and control of the Party Conference," which meets annually in February.[33] In addition to a number of direct members, the conference is composed of delegates nominated by registered area associations, women's associations and youth associations. The conference elects office bearers and an executive committee, which is empowered to maintain discipline among party members, appoint a nomination board or boards, and "to organize and maintain a Fund to finance the Parliamentary or General By-Elections."[34] The size of the Executive Committee has been greatly expanded, and unlike its predecessor it is a widely representative body. It consists of the office bearers of the party, members of the parliamentary party, ex-members of Parliament who have retained U.N.P. membership, and party members elected to the Colombo Municipal Council. In addition, each branch association, electorate youth association, and electorate women's area association is permitted to elect a member. One hundred other members are also elected by the annual conference.

The primary center of power in the U.N.P., however, is the Working Committee, which is appointed by the chairman of the party from members of the Executive Committee. Known informally as the "Friday committee" because it meets on the last Friday of every month, the Working Committee consists of the chairman, vice-chairman, secretaries, and treasurers of the U.N.P., all of whom are long-standing members of the party, and other members not exceeding forty. The committee is vested with all the powers of the Executive Committee. It is here that the parliamentary activity of the U.N.P. is co-ordinated with party policy, and the primary function of the committee has been to scrutinize the policy and action of the party. One observer notes that meetings of the committee are "fierce, frank and forthright" and that its members take seriously their supervisory role. He describes it as "a group striving to put cement, brick and concrete around the framework of democratic idealisms carefully put together after 1956." [35]

There is no question that the U.N.P. has become more sensitive to public opinion and more readily accessible to the views of its revitalized organization. One should not exaggerate, however, the extent of democracy in the U.N.P. organization. Like the organization of any party, it has oligarchical features. Policy is still primarily a function of the leadership, though the membership of the party has a much greater say than before. The Working Committee is no longer an "exclusive club" isolated from the organization and dictated to by a few leading men.

The branch associations have more of a role to play than before and electorally have become much more important units. While most of their funds come from central headquarters, they are permitted to levy a fee on their members, which is used for party work and organization in their respective electorates. Their role in party nominations has been increased. According to the constitution, nominations are to be made by a nominating board or boards appointed by the Executive Committee. In the process of nomination the board is to decide on candidates in consultation with the branch associations concerned.[36] In spite of this provision, the chairman of the party has a great deal of influence regarding nominations, as it is he who administers the oath to party candidates. Depending on the situation and his own personal inclination, therefore, the chairman can still exert strong control over nominations. In the second election of 1960, for instance, Dudley Senanayake said that he would serve as a one-man nominating board.[37] The role that the branch associations can play in nominations is further limited by the need to nominate prominent men and by the special restrictions imposed on the party by the need to contest elections in coalition with others. In the 1965 election, for instance, the U.N.P. withdrew from contention in sixteen constituencies out of deference to its coalition allies. In these cases the Nominating Board may well have had to deny requests by its branch associations to run candidates. However, the party had no other recourse, since if it wanted to return to power it had to accede to the requirements of an electoral coalition. In several other cases the U.N.P. accepted the nomination of what might be called nonparty members who appeared to the party to stand the best chance of election. Here again the Nominating Board may have acted against the wishes of branch associations that had good party men available as candidates. But this has not been done on a great scale. In the March, 1960, election the U.N.P. accepted the nomination of four candidates who had previously run as independents. In July of that year it gave its label to six candidates who had previously run as independents and to two who had run before under the label of other parties. In the election of March, 1965, six of the candidates it nominated had defected from other parties and two had previously contested as independents. Thus, while the needs of political contest in Ceylon still compel the U.N.P. to by-pass its local associations occasionally, the organizational growth of the party and other factors have lessened the frequency with which this has to be done. Much more than previously, the branch associations are consulted in the nomination of candidates, and for the most part, it is regular party men who are given nomination.

The U.N.P. has become much less dependent upon a personal-influence structure, and the party organization now provides a much greater electoral force than before. Administrative reform has to a great extent terminated the use of government personnel as agents in the mobilization of voters, and restrictions on the use of vehicles to convey voters to the polls has prevented the U.N.P., and any government party, from using government-owned vehicles for this purpose. The personal influence of local candidates is still an electoral factor, as it is anywhere, but party organization is fast becoming a much more decisive electoral factor. Many observers credit the organization of the U.N.P., especially its Youth League, for its victory in 1965. The party, primarily through its youth training program, has created a bloc of supporters among the younger voters, and the Youth League has provided the party with an active and efficient campaign organization. Because of this, the local organizations of the U.N.P. are now not as much under the control of local notables as they were previously. Defections are also not as easy now as they once were, as candidates have become increasingly dependent upon the party label and organization for election. All this has made the U.N.P. a much more disciplined and cohesive party than it was prior to 1956.

The organizational development of the U.N.P. has thus seen its gradual transformation from a party of notables relying heavily upon a personal-influence structure to a party whose formal organization, through its youth leagues and branch associations, actively and directly links the party to the voter. While the party has not dispensed with personal-influence structures committed to its notables, it is not as dependent upon them for electoral success as it once was. The ideological commitment of the U.N.P. has given it a mass-oriented image that the formal party organization can transmit to the voter. The U.N.P. has thus evolved an ideology and built an organization that is mass oriented and capable of mobilizing the voters. Links to pressure groups have also become less personal. Initially linkage was provided by the integration of communal leaders within the hierarchy of the party, the utilization of communal organizations committed to such leaders, the nomination of local and area notables supported by local and area interest groups, and by direct consultation between party and pressure-group leaders. While this personal linkage has been partly retained, the primary connection between the U.N.P. and pressure groups derives more now from the party's adoption of policies geared to the interests of important groups on the island, and by the formation of more impersonal links to organized pressure groups, such as the party's Buddhist Advisory Board. Now, policy, communicated to voters and pressure groups through the organization of the U.N.P., directly links the party to the voter and interest groups. This has enabled the party to become less dependent upon a cadre of notables and has allowed it to open up decision making within the party to wider participation by regular party members.

While the formal organization of the U.N.P. has not yet fully succeeded in replacing the influence of personalities in elections, it has nevertheless made a good deal of progress in this direction. As the image of the U.N.P. has become more distinctly personal to the voter, the local organization of the U.N.P. has been able to become more impersonal. This has given more power to the formal organization in shaping policy and has enlivened the whole organization of the U.N.P. If the U.N.P. can confirm its image by good government now that it is back in power, it is likely that the party will become less and less dependent upon notables for electoral success.

THE SRI LANKA FREEDOM PARTY

The S.L.F.P. was the child of Bandaranaike and the instrument through which he hoped to obtain power. Those who were associated with Bandaranaike in its founding also discerned in it the possibility of satisfying their ambition for power. Thus the S.L.F.P. had its origin in the same sort of personal ambition that had attended the birth of the U.N.P. some years earlier. It began as an association of notables united in a common antipathy to the U.N.P. and a common aspiration to power. While the U.N.P. had rationalized its formation on the grounds of a need to provide a government for independent Ceylon, the S.L.F.P. justified its formation on the basis of a need to provide an alternative to that government. At the First Annual Conference of the S.L.F.P., in December, 1952, Bandaranaike stated: "The appearance of our party did a great service to the cause of democracy in this country by providing a democratic alternative to the Party in power, and by affording the people who, while being dissatisfied with the policies and programs of the Government, wished to make a change that was neither revolutionary or extreme, the opportunity of doing so." [38]

The origin of the S.L.F.P. as an opposition party that aspired to become the government party stamped it with a character that it has not altogether been able to change. Now, as at its inception, the S.L.F.P. organization is receptive to the politically ambitious notable in search of a party, and its ideology is responsive to the claims of a variety of interest groups in search of a spokesman. As a result, the S.L.F.P. has not yet become, either ideologically or organizationally, a fully cohesive unit, and its career has therefore been characterized by a search for an ideological position that is acceptable to its many notables and electorally profitable in respect to the wide social base it seeks to mobilize. It has not found this easy, for while it has been able to generate enough electoral support to become a government, it has repeatedly suffered the erosion of its parliamentary majority through the pressures of governing. The reason for this is that the policy objectives set forth in its ideology are not supported by an organization capable of ensuring the votes of its elected M.P.'s. Its ideology can mobilize the voters, but its organization cannot always mobilize its parliamentary members.

Organization

The organization of the S.L.F.P. has not advanced substantially since its inception, and in many ways is similar to that of the U.N.P. prior to 1956. At the local level, the organization of the S.L.F.P. is not a great deal more than a network of *ad hoc* associations between the party and locally influential personalities who join at election time in a mutually exploitive arrangement. The party obtains organization, influence, and the potential of government through such association, while the candidate acquires the label and image of a popular party, the help of its nationally prominent leaders, and the opportunity of participation in a potential government. The opportunism of these associations is transmitted to Parliament, where the combined ambitions of party and notable seek realization in the formation and operation of a government. Posts as cabinet ministers and as parliamentary secretaries are distributed among the important leaders to galvanize the electoral coalition into a working arrangement in Parliament. Policy decisions become a function of the party caucus, where ministers and the Cabinet as a whole seek support among the members and blocs of the party backbench. Support from this backbench has often been precarious, and divisions in the Cabinet, personal conflicts among its members, and policy differences have led to courting the backbench in search of a factional base of power. Factionalism and indiscipline in Parliament have been the price that the S.L.F.P. has had to pay for its lack of an organization.

The S.L.F.P. is thus a party of notables at both the electoral and parliamentary levels of its organization. Its outstanding characteristic is its need to conduct a constant search for electoral and parliamentary majorities. In elections this means the filtering of applications from prospective candidates so that nomination can be given to the one most likely to succeed. In Parliament it means the consolidation and reconsolidation of a majority, and this in turn has necessitated the shifting of posts in the Cabinet and the frequent reconsideration or abandonment of policy proposals. Additional strains on the party have been imposed by the fact that the S.L.F.P. has become increasingly dependent upon the Marxist parties. A no-contest arrangement with them has become essential to the electoral success of the S.L.F.P., as well as to the realization of a stable majority in Parliament. As one S.L.F.P. minister recently observed, "the S.L.F.P. cannot do without the Left and the Left cannot do without the S.L.F.P." [39] This too, then, involves mutually exploitive arrangements. While the party draws strength from the series of mutually exploitive arrangements on which it is built, the whole structure is basically anarchical. When an S.L.F.P. government begins to move beyond the area of policy consensus that loosely binds its members into a working combination, or when the personal ambitions of its leaders are frustrated in competition with others, anarchy begins to appear. Thus, while a highly personal organization may be an electoral asset, it inevitably becomes a parliamentary liability. Almost every policy considered or presented by the Cabinet or a minister involves a campaign among the backbench constituents of the party, and decisions of an S.L.F.P. government are often the product of a "primary election" held among its own members.

The S.L.F.P.'s lack of a strong formal organization, and its resulting difficulty in maintaining cohesion in Parliament, is due largely to a situation that was also seen earlier in the U.N.P.: an informal personal-influence structure has served as a substitute for, and inhibited the growth of, a formal organization. While access to a personal-influence structure can serve initially as an asset that facilitates the construction of parties, it eventually becomes detrimental to their further growth. It was access to a personal-influence structure that originally enabled Bandaranaike to form the S.L.F.P. Bandaranaike came from a family of wealth and influence in Ceylon and thus had easy access to the political life of the island. His membership in the Ceylon National Congress, his formation of the Sinhala Maha Sabha, and his post as Minister of Local Government in the State Council gave him a wide range of influence before Ceylon became independent. After independence his cabinet post as Minister of Local Government and Health, his continuance of the S.M.S., and his presidency of the All-Ceylon Village Committee's Conference all gave him an island-wide network of contacts that served as a valuable personal-influence structure upon which to build the S.L.F.P. Once the S.L.F.P. was formed, it served as an agency receptive to all those groups and notables alienated from the U.N.P. for personal or policy reasons and disgruntled with its conduct of state. All those who joined the S.L.F.P. expanded the personal-influence structures on which the party was based and provided the links with the voters necessary for electoral success. Bandaranaike devised policies geared to the interests of the groups that followed notables coming into the S.L.F.P., and thus he supported the notables' personal-influence structures at the same time he was gaining a mass base of power for the party. What formal organization the S.L.F.P. did have served more as a center for the co-ordination of all these influence structures than as a major election machine in itself.

When Bandaranaike organized the S.L.F.P. in 1951 he had little time to prepare the party for the general election that took place some nine months later. It had no electoral associations other than those which its candidates could quickly mobilize behind them, and a storefront in Kotte and then Bandaranaike's home on Rosemead Place in Cinnamon Gardens was all the party had as a central headquarters. The task of co-ordinating and directing party activity was done by Bandaranaike with the help of a few honorary secretaries, as the party had no paid staff. Party propaganda was printed by a firm in nearby Slave Island, and nearly all the party funds came from Bandaranaike's personal fortune.[40] S.L.F.P. candidates in 1952 had to be self-supporting, since the party headquarters could offer little more than the services of Bandaranaike himself to help them. Even so, the S.L.F.P. won nine seats in that year and took 361,250 votes, a fact that attests to the strength of the personal-influence structure of the party.

The party was, however, able to publish a joint manifesto and constitution in 1951, and it was evident in both that the S.L.F.P. anticipated mass status. Its constitution provided for direct membership in the party for all adult nationals of Ceylon who subscribed to its principles and adhered to its discipline. The general policy of the party was to be decided at an annual conference, to which branch associations, women's associations, and youth leagues were to send delegates. In addition, each branch association elected two of its members and every women's association elected one member to sit on the General Committee. S.L.F.P. members of Parliament also sat on the General Committee. This committee met every four months or when called into session by the Working Committee. In a meeting prior to the annual conference, the General Committee elected the party president, secretary, two associate secretaries, a treasurer, and ten others from its members, all of whom comprised the Working Committee of the party. The Working Committee was the "Executive Authority of the Party" and was intended to be the primary organ of power. It could meet as frequently as it wished as long as it had a quorum of seven. It was empowered to summon the General Committee, whose agenda it determined. If the Working Committee rejected any matter for inclusion in the agenda, the General Committee could override it only with a two-thirds vote of those present and voting. The Working Committee also had control of the party fund and was permitted to form or promote associations of youths and adults. It was responsible, after consultation with branch associations, for the nomination of party candidates, and, in agreement with a branch association, it could decide to support the candidacy of independents or members of other parties instead of presenting candidates of its own.[41]

After 1952 the S.L.F.P. gave some effort to building its organization through the multiplication of branch associations and the expansion of its youth league. But by 1956, while its membership had increased, the formal organization of the S.L.F.P. had not developed appreciably. By then it had a central office in Maradana near the Town Hall, but this only consisted of two rooms in the annex of a photography store. Routine party work was handled by a paid staff of six or seven workers. Just prior to the election the party fund consisted of only Rs. 24,000. Most of the cost of advertising and other expenses incurred at central headquarters had to be borne by Bandaranaike, who spent, according to an intimate acquaintance, $200,000 of his own money before and during the campaign. The greatest asset that the party had was Bandaranaike, who traveled throughout the island in a truck in which he ate and slept, speaking to mass audiences in support of the candidates of his own and allied parties.

The lack of an organization and of funds, among other things, made it mandatory that the S.L.F.P. nominate local personages who could finance their own campaigns, mobilize support through their personal influence, and provide effective electoral organizations by means of familial and personal contacts. Weerawardana found that, in 1956, except for the Marxist parties, the candidate himself was "the pivot of a party organization in a constituency."[42] This was especially true of S.L.F.P. candidates, as the S.L.F.P., almost alone among the Sinhalese parties, gave no financial support to its candidates.[43] The nomination of candidates by the S.L.F.P. was particularly arduous for a number of other reasons as well, and Bandaranaike himself had the major voice in their selection. Association in the Mahajana Eksath Peramuna and the conclusion of no-contest pacts with other parties compelled Bandaranaike to refuse nomination in some constituencies to loyal party members anxious to run and having the backing of branch associations of the party. In other cases, according to Weerawardana, the "problem before the S.L.F.P. was to find a sufficient number of candidates with a reasonable chance of electoral success."[44] The problem was made acute by the desire of many prominent notables to run as independents and by the effort of the U.N.P. to persuade prospective S.L.F.P. candidates who appeared likely to win to run under its label.[45] In the end, those whom the S.L.F.P. nominated were mostly those who failed to obtain U.N.P. nomination, independents who consented to run under the S.L.F.P. label, or other locally prominent men. This meant that the S.L.F.P. had to disregard whatever branch associations it had and rely upon the ability of its prominent associates to win election.

The success of the M.E.P. in 1956 was beneficial to the development of the S.L.F.P. because it confirmed the ability of the S.L.F.P. to obtain office for its notables and implement policy for the groups that supported it. It had, by its success, rewarded the personal-influence structure on which it was based. Since the S.L.F.P. was in a coalition, and since it was a party of notables at the top and bottom, Parliament necessarily became the body in which its decisions were made. Policy was decided upon in cabinet meetings and subsequently in parliamentary caucus and was transmitted to the S.L.F.P. through its Working and General committees. The annual conference of the S.L.F.P. simply ratified policy decisions. Only the Working Committee of the S.L.F.P. participated in party policy decisions, and most of its members had seats in Parliament. Disputes between cabinet ministers inevitably arose, and Bandaranaike sought to resolve them within the secrecy of the cabinet meeting so as to prevent disunity from developing in the backbench and among other members of his party. This worked well as long as consensus could be achieved in the Cabinet and it could present a united front. It was inevitable, however, that both personal and ideological disputes should arise in the Cabinet, partly because its members' ideologies varied and partly because each member had won election on his own merits and had his own blocs of supporters among the backbenchers and the general public. Soon personal and ideological disputes within the Cabinet were brought to the attention of the backbench as ministers sought bloc support in their disputes with other ministers. As a result, factions formed in both the Cabinet and the backbench, where a "Forward Bloc" emerged in support of Philip Gunawardena's faction in the Cabinet. The more conservative ministers took their fight to the Working Committee of the S.L.F.P., where pressure was exerted upon Bandaranaike to break with his more radical allies. The executive apparatus of the S.L.F.P. was in the hands of the more moderate section of the party, and it was evident that once disunity arose in the Cabinet the conservative ministers would carry the dispute to the party. Disunity at the top of the party apparatus shifted power downward to the General Committee and the annual conference, which would be the final arbiter in the dispute at the top. With Bandaranaike supporting the conservatives, the S.L.F.P. conference in 1959 adopted a resolution avowing a non-Marxist policy orientation, and most of the Marxists in the S.L.F.P. were expelled or withdrew.

This and the subsequent assassination of Bandaranaike nearly ruined the S.L.F.P. as a party. Defections in its parliamentary ranks led to dissolution a few months after the assassination, and the delicate structure of personal influence put together by Bandaranaike began to disintegrate. Several leading members of the S.L.F.P. organized their own parties, and many previously S.L.F.P. M.P.'s and supporters went with them. Others joined the U.N.P. or the Marxist parties. This left the personal-influence structure of the S.L.F.P. in disarray, as the movement out of the party by many of its notables removed their local influence and organizations. The formal organization of the S.L.F.P. was similarly destroyed. The secretary of the Youth League, for instance, formed his own party, and the league was decimated by the withdrawal of Marxists from the party. The condition of the S.L.F.P. in 1959 was thus similar to that of the U.N.P. in 1956.

The S.L.F.P. had to search for new candidates for the election of March, 1960, and less than a fourth of the nominees it chose had contested the 1956 election as S.L.F.P. candidates. As before, the S.L.F.P. named as many locally influential persons as would accept nomination, but on the whole they were not as influential as those who had competed under the S.L.F.P. label in 1956. In spite of this, the S.L.F.P. won forty-six seats, and its survival as a party was assured. To a great extent the survival of the S.L.F.P. was due to the fact that Mrs. Sirimavo Bandaranaike had become its patron and thus conferred validity upon the S.L.F.P. as the party of her dead husband. Popular feeling for Bandaranaike also contributed to the survival of the S.L.F.P., as did the energy and influence of other leaders in the party who remained with it at this time. Another factor in its survival was the persistence of popular distrust of the U.N.P. and the rejection of the Marxist parties, as well as of the other, personality parties that sought mass support. After the March election the comeback of the S.L.F.P. was aided by a number of factors. The resurgence of the U.N.P. aroused fear in the Marxist Left, which became receptive to a no-contest pact with the S.L.F.P., primarily to prevent the U.N.P. from obtaining power. The failure of the Marxist pretense to majority status in the March election was also a factor. Also, the survival of the S.L.F.P. in the March election and the consequent assumption of active party leadership by Mrs. Bandaranaike had again made it attractive as a vehicle of power. Many who had defected from the party rejoined it and ran under its label in July, especially those who had run as candidates of the L.P.P. and the M.E.P., both of which parties suffered badly at the polls. As these defectors returned to the party, the S.L.F.P. regained its personal-influence structure. In any case, events had shown that the S.L.F.P. was dependent upon such a structure, and that many notables were likewise dependent upon an effective party label. The events of 1960 indicated that the S.L.F.P., in spite of lacking an organization, had developed an image that was itself of electoral consequence.

The S.L.F.P. remained largely a party of notables. Policy decisions of the Sirimavo Bandaranaike government were still a function of the cabinet meeting and parliamentary party caucus, as they had been under the previous Bandaranaike government. Except at the top, the formal party organization was not a center of policy decision. Disputes in the Cabinet were reflected in dissension in the backbench and within the party, and shuffling and reshuffling of cabinet posts was used to placate the disputants. This was not always effective, and defections of prominent members in Parliament repeatedly occurred, because of policy disagreement, or the frustration of personal ambitions, or both. The defection of such men was often caused by the Government's pursuit of policies they considered detrimental to the interests of their constituents or to the local network of influence from which they draw their strength. Often defections are encouraged by the fact that the M.P.'s consider their local influence sufficient to assure them a relatively safe seat. This is not always the case, and some notables who defected and ran as independents were subsequently defeated. This is one indication that the party has made progress in its move to replace personality as a primary determinant of voting behavior. What often happens, however, is that notables defect from the S.L.F.P. and obtain entry into other parties. In any case, the unity of the S.L.F.P. in Parliament has been made difficult by its reliance on notables and by the broad ideological spectrum that its members cover. Its leading notables have the support of personally or ideologically committed blocs in both the backbench and the party as a whole. These include the "Forward Bloc," which backed Philip Gunawardena in his conflict with the more conservative members of the M.E.P.

cabinet, and the so-called Ginger Group, formed in both the backbench and the Senate in 1965 "to safeguard the principles of the SLFP and to maintain its identity."[46] It was conflict between leading personalities and blocs that led to the erosion of the S.L.F.P. majority in 1964, when C. P. de Silva and his followers crossed the floor and the Government fell. Subsequently De Silva formed his own party, which in coalition with the U.N.P. in 1965 was able to return members in some areas.

The S.L.F.P. still depends a great deal on the influence of its candidates. In the election of 1965 the S.L.F.P. returned 41 of the 101 candidates who ran under its label. Of its 101 candidates, 41 were running under the party label for the first time, and only 14 of these were returned. Of these, 11 had run previously, either as independents or as candidates of other parties. Fifty-nine of the S.L.F.P. candidates had run under the S.L.F.P. label in 1960, and of these, 27 were returned. This may be one indication that the influence of its notables is still of considerable consequence. However, the importance of the S.L.F.P. label should not be denied. In spite of organizational deficiencies, the party's image seems to have become a definite electoral factor, for many independent candidates were defeated who had previously won election under the label of the party.

The S.L.F.P. has made some effort to build a formal organization. In June, 1963, the S.L.F.P. Women's Organization was instituted to organize work centers throughout the island.[47] The work centers are intended to engage in social work and thereby increase the influence of the party. The Youth League has also been expanded, but defections by its secretaries and the gravitation of many of its branch associations to the Marxist parties have absorbed a good many of the gains that the S.L.F.P. may have derived from its expansion. The Youth League was not particularly helpful to the party in the election of 1965, and its leadership is so decentralized and personalized that its role as an ancillary to the party is severely limited. While the party has formed branch associations almost everywhere in Sinhalese areas,[48] it is questionable whether their loyalty goes to the party or to the S.L.F.P. notables who represent constituencies in which they operate.

The S.L.F.P. adopted a revised constitution in 1963 in an effort to evolve a more democratic and effective organization.[49] The constitution provides for an annual general conference of delegates from the branch associations. The conference is empowered to decide on the general principles of the party. The new constitution replaced the General Committee with the Central Committee, which, like its predecessor, is to meet every four months or when summoned by the Executive Committee. It is composed of members appointed by local associations at the rate of two for every branch association and one for every women's society and youth league. In addition, all members of the party in Parliament, members of the Executive Committee, and seventy-five others elected by the general conference are members of the Central Committee. When it meets, the Central Committee must ratify all decisions taken by the Executive Committee. The Executive Committee is chosen by the Central Committee and consists of a president, a number of vice presidents not exceeding seven, a secretary, two assistant secretaries, a treasurer, assistant treasurer, and seventy-five other members chosen from the Central Committee. The Executive Committee meets once a month and exercises all the powers exercised by the Executive Committee of the previous constitution, including control of the party fund and nomination of candidates.

The major change in the organization of the S.L.F.P. is the expansion of the Executive Committee. It is now a much more representative body, and it is open to greater participation by party members. However, the Executive Committee cannot become a truly effective center for policy discussion and conflict resolution while the party organization under it remains immature electorally. The Executive Committee has to compete with the parliamentary party caucus for power, and as long as the party remains dependent organizationally and electorally on its elected notables, the caucus will remain the center of power in the party. It is unlikely that M.P.'s in the party will accept a transfer of their power to the Executive Committee when their support is essential to the electoral success of the party. Thus, for the Executive Committee to obtain power, the branch associations and other ancillary associations of the formal party organization must become a more efficient electoral force committed to the party rather than to personalities.

So far this development has been impeded by the inability of the central organization to provide funds for its branch associations and by the need of the S.L.F.P. to rely upon funds provided by its candidates for election campaigns. The wealthier pressure groups in Ceylon have not been anxious to contribute to the S.L.F.P. because it has implemented policies contrary to their interests. The cultural groups and indigenous pressure groups that do support the party are not affluent, and the party must raise funds through levies on its M.P.'s, membership dues, subscriptions, and contributions from its wealthier members. None of this amounts to a great deal. In addition, the informal personal-influence structure of the S.L.F.P. has been so effective that the growth of a formal organization has not been seen to be of critical importance. The party has had the services of a number of organized and amorphous pressure groups oriented to traditionalist interests, and these have provided the party and its candidates with a wide network of influence that has been invaluable in the mobilization of voters. A second personal-influence structure is provided collectively by S.L.F.P. candidates who in addition to their own influence are allied personally with locally influential interest groups. Whatever strength the formal organization of the S.L.F.P. has, has come primarily from the prominence of the national leaders of the party and the image the party has obtained because of the measures it has implemented as a government. It has been this image, more than anything else, that has enabled the S.L.F.P. to develop an identity in spite of its lack of an organization.

Ideology

The popular image of the S.L.F.P. has derived much more from what it has done as a government than from what it says it will do as a party. Thus, while the career of the party has been marked by some ideological confusion, the S.L.F.P. image has progressively become clearer both to itself and to the voter. The present ideological position of the S.L.F.P. is more radical than that which Bandaranaike had intended at the origin of the party. His objective was to organize an alternative to the U.N.P. that, while incorporating the fundamental political philosophy of the U.N.P., would better articulate the interests of groups that the U.N.P. neglected. The long-range objective of Bandaranaike was the foundation of a predominantly two-party system in Ceylon that would operate within the context of a broad ideological consensus. The examples of Britain and the United States were clearly in mind when Bandaranaike founded the S.L.F.P., and the ideological orientation of his party was toward the same Western political tradition as these, but readjusted to fit the peasant economy and traditional culture of Ceylon. Bandaranaike originally defined the S.L.F.P. as a "Social Democratic Party" that stood for "the preservation and fostering . . . of democratic ideals and freedoms." The first manifesto of the S.L.F.P. supported an approach to the solution of economic problems guided by what it vaguely termed "Socialist principles." The aim of the party, according to its original manifesto, was "to achieve a Social Democratic Society through a Government dependent upon the widest possible participation of the people." [50] In respect to the religion and culture of Ceylon, the S.L.F.P. announced its support of "a revival of our cultures and the use of our National Languages," as well as a policy that reflected the "spiritual values" of the people. [51]

The image of the S.L.F.P. was relatively clear when the party was formed. Bandaranaike was known among Westernized Ceylonese as a moderate socialist firmly committed to the values of Western democracy, and his entire background confirmed his dedication to the peasant and traditionalist element. The men who were associated with Bandaranaike in the formation of his party were similarly known, and the activity and personnel of the S.L.F.P. combined with its ideology to give the party a cohesive image. However, between 1952 and 1956 the S.L.F.P. sought an inclusiveness sufficient to give it a mass base of power, and the ranks of the party were thrown open to all who could assist the S.L.F.P. in gaining wide voter support. This move introduced a substantial Marxist element, and the S.L.F.P. became a composite party whose ideological spectrum had become so wide and so full of contradictions that the party image lost its clarity. Most importantly, events at this time gave the S.L.F.P. two heavily weighted wings, one radical and Marxist, and the other ranging from moderate socialism to traditionalist conservatism.

When the S.L.F.P. and its allies in the M.E.P. became the Government in 1956, the image of the party had become so unclear, except in regard to its language policy, that no one knew for sure how far to the left the Government would carry Ceylon. The party was composed of such disparate ideological elements that image clarification could only come from actual government. The experience of this period confirmed that the S.L.F.P. was the same moderate socialist and traditionalist party that Bandaranaike had originally intended it to be. Policy in the interest of the peasant and traditionalist class was implemented, and nothing was done to subvert democracy or private enterprise. A revival of indigenous culture was started, state enterprise was initiated, co-operatives were established, and welfare measures were introduced, but the economic order was not substantially altered. The moderation of the party was confirmed when, after the disintegration of the M.E.P., Bandaranaike denounced Marx-

ism and reaffirmed his party's commitment to "democratic socialism" at the annual conference of the S.L.F.P. in the spring of
1959. All this, as well as the ouster or withdrawal of Marxists
from the party, helped clarify its image.

However, the assassination of Bandaranaike, the temporary
assumption of power in the party by the right wing under Dahanayake, the dispersal of S.L.F.P. notables into various parties,
and all the confusion that preceded the March election of 1960
threw the entire S.L.F.P. into disarray. Whatever image the
S.L.F.P. had at this time came from its association with Mrs.
Bandaranaike, from the image of her late husband, from the
work the party had done for the country from 1956 to 1959, and
from the notables, particularly C. P. de Silva, who carried the
party banner through this period of trial. The reconsolidation of
the party at the time of the second election of 1960 and the
leadership of Mrs. Bandaranaike did not fully clarify the image
of the S.L.F.P., because, as before, open ranks had reintroduced
a substantial Marxist element into the party. Thus, in spite of
Mrs. Bandaranaike's repeated disclaimers of Marxist orientation
in the S.L.F.P., how far to the left an S.L.F.P. government would
go was again uncertain. But the image of the S.L.F.P. as a peasant-
oriented, traditionalist, and fundamentally populist party was relatively clear, and it was this, together with the influence of the
numerous notables who ran under the S.L.F.P. label in July, 1960,
that accounted for the success of the party in that election. Within a
year of the election the Finance Minister, Felix Bandaranaike,
sought to confirm the populist commitment of the party. He said
then that the party had a "simple standard; we stand by the interests of the rural people of this country." [52]

The measures implemented by the S.L.F.P. government between 1960 and 1965 involved an increasing amount of state economic initiative and ownership, the extension of social services
and welfare, land development, co-operative enterprise, emphasis
on indigenous culture, and de-Westernization of education and
the administrative services. Pushed by its radical wing, the Gov-

ernment indicated that it would take over the press and the parochial school system, and develop greater amounts of state-owned industry. As its majority eroded, the party decided that for survival it would have to enter a coalition with the Marxist L.S.S.P. This led, at the end of 1964, to a rupture in the party similar to that which it experienced in 1959. C. P. de Silva and fourteen others withdrew from the party. This faction represented the conservative and moderate wing of the party, and its withdrawal indicated the more radical position that the S.L.F.P. has adopted.

The official ideology of the S.L.F.P. is today similar to that of the L.S.S.P. except that it is more oriented to the peasant. It defines its ideology as "democratic socialism." This, it says, means maintenance of the political freedoms essential to democracy, such as freedom of speech and assembly, and a society of equal opportunities for all. The ultimate objective of this ideology is to create a classless society. This is to be achieved under "the aegis of a democratic institution" and without coercion, although the manifesto of the S.L.F.P. recognizes that some individual rights afforded under a capitalistic system may have to be denied or limited. What these are the manifesto does not specify. The other emphasis of "democratic socialism" is on the "revival and development of religious and cultural activities." The aim of the party is the achievement of a socialist state, which the S.L.F.P. expects to "develop systematically in accordance with the views and opinions of the masses." [53]

The S.L.F.P. has committed itself by its actions in office to an agrarian socialism, and by these actions and its official ideology the party aims at a classless, socialist state. This position facilitates coalition with the L.S.S.P., whose ideology similarly stands for the peaceful evolution of a socialist society based on the traditional culture of Ceylon. The party has become known for this, and its image as a socialist, agrarian, and traditionalist party has become visible. The problem with this image, however, is that the intended pace of movement toward a socialist state and what this movement may involve at any time is not known. While election platforms seek to specify this, the S.L.F.P. cannot guarantee their implementation because of the personal character of its organization. Policy decisions must be made in caucus after election, and only on broad questions of policy can agreement be assured. It is this organizational decentralization more than anything else that prevents full clarification of the S.L.F.P.'s image. In spite of this, the party has become known as a people's party with a more radical policy orientation than the U.N.P.

THE MARXIST LEFT

One observer has described Ceylon's Leftists as "the boisterous sons of University education and [of] the failure of the Government to give jobs to the English educated young men." [54] He was speaking of the conditions of the 1930's, out of which the leaders of the Marxist movement emerged. They were enthusiastic and visionary, and through the drama of the coming revolution they envisaged a utopia for Ceylon. As was true in the Second International, the Marxist leaders were absorbed in theoretical questions and fond of "interminable argument." [55] In time, theoretical conflict rationalized personal power struggles in the Marxist movement, and the divisions that resulted have never been healed. Every attempt since the division of 1939 to unite the Marxist parties has failed because of personal opportunism, ideological differences, and disputes over questions of tactics. The formation of the United Left Front in 1964 held the greatest promise of united action on the part of the Marxist parties, but this front soon crumbled, as the L.S.S.P. entered into coalition with the S.L.F.P. on its own. But while hopes of a new merger of the Marxist parties appear now to have faded, the C.P. and the L.S.S.P. have found more common ground for co-operation. They have also reached what seems a permanent no-contest arrangement with the S.L.F.P., and the potential of an L.S.S.P.-S.L.F.P. alternative government having the support of the C.P.

seems stabilized. The main divisive factor in the Left is not so much conflict between the Marxist parties as it is conflict within both the L.S.S.P. and the C.P. between the doctrinaire and the practical, the revolutionary and the parliamentary.

The Lanka Sama Samaja Party

The L.S.S.P., since its reunification in 1950, has moved from a revolutionary, radical socialism to a reformist, or evolutionary, socialism that accepts parliamentary action and multiparty competition. The two extreme ideological tendencies were evident almost from the beginning of the party, and the conflict between them has made it difficult for the L.S.S.P. to develop a definite image as a party. While the moderate wing under N. M. Perera has always been dominant, the L.S.S.P. has had to conciliate its revolutionary wing by retaining its revolutionary ideology. This has resulted in contradictions in its manifestos, and although N. M. Perera always argued for the defense of the democratic and parliamentary system, the electorate could not be sure of the nonrevolutionary character of the party. The L.S.S.P.'s left wing, whose base of power is in the trade unions, youth leagues, and the intellectuals who publish the *Young Socialist,* is so strongly antiparliament that it was an arduous task for N. M. Perera even to bring his party into no-contest arrangements with the S.L.F.P. But by 1960 the moderate group in the party had attained greater strength in the Central Committee and among the membership, and the manifesto of the L.S.S.P. that year reflected the moderation of this centralist group. Its program of nationalization was limited, and the attempt of the L.S.S.P. to obtain a parliamentary majority in that year was accompanied by a promise that it would guarantee the right of other parties to work freely in the country, and the right of the people "to turn us out of office if we fail them." [56] This was published despite the angry protest of the left wing, which, through the *Young Socialist* and its leader in Parliament, Edmund Samarakkody, advocated a policy of no compromise, and revolution. In 1964, when the Perera-dominated L.S.S.P. voted at its conference for a coalition with the S.L.F.P., the left wing condemned the action of the "reformists" as "a complete violation of the basic principles of Trotskyism on which the revolutionary program of the party is based."[57]

The rupture in the L.S.S.P. and the consequent participation of the main section of the party in a government coalition with the S.L.F.P. helped to clarify the image of the L.S.S.P. as a parliamentary party with a moderate socialist ideology similar to that of the Labour party in Great Britain. This was the type of ideology on which it ran its campaign in 1965. In that year its revolutionary section (L.S.S.P.-R.) ran four candidates, all of whom lost their deposits. One of them, Bala Tampoe, of Colombo Central, leader of the Ceylon Mercantile Union, obtained only 4,599 votes. In March and July, 1960, when he ran under the label of the L.S.S.P., he had received, respectively, 22,228 and 16,406 votes. In another constituency Meryl Fernando, a long-time notable of the L.S.S.P., received 1,048 votes, while the L.S.S.P. candidate got 16,020 votes. In the July, 1960, election Fernando, running under the L.S.S.P. label, had won his seat by a vote of 12,943. Most significantly, Edmund Samarakkody, leader of the L.S.S.P.-R. and one of the most prominent men in the L.S.S.P. almost since its inception, got only 278 votes, while the L.S.S.P. candidate carried the constituency with a vote of 13,023. In the July, 1960, election Samarakkody had won his seat as an L.S.S.P. candidate with a vote of 10,103. The electorate had totally rejected the L.S.S.P.-R., and the reformist policy of the L.S.S.P. was confirmed, not only by the electorate, but by disciplined party members who backed official party candidates.

Thus the L.S.S.P. has undergone an important ideological change over the years. It has dispensed with its extreme radicalism, dismissing its revolutionary wing from its ranks, and, as a whole, has adopted the strategy and policy of the center. This has been in response to the nonrevolutionary character of the masses and their orientation toward parliamentary action.

But at the same time the L.S.S.P. has had to accept its relegation to the position of a minor, coalition party. Its attempt toward a majority in 1960 met with disaster when it failed miserably in its attempt to get the rural vote.[58] One observer had remarked earlier, "its urban leadership lacks intimate contact with the masses who reside in the rural areas." [59] Thus the L.S.S.P. has remained a party of the worker, with few votes from outside the working class. But worker loyalty sustains it as a party and puts it into a position to enter into a coalition with the rural-based S.L.F.P., now that it has accepted parliamentary action as its political strategy.

The Marxist parties were for a long time the best organized parties in Ceylon, and the L.S.S.P., since its 1950 reunification, has been the best organized and most effective of all the Marxist parties. The L.S.S.P. has succeeded in developing an organization that operates with a good deal of democracy in the formulation of party policy, strategy, and tactics. As W. Howard Wriggins observed, "questions are aired and argued within the party with considerable vigor." [60] While the party has frequently suffered defections and splits as a result, the L.S.S.P. has nevertheless been able to contend against other parties with an organization that is both disciplined and resolute. While its influence with voters derives immeasurably from the popularity of its leaders and its expression of working-class interests, much also is due to its organization's efficient operation as an electoral machine. The trade unions of the L.S.S.P. give it a well-organized bloc of votes in those districts in Colombo and along the coast of the Western Province where the working class resides. Amalgamated into the Ceylon Federation of Labour, headed by N. M. Perera, the unions claimed a membership of about 112,000 workers in 1961.[61] The largest L.S.S.P. union is the Lanka Estate Workers Union, whose membership in 1959 was reported to have exceeded 60,000.[62] The most important of L.S.S.P. unions, however, is the Ceylon Mercantile Union, which at one time was under the control of the Labour party of A. E. Gooneshina. It claimed a membership of 15,000 in 1959,[63] and has branches in 150 firms in the Colombo area. Two other important unions of the L.S.S.P. are the United Port Workers Union, of 6,000 members,[64] and the All-Ceylon United Motor Workers Union, with a membership that exceeds 8,000.[65] In addition to providing an organized bloc of votes for the party, the trade unions of the L.S.S.P. are a source of some party funds. A union is legally permitted to establish a political fund for "the promotion of the civic and political interests of its members."[66] However, a majority of a union's members, present and voting, must first consent to the establishment of a political fund at a meeting called for that purpose. After that, contributions to it are voluntary, and the union is not allowed to use any other of its funds for political purposes. In addition to the campaign assistance provided by this political fund, union members are allowed to work on behalf of candidates endorsed by the union. This, perhaps more than the political fund, has been of value to the campaigns of L.S.S.P. candidates. The L.S.S.P. has not hesitated to employ its unions in political strikes against the Government. Several times L.S.S.P. unions have participated in general strikes, and often strikes are used to protest against what the party considers to be unjust actions of a government. Long after independence, and perhaps even now, the L.S.S.P. viewed its trade union members as a military reserve that could be activated if any government attempted to institute a dictatorial state.

The Youth League of the L.S.S.P. has been another source of organizational strength for the party, although that of the U.N.P. has become much more extensive. Founded in 1949, the Sama Samaja Youth League was defined as a "peripheral organization" open to those youths who accepted the leadership of the party, although they were not required "to conform to the strict rules which apply to party membership."[67] Philip Gunawardena was elected its first president at the All-Island Congress of Sama Samaja Youth Leagues in 1949. The league was disrupted when its president formed his own party one year later, but under the energetic direction of Robert Gunawardena and others it quickly recuperated. By 1956 it was able to provide considerable electoral assistance for L.S.S.P. candidates.[68] While the Youth League tends to be a center of radicalism in the party and to be more responsive to the exhortations of the left wing than is the formal party cadre, the leadership of the L.S.S.P. has managed to maintain control of it. At the annual conference of the Youth League in 1964, for instance, the centrist faction in the L.S.S.P. managed to oust the left wing from posts of leadership in the league.[69]

Membership in the youth leagues and trade unions of the L.S.S.P. does not automatically bestow membership in the party, although both the leagues and the unions have served as recruiting grounds for prospective members. The L.S.S.P. has preferred to remain a small and select group rather than to become a mass party—a choice that reflects the party's original revolutionary orientation. It has retained this elitist character partly because membership in the party is thereby made attractive and ambition-satisfying, which is necessary to a party that cannot offer the reward of political office to its members. Ideological indoctrination and the hierarchical structure within the party, access to which depends upon the energy and discipline with which a member serves the party, have permitted the L.S.S.P. to maintain discipline in its ranks. Before an applicant can be proposed for membership he must either have served as a member of the Youth League or have worked for the party in other ways, such as working for an electoral association or a trade union, or helping in the production or distribution of party publications. The purpose of this requirement is to enable a prospective member to demonstrate the sincerity and strength of his desire to serve the party and to break down any "petty bourgeois" attitudes that he might have. It also gives party regulars ample opportunity to gauge his worth. The applicant is proposed by a party member of a local organization who knows him well. The application is then sent on to the District Committee, which, after its endorsement, transmits it to the Organizational Bureau (Orgburo) for approval. This bureau is composed of about ten of the most important leaders of the party, who weigh the application of a prospective member on the basis of his record of work done for the party. This is one means that the party leadership has of disciplining its youth league members, as well as the members of other ancillary organizations who aspire to membership in the party, although the executive officers of the ancillary organizations can also take disciplinary steps against recalcitrant members. The role of the Orgburo in regard to party membership has doubtless been of importance to the party leadership, and probably partly explains the control it has been able to maintain over its more radical Youth League, whose officers the party leadership has been able to overthrow by a vote of the league conference if they refuse to follow the party line.

After review and consent by the Orgburo the application is sent back to the local organization, and the candidate is brought into one of its meetings. Here he makes a solemn pledge to abide by the constitution of the L.S.S.P. After this the candidate serves a probationary period that ranges from three months to a year, depending upon his ability and the quality of his work. His application is then reconsidered, and if the judgment is favorable, the candidate becomes a full-fledged party member. The whole procedure is designed to provide the party with dedicated members who are ideologically indoctrinated, committed to the party, and responsive to the discipline that is so vital to the effective functioning of the party. Such training as this is essential to a party like the L.S.S.P., which must maintain discipline without being able to provide the access to political patronage that other parties such as the U.N.P. and the S.L.F.P. can offer to members. Because of this, ideological devotion and sincere commitment must be instilled, and elevation within the party structure must replace patronage as a reward for service and an instrument of discipline. Now that the S.L.F.P. has become dependent upon the L.S.S.P., the party may have more access to patronage, and this may have the effect of strengthening the moderate section of the party leadership that advocates a parliamentary orientation.

While information on the size of the party is not available to the public, it is estimated that there are no more than four thousand members.[70] About one thousand delegates now attend its annual conference, and these are chosen from the local organizations at the rate of one for every three to five members. The conference is, therefore, a widely representative organ and, according to the rules of the party, is the main decision-making body. Decisions taken by the higher organs of the party must ultimately be ratified by the conference, and in the past it has not hesitated to exercise its authority. The conference elects the Central Committee of the party, which in 1964 consisted of forty-five members. This committee exercises all the powers of the conference between its sessions, and like the conference, it is a broadly representative body that includes working-class elements as well as intellectuals. At the apex of the party structure are the Politburo, which is responsible for political decisions, the Orgburo, which supervises the party organization, and the Trade Union Bureau, which links the L.S.S.P. trade unions to the party structure. Each of these organs has about ten members, who, collectively, are the most powerful men of the party. The Politburo is the most important of these units, and the most powerful leaders occupy seats on it as well as on the two other executive organs and the Central Committee. Power in the party derives from, and is indicated by, membership on these executive organs joined to a post as secretary or president of one of the more powerful trade unions of the party. A parliamentary seat and national prominence are additional symbols and sources of power in the party, and its leading members usually have all of these. As far as the party is concerned, the Politburo is the organ of the most power and prestige. In 1964, just prior to the outbreak of conflict in the leadership, the Politburo consisted of

N. M. Perera, Colvin R. de Silva, Leslie Goonewardene, Bernard Zoysa, Edmund Samarakkody, and Anil Moonesinghe—all of whom were heads of L.S.S.P. trade unions and members of the House of Representatives—and Bala Tampoe, head of the powerful Ceylon Mercantile Union, and D. G. William, vice-president of the Ceylon Federation of Labour, and G. P. Perera. The Politburo meets every Friday to review the political situation, and any decisions it makes must be ratified by the Central Committee. While all bodies but the conference are expected to act under the discipline of "democratic centralism," divisions within the Politburo have been reflected in equivalent divisions in the Central Committee, and a majority vote in the former must be overwhelming if the latter is to abide by it without division.

Unlike the U.N.P. and the S.L.F.P., the L.S.S.P. has its vital centers of political decision and conflict resolution in the party organs, rather than in the party caucus. Policy decisions and the resolution of disputes are handled in the higher organs, and the lower organs effectively participate only when divisions in the higher organs prevent decision or resolution. Dissension in the higher echelons inevitably leads to a downward shift in decision making. If the Politburo decision is unanimous or if the most powerful members agree, then the Central Committee or the conference will almost automatically concur with the decision. However, if there is a significant split in the leadership or if the issue at stake is particularly divisive, then a battle between leaders and factions will ensue at lower levels. On several occasions the conference has had to act as final arbiter in disputes at the top. Such was the case in 1953, for instance, when the issue of Leftist unity nearly split the party asunder. The negative view of unity held by N. M. Perera and a majority of the Politburo was finally sustained by the conference by a vote of 259 to 125 after a long and bitter struggle.[71] So divisive was this issue that after the decision of the conference one-third of its members walked out and formed their own section of the party. A rupture of this sort, however, has come to be the exception, although recalcitrants have frequently been expelled.

Each leader in the Politburo has his own personal bloc of support in the lower organs of the party, as each has his own trade union, electoral, and ideological constituency within the membership. The size of these personal constituencies varies with the prominence and charisma of the leader and the extent to which he occupies posts of power in the trade unions and party organization. No one man has the power to dictate to the party, though outstanding leaders like N. M. Perera and Colvin R. de Silva can count on the support of significant constituencies in the party on their own. Top-level decisions in the party can only be made if there is agreement between at least a few of the most powerful leaders, especially Perera, De Silva, and Leslie Goonewardene. The strong dissent of any one of these, together with a lack of unanimity among the other Politburo members, means that a divisive party struggle will ensue.

To an extent, therefore, each of the dominant leaders of the L.S.S.P. has a personal-influence structure within the party organizations and trade unions similar to an "extended family." There are lesser leaders who have "extended family" relationships in the trade unions. The influence of the "families" is brought to bear at decision-making centers within the party in almost the same way as notables in the S.L.F.P. apply the support of their personal blocs to the contests that occur within the meetings of the parliamentary caucus. L.S.S.P. members are subject to the same manipulation and mobilization as are members of the backbench and of personal local organizations of the S.L.F.P., and, for that matter, the U.N.P. prior to 1956. All are related to their leaders through personal-influence structures within the formal organization of their party.

The extent of personal blocs should not be exaggerated, however. There is always a number of free-floating members within the lower organs of the party who are not firmly committed to any leader, and it is to these that leaders must often appeal. This is especially true when divisions appear in the Politburo, because dissension here is reflected in confusion below. Absence of a firm decision above gives the lower organs greater freedom of decision, and this increases in direct proportion to the seriousness of the conflict in the higher organs. In these instances, particularly, the resolution of disputes depends upon the ability of leaders to convince their peers and followers of the correctness of their positions. Thus, while leaders may possess stable blocs of support in the party, their leadership also depends on "their intellectual kudos and talent for debate." [72] Often, to win a point a leader must argue incessantly, give repeated talks and lectures to meetings of party members, youth leagues, and trade unions, and ultimately engage in debate before the Central Committee and the conference. At the same time he must work behind the scenes to mobilize his followers and exert pressure on others in the party and trade unions. This can be an arduous and long task. Even N. M. Perera must fight long and hard at times to assert leadership. His decision to enter a coalition government with the S.L.F.P. in 1964 provides an illustration of the process of decision making in the L.S.S.P.

Leader of the moderate wing of the party, Perera decided that the best strategy for the L.S.S.P. was to accept partnership in a government with the S.L.F.P., whose majority was gradually eroding in Parliament. Consequently he entered into negotiations with the Prime Minister. A divided Politburo refused to sanction the negotiations, although Perera had the support of most of the parliamentary members of the L.S.S.P. A left wing formed in the Politburo, consisting of Bala Tampoe and Edmund Samarakkody, who violently opposed the "parliamentary reformism" of Perera's coalition attempt. A so-called centrist group also emerged, consisting of Colvin R. de Silva, Leslie Goonewardene and Bernard Zoysa. While they were receptive to parliamentary action as one means of achieving socialism, they were opposed to an "unprincipled" or "opportunistic" alliance. Their initial reaction to Perera's proposal was negative.[73] This left the so-called right wing of Perera in the minority in the Politburo. Perera next took his fight to the Central Committee, where a circular had been

distributed by the left wing attacking the Perera group as be-
trayers of the party. This had been signed by fourteen members
of the Central Committee.[74] When the Central Committee met,
it voted 22 to 19 against coalition, three of its members being
absent and one abstaining.[75] It was obvious that to obtain the
backing of his party for coalition, Perera would have to persuade
the centrists to support him. This support was provisionally won
by his agreeing with the centrists on a number of additional
demands to be made on the S.L.F.P. as a price for coalition.
With this support, Perera's resolution was accepted by the Central
Committee on May 10, 1964, against the wishes of twelve adamant members of the left wing.[76] Perera also succeeded in having
a special party conference summoned for June to appoint a new
Central Committee more receptive to coalition. The month before the conference was marked by speeches, maneuvers, lobby-
ing, and negotiations by the three factions to mobilize support
for the decisive session of the conference. Perera negotiated with
the S.L.F.P. to obtain the concessions necessary for the support
of the centrists, and at the same time he tried to persuade the
centrists to modify their demands so as to make them acceptable
to the S.L.F.P. In the struggle Perera succeeded in splitting the
unity of the centrists. While there was speculation that Perera
would have a majority among the more than nine hundred
delegates at the conference, by whose decision the centrists promised to abide, nothing was certain until the conference met. When
it did, it voted for a new Central Committee favorable to coalition, with only about 150 hard-core members of the left wing
voting against it.[77] Shortly after this, many of the left wing
either withdrew or were expelled from the party for not abiding
by a decision of the conference. Subsequently, many were ousted
from their positions in the trade unions and youth leagues by a
similar process.

While most decisions of the party are not this difficult, the case
illustrates the role that lower organs can play in the decision-
making process when issues are divisive. When they are not, and

when leaders agree, policy and decision in the party are transmitted from the top down. If internal opposition endangers the party, severe disciplinary measures are available to the leaders and are supported by a disciplined cadre. However, criticism is always permitted within reason, and as long as their activity does not threaten to injure the party, members are allowed a relatively free voice in most matters. This has resulted in a spirited membership that actively supports the party. Unlike the U.N.P. and the S.L.F.P., the L.S.S.P. reserves nomination as candidate for those who are loyal party members. Branch associations are consulted in the nominating process, and all candidates chosen by the party must first of all have performed services to the party in the past. The party then seeks to select from among this list a local candidate who has influence in the constituency in which he will run. The fact that while the L.S.S.P. takes the influence of a candidate into account, it considers his loyalty and service first, increases the spirit of the party and the vitality of its branch associations.

The only organizational weakness of the L.S.S.P. is its lack of funds. While its leaders are wealthy, the party is not, and in many cases L.S.S.P. candidates must supply their own funds. What funds the party has are drawn from the political funds of its unions, membership subscriptions, levies on its parliamentary members, sales of its publications, election subscriptions, and contributions from its wealthier members. This income does not amount to a great deal, and for election campaigns the party does not contribute much more, materially, than literature and posters. Its greatest contribution to its candidates is the efficient organization it can put at their disposal. A great many workers, drawn from its trade unions, youth leagues, and party organization, are available to assist in the campaigns of L.S.S.P. candidates. However, this assistance is limited to areas where the L.S.S.P. is well organized. When the party runs candidates all over the island, as it did in March, 1960, it is unable to supply an efficient organization for all of them. Ideologically limited to the working class, the party is organizationally restricted to working-class areas. Thus, while the L.S.S.P. has developed a mature organization, it is one that fits a minority party. In this capacity it serves well. But if the party is to expand, not only must it develop a mass ideology, it must also become a mass party organizationally. From its recent activity, it appears that it has decided against mass orientation.

The Ceylon Communist Party

The Ceylon Communist party has experienced the same intra-party tension as has the L.S.S.P. It has had its revolutionary and parliamentary wings, and there has been constant contradiction between its actions and statements in Parliament, on the one hand, and the revolutionary stand it has taken in its manifestoes and public statements, on the other. In the House of Representatives it has always stood firm for the privileges of democracy and the rights of Parliament, and it has used the power of the political strike to oppose what it considered to be undemocratic actions on the part of the Government. Of all the parties, the U.N.P. was the one most feared by the C.P., and as a result the C.P. was a prime force in negotiations for Leftist unity against the U.N.P. Like the L.S.S.P., the C.P. kept its well-organized union members as a defense force against a potential coup by the Government. But while the C.P. fought for the preservation of democracy, and while its leaders, especially Pieter Keuneman,[78] have been among the best parliamentarians in the House, the revolutionary ideology and orientation of the C.P. have contradicted and confused its image as a democratic and parliamentary party.

As in the case of the L.S.S.P., however, the C.P. made a gradual movement over the years toward the center, a move that was climaxed in the expulsion of the party's radical, revolutionary wing in 1963. After its attempt to gain major-party status failed in 1960, the strategy of the C.P. tended to de-emphasize revolution and stress co-operation with "progressive forces" in Parliament. The debacle of 1960 was final proof that the revolutionary ideology of the C.P. was inconsistent with the temper of the people. The party's movement away from revolution was also a reflection of the parliamentary orientation of its main leaders, who preached revolution, not so much out of dedication, as because of their entanglement in dogma and their need to convince the rank and file of the party of their dedication to Marxist theory and strategy. Also, the leaders have tended to become more conservative with the passage of time. Adherence to orthodox Marxist ideology and revolutionary dogma have become characteristic of a younger generation of Communists.

The rupture in the C.P. occurred in 1963, when its Central Committee expelled N. S. Shanmugathasan, general secretary of the Communist Ceylon Trade Union Federation (C.T.U.F.), from the party. The expulsion was due to Shanmugathasan's support of the Chinese position in the Sino-Soviet conflict, his opposition to the United Left Front, and his persistent condemnation of the C.P.'s orientation to Parliament and its turning away from revolution. As a result of the expulsion both the C.P. and the C.T.U.F. split, and in the early part of 1964 the two factions held separate congresses, each called the Seventh Congress of the Ceylon Communist Party. The China faction met in January and condemned the Soviet faction for revisionism and its denial "of the non-peaceful transition to socialism."[79] Later it condemned both the Soviet faction and the L.S.S.P. for their adoption of parliamentarianism.

The bulk of the Communist membership remained with their old-guard leaders, and the moderate group retained control of the party. Under the leadership of the moderates, the C.P. advocated co-operation with the S.L.F.P. government and conducted its 1965 campaign in coalition with the L.S.S.P. and the S.L.F.P. The C.P. (China Wing) ran four of its own candidates in the 1965 election, all of whom lost their deposits. They included Shanmugathasan, who polled only 2,427 votes in the Communist stronghold of Colombo Central. Pieter Keuneman, who had represented the constituency ever since 1947, was again returned, with a vote of 41,478. Thus the revolutionary section, none of whose leaders has ever sat in Parliament, was rejected.

The organization of the C.P. is not as extensive as that of the L.S.S.P., and it is apparently more centralized. The Politburo is the focus of power in the party, and leadership in this organ is exercised by three men: Pieter Keuneman, who is general secretary of the party and president of its Ceylon Federation of Trade Unions (C.F.T.U.), Dr. S. A. Wickremasinghe, who is president, and M. G. Mendis, who is general secretary of the C.F.T.U. The Central Committee of the party is directed by the Politburo and appears to act under its discipline. On the advice of the Politburo it voted to expel Shanmugathasan, with only two opposing votes.[80] The congress of the party elects the higher organization and is constitutionally the supreme organ of power. Provision has not been made for an annual meeting of the congress, however, and its ability to exercise its authority is thereby limited. The Central Committee is empowered to summon a congress, but in spite of a resolution adopted at the Sixth Congress, in 1960, that recommended its convention again in 1962, the Seventh Congress was not summoned until the spring of 1964. This interval may have been due to the need to rearrange and mobilize power blocs in the party in preparation for the confrontation between the Peking and Moscow wings of the party.

While the membership of the C.P. is not large, its ancillary organizations greatly extend its popular influence and organized strength. The party obtains much support through its comparatively large youth league and especially from its well-organized and powerful unions. At the Fourth Annual Congress of the Ceylon Communist Party Youth Leagues, in June, 1964, a thousand leagues were expected to be represented, with a total of five thousand delegates in attendance.[81] The trade union strength of the C.P. is second only to that of the Ceylon Indian Congress in number and influence. In 1963 the unions of the C.P., amalgamated into the Ceylon Trade Union Federation, had a membership of over 130,000.[82] The party split of that year temporarily disrupted the trade unions of the party and led to a bitter contest for their control. Shanmugathasan, following his expulsion from the party and his formation of the Communist party (China Wing), brought the C.T.U.F. over to his party as an ancillary organization. M. G. Mendis was president of the C.T.U.F., and he remained loyal to the C.P. and its leaders, with whom he had been associated for so long. The Ceylon Federation of Trade Unions (C.F.T.U.) was quickly organized, with Pieter Keuneman as president and M. G. Mendis as general secretary, and a battle ensued between the C.T.U.F. and the C.F.T.U. for control of Communist unions. While the Shanmugathasan faction seemed to succeed initially, the C.F.T.U. under the energetic direction of Keuneman and Mendis gradually began to recapture the unions. At a conference of the C.F.T.U. held a few months after the breakup, Keuneman, in his presidential address, reported that between 70 per cent and 80 per cent of the members of the Communist unions had joined the C.F.T.U. At the same congress M. G. Mendis claimed that ten Communist unions with their officers and members had recently joined the C.F.T.U. and that the unions affiliated with it numbered eighteen.[83] This movement continued, and two years after the split the *Ceylon News* reported that Shanmugathasan's unions were "in complete disarray."[84] However, Shanmugathasan has been able to maintain at least a minimum trade union base for the party that he formed, and this is crucial, since he has little electoral or organizational strength other than this. In 1967 his C.T.U.F. had about ten thousand members, organized in thirty-four firms.[85]

Trade unions are the primary source of power of the C.P., and its success in recapturing them testifies to the firm integration of the party and trade union structures, the popularity of party leaders, the discipline of party members, and the more attractive ideological image of the C.P. At the same time, however, the rupture demonstrated the power that leaders of a peripheral organization of a party have, especially when the membership of the party is small and when its influence upon voters is more dependent upon the personality of its leaders and the influence of its ancillary organizations than upon the party organization itself.

Thus the leaders of the C.P. have moved toward a more moderate position in the political spectrum and have carried the bulk of the party and trade union members with them. Like the L.S.S.P., the C.P. has expelled its radical wing and has come to accept parliamentary action. It has also accepted evolutionary socialism and has all but denounced revolution. In many ways its evolution has reflected that of the Soviet Union, whose radical ideology has been tamed with the years. The C.P. leaders fit comfortably into Parliament, and they appear to accept the current status of the C.P. as a minor party, receptive to electoral, and perhaps parliamentary, coalition with "progressive forces." The C.P., like the L.S.S.P., however, still uses its unions as a political weapon to harass conservative governments, and strikes are employed to indicate its opposition to particular legislation. The C.P., like other Marxist parties, co-ordinates its parliamentary activity and the strike action of its trade unions. Periods of intense strike activity coincide with the opposition of the C.P. in Parliament to the Government, while there are relatively few strikes by unions affiliated with the C.P. when the party leaders support the Government. Strikes serve the dual objective of reaffirming a leader's commitment to the interests of organized workers and of mobilizing support behind the party in periodic displays of power. Unions of the C.P., as well as those of the L.S.S.P., are thus employed to pressure governments into adopting policies more beneficial to the working class and to augment the political power of the C.P. much beyond that which it obtains from the small number of seats it occupies in Parliament.

The Mahajana Eksath Peramuna

The M.E.P. is the party of Philip Gunawardena and his personal retinue. It amounts to little more than this. Gunawardena is the outstanding political maverick in Ceylon, and his apparent opportunism is tempered by his deep devotion to the peasants, whom he and his party seek to represent. One of the founding members of the L.S.S.P., Gunawardena has tried to adapt Marxism to the peasant economy and culture of Ceylon, and has been more successful than any of the other leaders of Marxist parties in this respect. However, he has not succeeded in developing a mass peasant base for his party or himself, in spite of the fact that as Minister of Agriculture in the Bandaranaike government he did more for the peasant than the ministers of any previous government. His actions on behalf of the peasant from 1956 to 1959 caused him to anticipate the reward of votes in 1960. Consequently he ran eighty-nine candidates under the M.E.P. label, only ten of whom were returned in the March election. Only three were returned in the July election of that year. This rejection left him undaunted, and he persisted as a strong advocate of peasant and traditional interests. He sought in the United Left Front another road to power, which came to an abrupt end when the L.S.S.P. went into coalition with the S.L.F.P. This led him into an electoral pact with the U.N.P. in 1965, and seventy candidates ran under the M.E.P. label in areas of Leftist power. His purpose was to split the Leftist vote and to aid the U.N.P. candidates. As a reward, Gunawardena was given a post in the Cabinet of Dudley Senanayake.

The M.E.P. cannot be dissociated from the personality of Gunawardena. It is at any moment what he makes it. The power of the party derives from little more than the prominence of its leader and its trade union base. In 1961 the Central Council of Ceylon Trade Unions, controlled by Gunawardena, had a membership of around thirty thousand.[86] However, the influence of the M.E.P. with the working class is limited by competition from the larger unions of the L.S.S.P. and the C.P., and the peasant base of the party is restricted by the greater influence of the S.L.F.P. and the U.N.P. on the peasant. Thus, in spite of Gunawardena's ideological and personal opportunism, his hard and diligent work as an individual and minister, and the expenditure of his once considerable fortune, his M.E.P. has remained a minor party, receptive to offers of coalition with any party willing to give him a cabinet post.

COMMUNAL PARTIES

The Tamil areas of the north and east were alienated from the mainstream of national politics when the language question emerged in 1956. Since then the Federal party has dominated Tamil politics. Its original demand for a federal state has not been altered, and in 1960 it declared that it "concentrates all its attention to achieve freedom for the people whom they [sic] represent." Since its origin the F.P. has been isolated in Parliament, unwilling to co-operate with any Sinhalese party and unable to find a Sinhalese party willing to co-operate with it. While it has promised to "support all progressive measures in the economic and social sphere introduced by any government in office,"[87] the F.P. has repeatedly announced that it will support no government unless certain demands, including establishment of a federal state, are met. Attempts at coalition with either the U.N.P. or the S.L.F.P. came to nothing in 1960 because of inability to find a common basis of agreement for co-operation.

Since 1956 most of the activity of the F.P. has taken place outside of Parliament in satyagraha and disobedience campaigns. However, the closeness of the 1965 election gave the F.P. an opportunity to use its bloc of seats in Parliament as an enticement, and agreement was reached with the U.N.P. to form a national government. Thus its demands for coalition have been modified, and the F.P. has been able to bring itself into a more effective position in Parliament. This constitutes a major change in the F.P. and may indicate its acceptance of the fact that federalism is an aspiration above realization. If this is so, then it can be said that the F.P. has modified its radicalism and consequently has succeeded in bringing itself and the Tamils back into the main arena of Ceylonese politics. If the Tamil Congress, whose limited resurgence in 1965 may have been chiefly due to the prominence of its candidates, can survive and grow, then organized party competition may be introduced into Tamil areas.

The emergence of the communal division in Ceylon has not only restricted party competition in Tamil areas; it has also inhibited the organizational development of Tamil parties. Lack of effective competition has made it unnecessary for the F.P. to construct much of an organization. Its candidates are all locally prominent men whose personal-influence structures in their constituencies serve to mobilize voters behind them. Their association with the F.P. is loose, though it is a definite electoral asset because of Chelvanayakam and because the party has developed a reputation as a defender of Tamil interests. To the voter, the image of the F.P. is little more than this, as the party has never had to commit itself on matters of caste or economic or social policy. The intensity of communal conflict has enabled the F.P. to generalize on these matters, which, if they had to be specified, might split the unity of the party. The only decisions that have to be made by the party relate to strategic questions involving the interests of the Tamils as a communal group. Decisions of this sort are primarily a function of the party caucus. If the intensity of communal discord subsides, as appears likely, the F.P. will be confronted with the need to define its views more specifically on a wide range of matters, and this may entail defections from its ranks. How seriously this will affect the party remains to be seen, for while the party has an image that is electorally profitable, it has an organization that is highly personalized at the local level and one that discourages the development of a formal party organization.

The party system in Ceylon has experienced several important changes since its emergence in 1947. Parties have undergone ideological and structural changes; the independent has declined and the party has risen as the vital unit in politics; the major, or established, parties have confirmed the bases of their social support; and parties have achieved a sufficient consensus for co-operation. Consequently the entire operation of the party system has been transformed. In their totality, these changes have stimulated and reflected the growth of party orientation on the part of the electorate, and are indicative of the progress Ceylon has made in the maturation of its party system.

DECLINE OF THE INDEPENDENT AND PERSONALITY PARTIES

In 1947 over half the candidates contesting the election were independents or attached to minor personality parties. This was to be expected, since the preceding political experience had emphasized the role of the independent, both for the elector, who had voted as an independent in 1931 and 1936, and for the candidate, who had acted as an independent in a State Council specifically designed to discourage party operation. Then too, the parties that were active in 1947 had no clearly defined programs to offer and were themselves unsure of their own programmatic personality. In such circumstances it was natural that the electorate should tend to vote for local notables regardless of whether or not they had any party affiliation. As one observer noted at the time, "When parties do not form according to principles, and when principles cannot keep track of parties, the void has still to be filled." In this situation, he concluded, "re-emerges the idea of an individual representative."[1]

But 1947 was the last big year of the independent. With the exception of the March, 1960, election and the election of 1965, the number of independent candidates has continuously declined, and both their total vote and their percentage of the vote have diminished. In 1947 half of the 360 candidates were independents. In 1952 only 85 of the 303 candidates, around 28 per cent, were independents. In 1956 the number of independent candidates dropped to 64 out of a total of 241 candidates, or about 26 per cent. In March, 1960, there was a tremendous increase in the number of candidates in competition. However, the ratio of independents to the total number of candidates continued its decline and fell to under 20 per cent. Among the 899 candidates in competition there were 167 independents. The election of July, 1960, saw the lowest number of independent candidates. There were 39 out of a total of 393 candidates, slightly less than 10 per cent. In 1965 there was an increase, as 106 out of 495 candidates were independents, just over 20 per cent. The reason for this increase was a corresponding decrease in multiparty competition and the inability of many aspirants to obtain party nomination. There is also the possibility that many of these independents were encouraged to run by major parties in order to divide the vote of their opponents. In any case, as will be shown, the debacle of the independent that occurred in 1965 was further evidence of his gradual movement out of politics in Ceylon.

The vote received by independents has shown a similar decrease over the years (see Table 2). In 1965 it was less than half of what it had been in 1947, a decline made more significant by the fact that the total vote had more than doubled. The independent vote declined from 1947 to July, 1960, and then rose somewhat in 1965. Except for 1965 the percentage of the total

TABLE 2. Popular Vote for Independent Candidates, 1947–65

Election	Total Vote	Independent Vote	% of Total Vote
1947	1,881,372	549,381	29
1952	2,327,627	326,783	14
1956	2,616,759	289,491	11
1960 (March)	3,093,996	282,797	9
1960 (July)	3,043,532	183,728	6
1965	4,046,720	259,960	6

Source: For 1947, 1952, and 1956 elections, Ceylon Daily News, *Parliaments of Ceylon, 1960*, p. 221; for 1960 elections, *Sessional Paper II of 1962*, pp. 115–16; for 1965 election, *Sessional Paper XX of 1966*, p. 30.

vote taken by independents has steadily declined. The average vote for independent candidates was lower in 1965 than in 1947, while the average vote for major-party candidates had substantially increased and was almost four times as large as the average independent vote (see Table 3). If the votes for a few really

TABLE 3. Average Vote for Independent Candidates and Candidates of Major and Minor Parties, 1947–65

Election	Independent Candidates	Major Party Candidates[a]	Minor Party Candidates
1947	3,035	7,630	1,069
1952	3,844	9,635	3,765
1956	4,523	12,806	3,083
1960 (March)	1,620	4,422	1,782
1960 (July)	3,603	8,488	5,001
1965	2,452	9,678	1,879

Source: For elections of 1947 to July, 1960, Ceylon Daily News, *Parliaments of Ceylon, 1960*, pp. 220–21; for 1965 election, *Sessional Paper XX of 1966*, p. 30.
[a] Includes candidates who ran under the following party labels:
        1947 – U.N.P., C.I.C., L.S.S.P., C.P., B.L.P., L.P., T.C.
        1952 – U.N.P., S.L.F.P., L.S.S.P., C.P.–V.L.S.S.P., T.C., F.P.
        1956 – U.N.P., M.E.P., L.S.S.P., C.P., T.C., F.P.
March, 1960 – U.N.P., S.L.F.P., F.P., L.S.S.P., M.E.P., L.P.P., C.P.
  July, 1960 – U.N.P., S.L.F.P., F.P., L.S.S.P., M.E.P., C.P.
        1965 – U.N.P., S.L.F.P., M.E.P., L.S.S.P., L.P.P., F.P., C.P., T.C.

powerful independents were subtracted from the total votes of the independents, the ratio would be even more in favor of the major-party candidates. In fact, the votes for independents have become so low that in 1965 over two-thirds of the independents lost their deposits, since they polled less than one-eighth of the total vote in their constituencies (see Table 4).

The number of seats won by independents and the ratio of this number to the total number of elected seats in the House of Representatives have steadily declined. In 1947 the independents formed an impressive bloc of 21 seats in the House. By 1952 this bloc had declined to 12, by 1956 to 8, and by March, 1960, to 7. In the elections of July, 1960, and 1965, 6 independents were returned. The ratio of independents to the total number of seats in the House has dropped considerably. In 1947 the independent bloc held 20 per cent of the seats. In 1956 this bloc dropped to 8 per cent, and it has won about 4 per cent of the seats in elections since then.

Thus the independent has suffered a serious setback as a vital unit in Ceylonese politics. After 1947 he survived only in certain provinces where certain prominent men decided to remain unattached to parties. Independents have had almost no success in the Western, Central, North Central, Southern and Sabaragamuwa provinces and have been only sporadically successful in Uva Province. The North Western Province has consistently returned two independents. Independents have been most successful in the Northern and Eastern provinces, although in 1965 the Northern Province returned party members only, for the first time. Communalism and the lack of party competition mainly account for the past success of independents in the Tamil Northern Province. In 1947 the Tamil Congress was the only organized Tamil party, and although the Federal party emerged in 1952, it competed with the T.C. in only a few constituencies. After 1956 independents provided the only competition for the F.P., as the T.C. suffered the disgrace and disaster of its association with the U.N.P. The re-emergence of the T.C. in the 1965 election resulted

TABLE 4. *Number of Independent Candidates (Ind.) and of Independent Candidates Who Lost Deposits (Ind. L.D.), 1947–65*

Province	1947 Ind.	1947 Ind. L.D.	1952 Ind.	1952 Ind. L.D.	1956 Ind.	1956 Ind. L.D.	March, 1960 Ind.	March, 1960 Ind. L.D.	July, 1960 Ind.	July, 1960 Ind. L.D.	1965 Ind.	1965 Ind. L.D.
Western	40	27	13	11	17	17	31	30	15	13	24	23
Central	34	18	17	12	4	3	25	19	5	4	9	8
Southern	30	17	7	4	5	2	22	16	3	3	12	11
Northern	14	8	12	3	8	0	23	15	2	0	8	5
Eastern	14	2	8	0	9	3	18	10	6	2	12	4
North Western	13	5	9	3	5	1	18	12	4	1	10	8
North Central	4	0	2	1	2	2	7	6	1	1	4	3
Uva	13	5	10	8	2	1	14	14	1	1	8	5
Sabaragamuwa	18	14	2	1	4	4	12	9	3	2	6	3
Total	180	96	80	43	56	33	170	131	40	27	93	70

SOURCE: Data obtained at Office of Commissioner of Elections, Colombo.

in the eclipse of the independent in the Northern Province. It is too early (in 1968) to say whether or not this eclipse will be permanent. To a great extent it depends upon the viability of the two Tamil parties, whose competition may now dominate politics in the Tamil north. In any case, the role of the independent there now is minimal, for some once-outstanding independents in the Northern Province have been defeated.

Independents have survived in the Eastern Province, although in 1968 they held only two seats there. Independents have usually won in Tamil-speaking Muslim constituencies where voters seek to disassociate themselves from the communalism of the north yet do not fit comfortably into the Sinhalese-dominated party system. They are pulled one way by their language interests and another by their religious affiliation. The Muslims have never been sufficiently alienated to form their own party and have sought to maintain a neutral position by returning independents. In other provinces the few independents who have been returned have been outstanding men in their area who for one reason or another refused to join a party. R. G. Senanayake has consistently been returned by wide margins in the North Western Province and has preferred the role of political maverick since his defection from the U.N.P. It can be expected that when men such as he withdraw or retire from politics, independent representation of Sinhalese areas will disappear completely. Except in the Northern, Eastern, and North Western provinces, which together significantly increase the national vote for the independent, the ratio of the independent vote to the total vote is very small. Many who once ran as independents have since been incorporated into the party system. The day of the independent is over in Ceylonese politics (see Table 5).

There are several reasons for the decline of the independent. The cost of election has led to the absorption of many former independents into the party system. In the first place, the deposit for a party candidate is less than for an independent. Originally, every candidate had to deposit Rs. 1,000 ($210) which was for-

TABLE 5. *Percentage of Total Vote Won by Independents, 1947–65*

	1947	1952	1956	March 1960	July 1960	1965
Province:						
Southern	26	11	8	7.2	0.4	3
Sabaragamuwa	15	3	0.4	4	1	5
Uva	32	15	2	8	0.7	14
North Western	44	20	26	9	1	10
North Central	21	9	0.8	5.5	0.2	4
Eastern	72	61	22	44	21	22
Northern	21	23	31	21	6	9
Western	16	5	6	3	2.6	1.5
Central	40	10	2.3	6	5	4
All provinces	29	14	11	9	6	6

SOURCE: Data obtained at Office of Commissioner of Elections, Colombo.

feited if he failed to obtain one-eighth of the votes cast in his constituency. This was changed in 1959, apparently in order to discourage independents and to aid the development of parties. Under the provisions of the new act, the deposit was lowered to Rs. 500 for the candidate of a "recognized political party," and in 1964 it was further reduced to Rs. 250.[2] The deposit for non-party candidates remained at Rs. 1,000. A recognized political party was defined as one that had been in existence for at least five years or of which at least two members were or had been members of Parliament.[3] This definition of "political party" was designed specifically to inhibit the mushroom growth of personality parties, which might be formed as a means to avoid the extra expense of contesting as independents. While this amendment had no effect in the March, 1960, election in restraining independent candidates, its long-range effect, especially in view of the many who are compelled to forfeit their deposits, may be to discourage the independent candidate.

However, other provisions of the act may have helped independent candidates, although designed to limit the political advantage derived by the U.N.P. due to its greater access to funds. One provision of the act states that no one may "let, lend, employ, hire, borrow or use any vehicle, vessel or animal for the purpose of conveying any voters to or from the poll."[4] Freedom to do this previously had been of benefit to the U.N.P., which had more vehicles at its disposal than its rivals. In addition, the act provided that every candidate would be allowed to send, free of charge, one postal communication concerning the election to each elector in his constituency. Provision was also made to limit the amount that a candidate could spend in his campaign. According to the amendment, no candidate can spend or cause to be spent an amount "in excess of seven thousand five hundred rupees or of an amount equal to thirty cents for each elector on the register."[5] This does not include Rs. 1,000 that a candidate is permitted to spend for an election agent and Rs. 2,000 for his personal expenses. While these provisions have perhaps been of benefit to major parties with limited funds, such as the L.S.S.P., they also have helped the independent. On the other hand, the limit on campaign expenses is high in terms of income in Ceylon, and candidates of organized parties that finance or defray the campaign costs of their members have an advantage over the independent. According to the Commissioner of Elections, from Rs. 3,000 to Rs. 4,000 was spent by most candidates in the 1960 election. The average was below Rs. 2,000 in the Eastern and North Central provinces, a little below Rs. 3,000 in the Northern Province, and over Rs. 3,000 in the others.[6] Few independents can afford such amounts, and this has helped to reduce the number of independent candidates, has limited their ability to run effective campaigns, and has given the party candidate a definite electoral advantage.

Personal ambition, however, has been the primary incentive driving independents into parties. Almost from the beginning the independent member has been isolated in the House. A few Tamil independents succeeded in obtaining cabinet portfolios in the first U.N.P. government, but since then the participation of independents in a government has been restricted to membership in the government parliamentary party and an occasional appointment as parliamentary secretary. Except for 1947, when a large bloc of independents was returned, the independent has not been able to contribute much to the construction of government coalitions, and governments have consequently not reciprocated in the allocation of posts. This has led many independents to join a party, where there is more opportunity for personal gain and advancement. Another factor is that the isolation of the independent has made him less effective as a representative of his constituency, for governments have been prone to respond more readily to the needs of constituencies from which they draw their strength. Both the parties and the press have continually stressed that the independent is a less influential member of Parliament and that it is in the interest of the electorate to vote for major parties, with their greater potential for government. The voting statistics of elections since 1947 suggest that the electorate has responded to this advice.

The emergence of the Sri Lanka Freedom party was a major cause of the decline of the independent. In the first place, it absorbed many independents into its ranks. Prior to its emergence the moderate who had found no room for himself in the United National party or had become disenchanted with the U.N.P. had no choice but to remain independent. The S.L.F.P. provided a refuge for many such independents and, as a party that might possibly obtain power, seemed to offer greater opportunity for personal advancement. Secondly, the rise of the S.L.F.P. undercut the independents' claim to votes as the only non-Marxist alternative to the U.N.P. Not only did the S.L.F.P. provide a non-Marxist alternative to the U.N.P. but it also emerged as a possible alternative government to the U.N.P., which the independents could not claim to be. It was more profitable for those dissatisfied with U.N.P. rule to vote for the S.L.F.P. or the M.E.P. in 1956, in terms of political effect. And since this time, the electorate has had the opportunity of choosing among a number of parties. This choice has eliminated the primary role that independents once played.

Other factors have also been involved. The opportunism of parties has made them welcome notable independents as members in an attempt to widen their power base and increase their numbers in Parliament. Parties have been as eager to bestow their label on potential winners as independents have been to join parties. In addition, there has been a definite nationalization of politics in Ceylon, as both party and national party leaders have become crucial electoral factors. To a great extent, this has been due to the fact that parties have become more identifiable as units, and the people are now able to associate an ideology or policy orientation with them. The decline of the independent has thus both contributed to and reflected the growth of party orientation on the part of the people.

The refusal of the electorate to consider seriously the pretense of personality parties to major status is another indication of its party orientation. The S.L.F.P. is the only new party that has been able to establish itself since 1947, except for the Federal party in Tamil areas. The Mahajana Eksath Peramuna of Philip Gunawardena is an organizational offshoot of the 1947 Trotskyist division, which adopted the name originally used for the coalition of 1956. Its base of power is small, and it has made no progress in its efforts to extend itself. It is the most enduring of the personality parties, and its relatively minor strength derives from the local prominence of its leader and its trade union connections. Neither the Communist party nor the Lanka Sama Samaja party has been able to widen its popular base of power, and the attempt of each to attain major-party status was crushed in 1960. Just as the electorate has discouraged the growth of Leftist parties to major status, so it has discouraged the efforts of any other party to establish itself. The L.P.P., or Ceylon Democratic party, and the People's Socialist Front (S.M.P.) both met disaster in March, 1960, and most of their candidates lost their deposits. The best any other emergent party could do in that year was to return its leader. Provincially confined parties have also failed. The Jatika Vimukthi Peramuna has never had more than two seats, and its attempts in 1960 and 1965 to increase its number of seats failed when even its leader was defeated. The Sri Lanka Freedom Socialist party, formed in 1965, was a group of notables organized by right-wing defectors from the S.L.F.P. It later merged with Dahanayake's L.P.P. and has taken the name of that party. Its few seats are occupied by, and its base of power is confined to, the nationally prominent men who organized it. Its eventual movement into the U.N.P. is not unlikely. In any case, it has no real pretense to being a party, for it has no organization or aspirations.

In short, the electorate has clearly demonstrated its confidence in the established party system and has indicated a definite preference for party candidates. This is further substantiated by the fact that elections in almost all the Sinhalese constituencies are dominantly biparty contests. There is now little place in Ceylonese politics for independents or new, personality parties. The ideological spectrum is adequately spanned by established parties, and every social group in Ceylon can find its interests articulated by one of them. There is no void to be filled as there was in 1947. While a prominent notable is able to organize and lead a new party, he can carry few other candidates with him into the House of Representatives. Election returns have demonstrated that support for notables is confined to their own or, in some cases, surrounding areas. Thus their impact is slight, and that it cannot be greater was demonstrated by the disasters met by new parties in March, 1960. This election marked the end of most personality parties. Like the independents, they have been rejected by the Ceylonese electorate. In so far as personality is still a factor in Ceylonese politics, it operates almost entirely within the party system.

THE CONFIRMATION OF ESTABLISHED PARTIES

Another indication of the party orientation of Ceylon's electorate and the stabilization of the established parties is the consolidated base of power that each party has obtained, as demonstrated by the persistence of voting patterns. In the first place, between 1947 and 1965 established parties increased their percentage of the national vote (see Table 6). The S.L.F.P. and the U.N.P. are the dominant parties and between them share about two-thirds of the total vote. The U.N.P. started out with about 40 per cent of the popular vote, in 1947, and in 1956, in spite of its disaster, it still took about 27 per cent of the vote. Since then the U.N.P. share of the vote has increased, and the party now appears to have a stable voting bloc of slightly over one-third of the total vote. The percentage of the vote for the S.L.F.P. is a little less than this. The S.L.F.P. grew from a minor party in 1952, when it took about 15 per cent of the vote, to a major party in 1956, when it and the M.E.P. coalition took almost 40 percent of the vote. Its percentage decreased in March, 1960, because of the disintegration of the M.E.P., multiparty competition, and the lack of a no-contest arrangement with the Left, and then rose again. The S.L.F.P. appears to have developed a stabilized voting base of a little under one-third of the electorate.

The percentage of the popular vote taken by the Marxist parties decreased from 1947 to 1965. Except for the election of March, 1960, when each of the Marxist parties ran a large number of candidates, the vote of Marxist parties has decreased a few percentage points with each election. The decline of the Marxist vote appears even more striking if the vote for the M.E.P., which is really a personality party, is subtracted from the total Marxist vote. Excluding the M.E.P., the Marxist parties took only 10 per cent of the vote in 1965, less than half of the percentage of the vote they took in 1947. However, the concentration of the Leftist votes in certain areas guarantees them the return of a minimum number of M.P.'s, and the number of seats held by the Marxist parties has not substantially decreased since 1947.

The main base of power of the U.N.P. is in urban areas, where it gets the backing of almost all the Westernized population,

TABLE 6. *Number of Votes and Percentage of Total Vote Won by Major Parties, 1947–65*

Party	1947 Votes	1947 % of Total Vote	1952 Votes	1952 % of Total Vote	1956 Votes	1956 % of Total Vote	March, 1960 Votes	March, 1960 % of Total Vote	July, 1960 Votes	July, 1960 % of Total Vote	1965 Votes	1965 % of Total Vote
U.N.P.	751,432	39.9	1,026,005	44.0	718,164	27.4	909,043	28.4	1,144,166	37.5	1,590,929	39.3
S.L.F.P.			361,250	15.5	1,045,725[b]	39.9	647,175	20.2	1,022,171	33.5	1,221,437	30.1
Marxist parties:												
L.S.S.P.	204,020	10.8	305,133	13.1	274,204	10.4	325,286	10.5	224,995	7.3	302,095	7.4
C.P.	70,331	3.7	134,528[a]	5.7	119,715	4.5	147,612	4.6	90,219	2.9	109,754	2.7
M.E.P.							324,332	10.4	106,816	3.5	96,665	2.3
B.L.P.	113,193	6.0										
Marxist total	387,544	20.5	439,661	18.8	393,919	14.9	797,230	25.5	422,030	13.7	508,514	12.4
T.C.	82,499	4.3	64,512	2.7	8,914	0.3	38,275	1.2	46,803	1.5	98,746	2.4
F.P.			45,331	1.9	142,036	5.4	176,444	5.5	213,733	7.0	217,914	5.3
Total	1,221,475	64.7	1,936,759	82.9	2,308,758	87.9	2,568,167	80.8	2,848,903	93.2	3,637,540	89.5

SOURCE: For 1947, 1952, and 1956 elections, Ceylon Daily News, *Parliaments of Ceylon, 1960*, p. 221; for 1960 elections, *Sessional Paper II of 1962*, pp. 115–16; for 1965 election, *Sessional Paper XX of 1966*, p. 30.

[a] Represents vote for C.P.–V.L.S.S.P.
[b] Represents vote for M.E.P. coalition.

especially people in the middle-income bracket and the owners of businesses and property. It also draws support from the Sinhalese middle class and Muslims. But it also gets the support of many peasants, although this support diminishes in areas closer to the interior of Ceylon, a fact that is probably explained by the poverty of inland peasants. An analysis of the political geography of Ceylon reveals that the U.N.P. draws its greatest strength from the Western, Central, North Western, Southern, Uva, and Sabaragamuwa provinces (see Table 7). These are the most developed, urbanized, and organized of the Sinhalese provinces, and most have Westernized elements. In the Western Province the U.N.P. draws its strength from the Catholic constituencies that lie to the north of Colombo and from the urbanized coastal area to the south. It is weakest among the peasants of the inland area, where the S.L.F.P. has strength, and it encounters heavy competition in the urban areas, where the Marxist parties are well organized. It also obtains the votes of minority groups such as the Malays, Burghers, Muslims, and English-speaking elements. The organization of the U.N.P. is more consolidated and politically relevant in the Western Province because of the population concentration there. The U.N.P. has also been powerful in the Central Province, where in 1965 it took nearly 50 per cent of the vote. Again its strength is in the urban areas, among minority groups, and among the more prosperous and Westernized members of the peasant and middle classes. It is also highly organized here, and its ranks contain numbers of local notables. It also has the support of the wealthy Sangha that is centered in Kandy. In the Southern Province the U.N.P. is strongest in the urbanized areas. The North Western Province has population concentrations where the more highly developed organization of the U.N.P. is an asset. This province, Uva, and Sabaragamuwa are prosperous, and the conservative appeal of the U.N.P. is effective. In these provinces there is little landlessness, and the property-owning peasant, contented with his lot, is not responsive to the S.L.F.P.

TABLE 7. Electoral Strength of United National Party, by Province, 1947–65

Election	Western		Southern		Central		North Western		North Central		Uva		Sabaragamuwa		Northern		Eastern	
	Seats Won	% of Vote	Seats Won	% of Vote	Seats Won	% of Vote	Seats Won	% of Vote	Seats Won	% of Vote	Seats Won	% of Vote	Seats Won	% of Vote	Seats Won	% of Vote	Seats Won	% of Vote
(Elective seats: 95)																		
1947	10	42	5	47	6	31	5	54	5	64	2	16	6	54	0	14	3	38
1952	12	41	5	41	11	54	7	53	4	54	5	51	7	61	1	8	2	41
1956	1	31	1	28	3	45	1	27	1	32	1	34	0	32				
(Elective seats: 151)																		
1960 (March)	18	35	7	33	9	29	5	33	1	27	3	31	7	35	0	3	0	5
1960 (July)	8	43	2	41	8	45	5	40	1	35	2	42	3	43			1	19
1965	14	46	8	34	17	49	12	52	1	28	3	33	8	44			3	24

SOURCE: Data obtained at Office of Commissioner of Elections, Colombo.
NOTE: In elections for which there are no entries the party ran no candidates.

The S.L.F.P. has strength in the same provinces as the U.N.P., but its power base comes from different social elements, the poorer peasant and the traditionalists (see Table 8). It is weak in the urban areas of all the provinces, and its success in the peasant areas is due not so much to organization as to its integration of notables. It competes in these areas with the U.N.P., and the decisive factor appears to be the degree of peasant discontent. Any increase in this increases the vote of the S.L.F.P. In addition, the S.L.F.P. has an ideology specifically designed for the peasant.

The Marxist parties are confined to areas where their unions provide an organized voting bloc and to the personal constituencies of their leaders. They have never been able to extend beyond these limits. Attempts at penetration of the Tamil or peasant areas have repeatedly failed, and even after the C.P. and L.S.S.P. adopted the policy of "Sinhalese only," they had no success among the traditionalists. The L.S.S.P. derives almost all its strength from the urban area of Colombo and the southern coastal areas of the Western Province, where it has well-organized unions. Its main base of power has always been here, and it takes about 14 per cent of the provincial vote. It also has a power base in Sabaragamuwa Province, where it organized estate workers and where N. M. Perera has a great deal of personal influence. It also has a minor base of power in the Southern Province, because of organization and the influence of a few L.S.S.P. notables. The Southern Province is the mainstay of the C.P., which draws about 10 per cent of the provincial vote. This is partly due to Communist organizations, but primarily it is because of the influence of Dr. S. A. Wickremasinghe, president of the C.P., who resides there. His influence extends to areas around his own constituency, and Communist strength is confined to these areas. In the Western Province, the strength of the C.P. is again largely personal, despite its union strength there. Pieter Keuneman has always been returned from the multimember Colombo Central constituency, more for his personal qualities

TABLE 8. Electoral Strength of Sri Lanka Freedom Party, by Province, 1952–65

Election	Western Seats Won	Western % of Vote	Southern Seats Won	Southern % of Vote	Central Seats Won	Central % of Vote	North Western Seats Won	North Western % of Vote	North Central Seats Won	North Central % of Vote	Uva Seats Won	Uva % of Vote	Sabaragamuwa Seats Won	Sabaragamuwa % of Vote	Northern Seats Won	Northern % of Vote	Eastern Seats Won	Eastern % of Vote
(Elective seats: 95)																		
1952	2	20	2	13	3	28	0	15	1	28	0	8	1	10				
1956a	8	33	10	56	12	57	6	45	4	61	4	33	7	51				
(Elective seats: 151)																		
1960 (March)	6	18	2	15	12	29	9	38	6	53	5	31	5	24			1	12
1960 (July)	15	31	11	36	15	48	10	46	6	59	6	32	10	37			2	12
1965	14	29	3	30	6	44	2	38	5	50	5	40	4	32			2	14

SOURCE: Data obtained at Office of Commissioner of Elections, Colombo.

NOTE: In elections for which there are no entries the party ran no candidates.

a Figures given are for M.E.P. coalition.

than for his party affiliation. This is also true of Philip Guna-wardena and his M.E.P. The seats it wins are usually from personal constituencies.

Thus each of the established parties has been able to stabilize its base of power. Only the U.N.P. and the S.L.F.P. have succeeded as mass parties, because only these parties have developed an appeal to which the peasant is responsive. The power of the S.L.F.P. depends only on the peasant, whereas the U.N.P. succeeds in integrating other elements as well. The Marxist parties have established themselves as organizations of the working class, and their being group-based parties has permitted their survival but prevented their expansion. The F.P. has established itself as the dominant Tamil party, and while it has been again challenged by the T.C., its power base (in 1968) appears secure. These are the parties of Ceylonese politics and each has been confirmed by an electorate that neither needed nor permitted any others.

COMPETITION AND COALITION

An adequate appraisal of Ceylon's party system requires an analysis of the degree and character of competition and coalition within the party system, since a multiparty system appears to be in operation. Yet, if an analysis in depth is made, it becomes clear that actually a biparty system functions in what is numerically a multiparty system. This biparty character is evident at both the electoral and parliamentary levels.

Electoral Competition and Coalition

Contrary to their multiparty appearance, elections in Ceylon are pre-eminently two-way contests. This has been true ever since 1947, and, except for March, 1960, when the number of candidates competing in the election rose sharply, the biparty nature of political contests in Ceylon has become ever more firmly stabilized (see Table 9). In spite of the fact that a large number

TABLE 9. *Vote and Per Cent of Total Vote Won by First Two Candidates, 1947–65*

Province	1947 Vote	1947 %	1952 Vote	1952 %	1956 Vote	1956 %	March, 1960 Vote	March, 1960 %	July, 1960 Vote	July, 1960 %	1965 Vote	1965 %
Western	458,922	86	639,042	89	776,411	93	777,254	76	965,797	96	1,228,162	97
Central	254,640	81	239,653	88	301,785	98	265,038	74	335,517	92	488,590	98
Southern	268,152	81	377,132	89	416,689	93	319,289	70	429,779	96	576,964	97
Northern	122,081	81	131,583	71	175,198	88	176,953	77	196,997	96	229,534	82
Eastern	64,436	75	92,345	90	97,722	85	174,007	85	197,528	98	229,713	86
North Western	137,936	89	242,846	94	284,017	97	240,096	72	311,562	95	436,868	97
North Central	27,202	80	44,979	87	68,931	94	77,626	85	89,979	99	119,881	95
Uva	84,413	89	71,793	80	76,959	91	73,304	72	99,831	98	139,612	93
Sabaragamuwa	167,904	86	247,385	95	293,834	98	214,133	72	278,760	95	387,231	95
Total	1,585,686	82	2,086,758	88	2,502,125	95	2,317,700	75	2,917,291	96	3,836,555	95

SOURCE: Data obtained at Office of Commissioner of Elections, Colombo.

of candidates compete in Ceylon's elections, the electorate has divided its votes, for the most part, between only two candidates. Recent elections have only confirmed this voting pattern at the constituency level and further stabilized the biparty character of electoral contests. In addition, except in a few instances, there has not been significant provincial deviation from the national average, and biparty elections appear consistently in all provinces. In 1965 every province except the Northern and Eastern gave over 90 per cent of its vote to the first two candidates in each constituency. The reasons for the lower percentage in the Northern and Eastern provinces are that the independent retains some strength there still and that in the multicommunal Eastern Province Sinhalese parties compete with both the F.P. and independents. However, in these provinces, as in the rest, elections are predominantly biparty contests. In addition, elections have been closer recently. In 1947 the winning candidate in each constituency received, on the average, 34 per cent more of the vote than the second candidate. By 1952 this winning margin had been reduced to 27 per cent. In 1956 it went up again, to 33 per cent, because of popular discontent with the U.N.P. In March, 1960, it was 20 per cent, in July, 1960, 21 per cent, and in 1965 it dropped to a low of 16 per cent.

The no-contest arrangements have been constructed on the basis of the biparty nature of electoral contests. In the peasant areas of the Sinhalese provinces electoral contest has been mainly a struggle between the U.N.P. and the S.L.F.P. since the S.L.F.P. was formed in 1951, although in 1965 the U.N.P. withdrew from electoral contest in some areas in deference to candidates of its political allies. In urban areas of the Sinhalese provinces electoral contests are more complex, but they are still fundamentally biparty contests. In the Western Province urban contests are usually between the U.N.P. and a Marxist ally of the S.L.F.P. In Sabaragamuwa Province the U.N.P. competes in most constituencies with the S.L.F.P. and in others with the L.S.S.P. In the Southern Province, except for 1965, when in some constituencies the U.N.P. bowed out to candidates of the S.L.F.S.P., elections have been primarily contests between the U.N.P. and either the S.L.F.P., the L.S.S.P. or the C.P. In all the other provinces elections are usually a struggle between the U.N.P. and the S.L.F.P., although in some constituencies in 1965 the J.V.P. or the S.L.F.S.P. was the opponent of the S.L.F.P. In the Eastern Province electoral contests may be between the U.N.P. and the S.L.F.P., or among the S.L.F.P., the U.N.P., the F.P. and independents, or between the F.P. and an independent. The number and party affiliations of contestants depend upon the communal texture of constituencies. Sinhalese parties compete in Sinhalese and Muslim constituencies, and the F.P. and independents compete in Muslim and Tamil constituencies. Following the disaster of the T.C. in 1956 contests in the Northern Province were between candidates of the F.P. and independents. In 1965 candidates of the T.C. replaced independents as the main opponents of the F.P. in several constituencies.

No-contest arrangements have thus reflected and organized the reality of the biparty character of elections in Ceylon. While these no-contest pacts or electoral coalitions are primarily motivated by political opportunism, they nevertheless required an ideological shift on the part of the members of the coalitions. This shift is most striking in regard to the Marxist parties, which had to pay the price of defections in their ranks for their decision to enter a coalition with a non-Marxist "bourgeois party." The same is true of the S.L.F.P., which suffered the loss of its conservative wing because of its decision to associate in a coalition with Marxist parties. But the S.L.F.P.-Left coalition had a firm base of power, and it was a natural coalition in that it united the working class and the poorer peasant, who share common problems and interests. It was also natural because it compensated for both the weakness of the S.L.F.P. in urban, working-class areas and the weakness of the Left among the peasant class. The U.N.P. coalition is of recent origin, and it seems likely (in 1968) that the U.N.P. will absorb at least its L.P.P. and

J.V.P. partners within its ranks. This would be natural because both junior partners are conservative. In any case, the L.P.P. and the J.V.P. are primarily personality parties that probably will not survive the retirement of their leaders. Unlike the S.L.F.P. and its Marxist allies, the U.N.P. is sufficiently comprehensive and has a strong enough organization to contest on its own.

Parliamentary Competition and Coalition

The biparty nature of electoral contests in Ceylon is reflected in Parliament by a bipolarized multiparty system. The party system now includes two major "center" parties about which minor parties can coalesce in the formation of a government. This was not always so, and the system took time to evolve. At one time only the U.N.P. was sufficiently strong to act as a nucleus around which a parliamentary coalition could form. Not only was there no other major party in competition but the parties in opposition to the U.N.P. had so many conflicts and were so antagonistic to each other that any organized action against the U.N.P. was impossible. The emergence and growth of the S.L.F.P. changed this, as did the gradual movement of the Marxist parties toward co-operation with each other and with the S.L.F.P. But the election of 1956 left the U.N.P. a fragment of itself and isolated in an unstable opposition that refused to work with it. In a short time the F.P. was also isolated. Thus in this period only the S.L.F.P. was capable of building a coalition, although because of its treatment of its Marxist components in 1959, its coalition potential had dwindled by 1960.

The first election of 1960 showed how difficult it had become for any party to obtain a majority by itself; and after the election the weakness of the U.N.P. as a coalition pivot was demonstrated as it looked in vain to other parties for support. The S.L.F.P. appeared capable of forming a government, but whether it could have done so is not certain, as a dissolution abruptly terminated its opportunity. The next election unexpectedly returned the

S.L.F.P. with a majority, although this was obtained by the aid
of a no-contest arrangement with the Leftist parties and sustained later by coalition with the L.S.S.P. At the same time the
July, 1960, election confirmed the resurgence of the U.N.P. as a
major party, and while it and the F.P. had to act alone in the
Opposition, the party system nevertheless now included the two
major parties needed for alternative coalitions. The major contribution of the election of 1965 was to prove that alternative
coalition government was possible. The U.N.P. was returned
as the pivot of a coalition, and with the support of the J.V.P.,
the S.L.F.S.P. (or L.P.P.), the M.E.P., and the F.P. it was able
to form a national government.

Thus 1965 confirmed the existence of a bipolarized multiparty
system. Two major parties existed, and the area of co-operation
in Parliament had sufficiently widened to enable each to act
as the center of a coalition. This required a great deal of ideological and personal adjustment on the part of parties and leaders.
All had to modify their extremism and move ideologically toward a central area where interparty agreement and co-operation
were possible. The Marxist parties had to adapt their revolutionary
ideology to co-operation in a parliamentary regime. The F.P.
had to forego its extreme demands and its refusal to co-operate
with Sinhalese parties. The U.N.P. had to move into the center
from the extreme position given the party by its right wing, and
other parties had to recognize its transformation and accept it.
In all of this movement and reshuffling political opportunism
was evident as parties acted in response to the needs of political life.

The nature of the two coalitions that the bipolarized multiparty system in Ceylon produced made possible alternative governments that differ organizationally and ideologically. The
S.L.F.P. coalition was based on the peasant and worker, and was
the more progressively oriented of the two in terms of policy.
In 1965 the S.L.F.P. and its allies took 40 per cent of the vote.
The members of the U.N.P. coalition took 53 per cent of the
vote in 1965 and collectively represented a wider social base than

the S.L.F.P. coalition. While its main power base was in the urban middle class and among the more prosperous peasants, the U.N.P. also drew backing from other social elements. The M.E.P. brought in some working class elements, and the J.V.P. and the S.L.F.S.P. widened its peasant base. The U.N.P. coalition included the F.P. and the T.C., and thus it brought the Tamils back into the active center of an operational party system.

The competition between parties and their coalitions is affected at both the parliamentary and electoral levels by the nature of the electoral system in Ceylon, as well as by the realities of the social environment that this system organizes. Because of this, aspects of Ceylon's party system cannot be fully appreciated without an understanding of the effects that the electoral system has on parties in Ceylon.

Party Competition and the Electoral System

With few exceptions, the electoral system in Ceylon is composed of single-member districts, election in which is based on a plurality of votes cast. Contrary to the contention of Maurice Duverger[7] that this type of electoral system encourages a two-party system, Ceylon has evolved a multiparty system. Its multipartism is primarily the result of communal pluralism, social divisions and tensions in Ceylonese society, and the maneuvering of politically ambitious men engaged in forwarding their careers. While the electoral system has neither determined nor seriously affected the number of parties, it has nevertheless had some influence on the shape and evolution of a party system in Ceylon. When an electoral system was designed for Ceylon, the most important decisions related to communalism, geographic variations in socioeconomic development, and cultural divisions in Sinhalese society. These considerations resulted in the construction of an electoral pattern that affects the voting strength of communal and cultural groups in Ceylon and one based on, for the most part, homogeneous districts.

The electoral system in Ceylon was designed to produce a communal pattern in the House of Representatives that reflected the communal texture of Ceylonese society. To achieve this, the Soulbury Commission recommended adoption of an electoral system that rejected communal representation but that "by no means conforms to the strict canons of territorial election and [that] it would not be unfair to describe . . . as a combination of territorial and communal representation."[8] In the first place, provision was made for the appointment by the Governor-General of six nominated members to the House of Representatives. These seats were intended to be reserved for the Burghers, Malays, and Europeans, none of whom had sufficient concentration of numbers to elect a member of their own. For the most part, the "appointed bloc" has been composed of representatives from these communities, although since 1956 one of the members has been a Sinhalese. In addition, since 1960 the disfranchised Indians have had representation here, with one Indian member being appointed in that year and two in 1965.

The Ceylon Tamils, Ceylon Moors, and initially, the Indian Tamils were expected to be able to elect members to the House of Representatives in proportion to their numerical strength on the island. The concentration of Ceylon Tamils in the Northern and Eastern provinces and the concentration of Moors in the Eastern Province meant that seats in those areas would be controlled by representatives of the two communities. In other areas communal constituencies were drawn wherever a communal minority was concentrated in sufficient numbers to justify a seat. The Order-in-Council of 1947 specified that where "it appears to the Delimitation Commission that there is in any area of a Province a substantial concentration of persons united by a community of interest, whether racial, religious or otherwise, but differing in one or more of these respects from the majority of inhabitants in that area, the Commission may make such division of the Province into electoral districts as may be necessary to render possible the representation of that interest."[9] In addition, the commission was empowered to draw multimember districts in areas where communal groups were too mixed to separate them electorally, so long as this did not alter the number of seats assigned to a province. At first these provisions applied to the Indian Tamils as well as to the other minorities, but this was changed after Indians were disfranchised in 1949. The Second Delimitation Commission of 1959 was empowered to draw multi-member constituencies only "where the racial composition of the *citizens* of Ceylon in that Province is such as to make it desirable to render possible the representation of any substantial concentration of *citizens* of Ceylon in that Province, who are united by a community of racial interest different from that of the major-ity of citizens of Ceylon in that Province." [10] As a result of this pro-vision there are five multimember districts in Ceylon returning eleven members to represent the racially mixed communities that vote in these constituencies.

The electoral system has thus been designed to ensure the re-turn of communal representatives in numbers proportionate to the size of the various communities they represent. The Ceylon Tamils and Moors have been able to obtain a number of seats that accurately reflects their population (see Table 10). The Sin-halese profit electorally from the disfranchisement of the Indians, as seats once controlled by Indians are now controlled by Sin-halese. Thus, over all, the electoral system does not affect com-munalism in Ceylon other than to ensure the control of a certain number of seats by Ceylon Tamils and Moors. It neither per-petuates communalism nor dictates the emergence of communal parties. The decision of the Tamils to form and support their own parties relates to communal strains and tensions that have endured in Ceylon, not to the electoral system, which, while it supports communal parties, does not necessarily encourage them.

The electoral system in Ceylon works to the advantage of some groups and to the disadvantage of others. It is not a perfect

TABLE 10. Distribution of Parliamentary Seats among Communal Groups, 1947–65

	Sinha-lese	Ceylon Tamils	Ceylon Moors	Indians	Other	Total
Seats due on population basis[a]	66	12	6	10	1	95
Seats won:						
1947	69	13	5	7	1	95
1952	74	13	7	0	1	95
1956	75	12	7	0	1	95
Seats due on population basis[b]	106	17	10	18	0	151
Seats won:						
1960 (March)	123	18	9	0	1	151
1960 (July)	122	18	10	0	1	151
1965	121	18	11	0	1	151

Source: Data obtained at Office of Commissioner of Elections, Colombo.
[a] *Sessional Paper XIII of 1946.*
[b] Based on 1953 census.

system, and it has resulted in a distorted pattern of representation, in which some areas and social elements are overrepresented at the expense of the underrepresentation of others. For the most part, this has been intentional, although slight distortions derive from the inevitable problems involved in the attempt to draw constituencies of approximately equal size in terms of population. Disproportional representation results from the use of "area weightage" and from a situation related to the disfranchisement of Indians: the assignment of seats to the provinces on the basis of "persons" while the electoral districts are drawn on the basis of "citizens." The use of these criteria means that citizens who live in the territorially large provinces and in those in which a large number of Indians reside have proportionally more representation than other citizens.

In the apportionment of seats to provinces, both area and

population are taken into account. The Soulbury Constitution stipulates that a province shall be given one seat for every 75,000 people and an additional seat for every 1,000 square miles of territory. The use of area weightage was intended to serve the dual objective of increasing the number of seats for the sparsely populated "backward" provinces, and increasing the number of seats for minority communities, like the Ceylon Tamils and the Moors, who would gain from the area seats assigned to the sprawling Northern and Eastern provinces.[11] In 1959, when the number of seats in the House of Representatives was increased, the Government retained the provision for area weightage in the provincial apportionment of seats. Prime Minister Bandaranaike explained that it was decided to continue to give one seat to a province for every 1,000 square miles of territory "because a certain weightage resulted from this provision, and if those areas which got benefit were deprived of it, it would not be altogether just, although purely theoretically, a pure and simple population basis naturally had certain attractions."[12] Sparsely populated but territorially large provinces, like the Northern, Eastern, and North Central, profit the most from area weightage, while the more heavily populated but smaller provinces, like the Western and the Southern, profit the least. The distortion intentionally introduced by using area weightage was further aggravated by the fact that in 1947 seats were assigned to provinces on the basis of population figures derived from the 1931 census. The use of an obsolete census was the major factor in the underrepresentation of populous provinces where population had increased substantially since 1931.[13] This factor, coupled with area weightage, resulted in some provinces having two to three times as many people per seat as other provinces. In 1947, for instance, each seat in the Western Province represented an average of 93,400 people, while in the North Central Province one representative was returned for every 27,900 people (see Table 11).

The provinces also have shown great disparities in the number of registered voters per seat. The disfranchisement of the Indians

TABLE 11. Provincial Population and Representation in Parliament, 1947

Province	Population	Area-based Seats	Population-based Seats	Total Seats	Population per Seat
Western	1,866,391	1	19	20	93,319
Central	1,131,107	2	13	15	75,407
Southern	961,534	2	10	12	80,128
Northern	479,835	4	5	9	53,315
Eastern	272,147	4	3	7	38,878
North Western	667,361	3	7	10	66,736
North Central	139,380	4	1	5	27,876
Uva	371,219	3	4	7	53,031
Sabaragamuwa	744,643	2	8	10	74,464

SOURCE: *Sessional Paper XIII of 1946*, pp. 19, 162.

contributed to such distortions. About 800,000 Indians were removed from the voting register, of whom 325,000 resided in the Central Province, 117,578 in Uva, 96,188 in Sabaragamuwa and 100,000 in the Western Province.[14] In 1952 there were over twice as many voters per seat in the Western Province as there were in the Central and Eastern provinces, and three times as many as in Uva and the North Central Province (see Table 12). While in some constituencies in the Western Province over sixty thou-

TABLE 12. Number of Registered Voters per Seat, 1947, 1952, and 1956

Province	1947	1952	1956
Western	43,400	45,850	51,850
Central	28,000	22,200	26,000
Southern	40,000	41,085	47,085
Northern	31,222	29,667	32,223
Eastern	21,143	20,714	24,857
North Western	31,700	35,100	41,500
North Central	13,480	15,280	20,840
Uva	17,471	15,228	19,071
Sabaragamuwa	30,840	30,210	34,670

SOURCE: Data obtained at Office of Commissioner of Elections, Colombo.

sand electors were on the register in 1952, those constituencies in the Central Province that had originally been designed to represent Indians, had under ten thousand apiece. In 1952 the electoral district of Talawakella had only 2,912 electors, while Katagala had 7,749, Nuwara Eliya had 9,279, and Maskeliya had only 8,703. Extreme distortions of this kind remained unchanged until 1959, when electoral districts were revised.

In 1959 a delimitation commission was appointed to reassign seats and redraw electoral boundaries in accordance with the Government's scheme for an enlarged House of Representatives. The number of elected members was to increase from 95 to 151. The major change in the method of apportioning the seats was that while the number of "persons," as well as the area size, continued to be used to determine the number of seats allocated to a province, an attempt was to be made to achieve an "equality of citizens" per seat within the province.[15] This meant that while Indians would be counted in determining the number of seats alloted to a province, most of them would not be considered in the drawing of constituency boundaries within provinces, since most of them were not citizens. Bandaranaike told the House of Representatives that while there had been "divergent views" over whether to use "persons" or "citizens" as the basis for determining the population of a province and the seats it deserved, "in the end it was felt that it was difficult or it would not be altogether equitable—that was the feeling of the majority of the Committee—merely to go on the basis of citizens, because those persons who are resident in an area too have their needs."[16] The logic of having Sinhalese represent Indians was challenged by one member of Parliament who suggested that Bandaranaike's proposal "gives the representation to those to represent those whom they most want to kick out."[17]

In any case, the combined effect of the disfranchisement of the Indians and the use of "persons" rather than "citizens" is to give proportionally more representation to citizens of those provinces in which Indians reside. The Delimitation Commission, while not making a judgment, noted that the Central Province, Uva, and Sabaragamuwa, where there are large concentrations of Indians, profit from the use of "persons."[18] While the use of more up-to-date census figures, especially, reduced some of the inequities of the first delimitation, there are still great disparities between provinces in the ratio of persons, voters, and citizens to seats (see Table 13). Within provinces, however, the Delimitation Commission has been able to obtain a fairly equal distribution of citizens per seat, although each province has a few cases of distortion. For the most part, disparities between electoral districts within provinces derive from attempts to shape constituencies about a concentrated minority group, the need to conform to geographical, transport or communication realities, or the concentrations of Indians.

Electoral Distortions and the Party System

The disproportionate representation in Ceylon affects the party system by artificially weighting the electoral power of certain social elements. Area weightage has helped the Tamil and Muslim communities by increasing the number of M.P.'s that each can potentially return. (This gain has been more than offset by the fact that the Sinhalese control more than their share of seats because of the Indian disfranchisement and the continued use of "persons" in the provincial assignment of seats.) The main advantage from the use of area weightage, however, has gone to the "backward" provinces, whose number of seats substantially exceeds that which they would have on a purely population basis (see Table 13). In contrast, the more progressive Westernized and urbanized provinces are put to great disadvantage. Because of area weightage, therefore, the peasant, rural, and backward areas have more representation than the more urbanized and prosperous areas. The Marxist parties in particular suffer because of this, since their main strength lies in the underrepresented Western and Southern provinces. Peasant-oriented parties, on the

TABLE 13. Number of Seats per Province under 1959 Delimitation, and Number of Persons, Citizens, and Voters per Seat

Province	Population	Citizens	Population-based Seats	Area-based Seats	Total Seats	Persons per Seat	Citizens per Seat	Voters per Seat
Western	2,547,500	2,392,200	34	1	35	72,785	68,348	32,145
Central	1,552,600	1,000,700	21	2	23	67,504	45,508	18,556
Southern	1,258,700	1,237,100	17	2	19	66,247	65,110	31,373
Sabaragamuwa	1,016,100	850,300	14	2	16	63,506	56,686	23,237
North Western	1,000,900	977,700	13	3	16	62,556	61,106	27,400
Northern	664,300	638,600	9	4	13	51,100	49,123	24,007
Uva	549,900	359,300	7	3	10	54,990	35,930	14,225
Eastern	496,200	487,300	7	4	11	49,109	44,300	18,127
North Central	275,100	270,600	4	4	8	34,388	33,825	15,362
Total	9,361,300	8,213,800	126	25	151			
National average						58,020	51,104	22,705

SOURCE: *Sessional Paper XV of 1959*, p. 11.

other hand, such as the S.L.F.P., profit under the present system. The U.N.P. loses in that the Westernized areas are underrepresented but profits in that it, like the S.L.F.P., depends upon peasant support. As far as the party system is concerned, the main effect of increasing the electoral weight of backward areas is to compel parties to articulate the social, cultural, and economic needs of such areas.[19]

The main distortion caused by the electoral system in Ceylon, however, is in the division of seats between the Kandyan and the low-country Sinhalese. In 1947 there were 1,695,416 Kandyan Sinhalese in Ceylon and 2,819,782 low-country Sinhalese.[20] If seats had been allotted purely on the basis of island-wide population, the Kandyan Sinhalese would have occupied 25 seats and the low-country Sinhalese 34 seats. If the province had been used as a unit without area weightage, the Kandyan Sinhalese would have been given 27 seats to 34 for the low-country Sinhalese.[21] As the seats were finally assigned in 1947, the Kandyan Sinhalese had 36 seats, and the low-country Sinhalese had 32. The First Delimitation Commission noted this disparity and explained, "This is not due to the adoption by us on behalf of the Kandyan Sinhalese of the special devices provided in The Order for increasing the representation of sections of the population, but is due to the factors inherent in the general plan for delimitation as contained in The Order."[22] While the distortion in 1947 was partly due to area weightage, which increased the number of seats assigned to provinces where the Kandyans reside, the disparity between Kandyan and low-country Sinhalese in regard to seats was to be made even greater in 1959 because of the disfranchisement of the Indians and the continued use of "persons." On an island-wide population basis, the low-country Sinhalese would have had 74 seats allotted to them in the electoral revision of 1959, while the Kandyan Sinhalese would have had 47. As the present system works out, the low-country Sinhalese have 56 seats while the Kandyan Sinhalese have 66. The Second Delimitation Commission observed that the overrepresentation of the Kandyan Sinhalese derived primarily from the use of "persons"[23] and noted that it expects the future registration of Indians as citizens to reduce the disparity.[24]

The present electoral system gives the Kandyans priority in Ceylonese politics. A major party must gain the votes of the Kandyan Sinhalese for electoral success, and this means an emphasis on the traditional culture and an articulation of the interests of influence groups that relate to this culture. The S.L.F.P. is the party that profits the most from Kandyan overrepresentation, since it was the S.L.F.P. that first made an effective ideological appeal to Kandyan interests. Since 1956 all Sinhalese parties have adopted ideologies oriented to Kandyan interests. Marxist parties have been hurt the most by Kandyan overrepresentation, because their strength lies in low-country Sinhalese areas and because until recently they have been noncommunalist. Thus, on the whole, the electoral system in Ceylon works against parties whose orientation is to the Westernized, urbanized, progressive, and low-country Sinhalese elements. The electoral pattern is such that the Kandyan Sinhalese, the peasants, and residents of rural and backward areas are given strength, and so also the parties that express their interests.

In Ceylon, delimitation commissions have been instructed to draw constituency boundaries wherever possible around "communities of interest," whether these be distinguished by their racial, caste, religious, economic, or occupational character. Assisted by the territorial concentration of such groupings, the delimitation commissions have been able painstakingly to carve out electoral districts that conform fairly well to communities of interest. The result is that most of the electoral districts in Ceylon are free from competition between social, communal, and religious groups. Minority religious and communal groups exist in almost every province of Ceylon. Only in the Northern and Southern provinces is there an appreciable absence of minority communal groups, and religious minorities exist in substantial number in every province except the Southern (see Tables 14 and 15). Thus a sociological basis exists in Ceylon for the operation of minority pressure groups that could make themselves felt at the constituency level. However, the electoral design, by isolating such groups within constituencies drawn on the basis of communities of interest, has largely militated against this.

In six of the nine provinces there is practically no competition between religious or communal groups within the electoral dis-

TABLE 14. Distribution of Population by Communal Group

Province	Low-Country Sinhalese	Kandyan Sinhalese	Ceylon Tamils	Ceylon Moors
Western	2,035,166	52,830	108,919	122,605
Central	149,659	691,114	45,918	82,833
Southern	1,182,371	6,473	7,721	33,223
Northern	9,260	7,425	597,469	23,349
Eastern	27,783	30,044	199,408	168,513
North Western	322,038	561,205	30,715	55,912
North Central	48,342	189,797	16,572	22,205
Uva	46,629	266,769	16,377	15,846
Sabaragamuwa	128,743	675,298	15,204	25,913
Total	3,949,991	2,480,955	1,038,303	550,399

SOURCE: *Sessional Paper XV of 1959,* Appendix VI.

TABLE 15. Distribution of Population by Religion

Province	Buddhist	Hindu[a]	Muslim	Christian
Western	1,779,007	159,726	169,126	434,107
Central	829,121	544,195	98,884	70,169
Southern	1,182,782	27,189	35,438	11,818
Northern	14,525	526,592	27,663	95,240
Eastern	53,941	187,194	170,900	27,524
North Western	756,724	32,317	61,879	148,585
North Central	236,218	17,231	24,072	5,847
Uva	312,314	200,511	19,944	16,327
Sabaragamuwa	794,985	162,140	30,569	26,834
Total	5,959,617	1,857,095	638,475	836,451

SOURCE: *Sessional Paper XV of 1959,* Appendix VII.
[a] Includes nonvoting Indian population.

trict.[25] In the Southern Province all the electoral districts except one have electorates that are over 90 per cent Buddhist and 90 per cent low-country Sinhalese, while in the Northern Province, Ceylon Tamils and Hindus comprise over 90 per cent of the electorate in all constituencies except three, where Christians, Moors, and Muslims provide some competition. In the Central Province most electoral districts are from 80 per cent to 90 per cent Buddhist and Kandyan Sinhalese, although in two there are substantial minorities of Christians, Moors, Muslims, and Ceylon Tamils. Akurana, which has a large concentration of Moors, was made into a multimember district. Uva Province is also free from religious and communal competition in elections. All the constituencies in this province are over 90 per cent Buddhist, and Kandyan Sinhalese comprise from 80 per cent to 90 per cent of the electorate in all districts except two. In the North Central Province, Kandyan Sinhalese form over 75 per cent of the electorate in most constituencies, and except for one, all districts are over 80 per cent Buddhist. Sabaragamuwa Province is largely dominated by Kandyan Sinhalese, who comprise over 80 per cent of the citizens in most constituencies. Low-country Sinhalese form minorities in most constituencies, though in only three do they exceed 20 per cent of the electorate. Except for one constituency, the electorate in every district is overwhelmingly Buddhist.

The religious and communal pluralism of the North Western, Western, and Eastern provinces is such that potentially they have highly competitive groups within the electorate. However, in all three provinces the meticulous carving of electoral districts and the creation of multimember districts has had the effect of limiting religious and communal competition in elections. In the North Western Province, while communal minorities exist in every constituency, the dominant community in most cases comprises over 70 per cent of the electorate. One district has almost equal numbers of Moors and low-country Sinhalese, as well as a substantial minority of Ceylon Tamils. Constituencies are from 80 per cent to 90 per cent Buddhist, except for four in which Buddhists, Christians, and Muslims reside in fairly equal numbers. In the Eastern Province there are almost equal numbers of Ceylon Tamils and Moors, as well as a significant Sinhalese minority. However, the creation of two multimember districts and the careful construction of single-member districts has separated these communities electorally. Only in one single-member district is there a fair balance between Moors and Tamils. Competition in the Western Province has also been similarly limited. The metropolitan area of Colombo is broken up into multimember and single-member districts, and this has electorally separated a communally and religiously mixed electorate. Buddhists and Roman Catholics in the areas north of Colombo have been fairly effectively separated, a task facilitated by the fact that Catholics reside in the coastal areas, while Buddhists inhabit the inland region. In spite of this, many districts in the Western Province are religiously and communally plural, and it has the most intergroup competition of any province in Ceylon.

In addition to concentrating communal and religious groups as far as possible within their own constituencies, delimitation commissions have sought to consolidate other kinds of communities of interest within electoral districts. In some cases efforts were made to create constituencies where the "depressed classes" would have a major voice in the election of parliamentary members. In many cases, "backwardness of development" served as a criterion for drawing electoral boundaries. The Second Delimitation Commission, for instance, stated that "in the interest of the development of such backward areas, we have deemed it necessary that they should be carved into separate electoral districts." [26] In others, such as the Galle district in the Southern Province, the commission "kept in mind the economic pursuits of the people." [27] An attempt was also made to carve constituencies made up of people engaged in maritime pursuits, agriculture, or other forms of livelihood.

Thus the drawing of electoral boundaries in Ceylon has been

guided by an effort to give almost every major group in Ceylon's plural society a share of parliamentary power commensurate either with its numbers or with its need to make itself felt in Parliament. The objective of the Second Delimitation Commission was to make certain that "Parliament would be a mirror of the will of the people." [28] While there is undoubtedly a great deal of merit in this, the method of creating electoral districts in Ceylon has resulted in the construction of constituencies that are largely homogeneous. This is especially so in regard to religious and communal groupings, but it is also true socially as well. The effect is that few members of Parliament have to represent a culturally mixed constituency and that most of them must speak in Parliament for the one interest group dominant in their constituency. The social patterns of electoral districts in Ceylon, therefore, do not encourage reduction or reconciliation at the constituency level of intergroup conflict, and Parliament necessarily becomes the arena where such conflict must somehow be worked out. Much of the tension and conflict that occurs in Parliament is at least partly due to this. The social makeup of electoral districts also explains some of the difficulties that parties have in maintaining cohesion in Parliament. Party members who are elected from largely homogeneous districts and who represent conflicting interest groups, are difficult to control through party discipline when questions arise that bear on the interest group dominant in their constituencies. The need to remain committed to the major interest at the constituency level often impels a party member to take an extreme position on certain measures lest he lose the confidence of his constituents and suffer the transfer of their support to someone else. Thus while the electoral system in Ceylon lessens intergroup competition and the need for compromise within constituencies, it heightens competition in Parliament by encouraging the return of group-oriented members.

CONCLUSION

The growth of parties in Ceylon has involved their transformation from notable-determined structures to voter-determined and socially responsive units. While the process is not complete, parties in Ceylon have made what Sigmund Neumann in his analysis of modern parties terms "a visible shift from loose parties of individual representation to powerful parties of social integration."[1] Parties become public organizations when they relate to their social environment as well as to their institutional environment. When parties relate only to the parliament and strive to obtain power for their members within this structure, they are personalistic. It is when they relate the voter to parliament and strive to obtain power in this structure for him as well as for the political careerist that parties become socially responsive organizations. The shift of parties from being personal to being public organizations involves their conversion from notable-determined into voter-determined structures. In the party that operates only for the purpose of obtaining power for notables, party ideology is shaped by the interests of notables and party organization consists primarily of the personal-influence structures of party notables. Parties that function to obtain power for voter blocs, develop ideologies expressive of the preferences of voters and construct organizations that extend into the electorate and link party, voter, and notable in a mutually exploitive and dependent relationship.

The process of party growth in Ceylon reveals that the transformation of a party from a personalistic to a public organization involves the displacement of notables as viable and self-sufficient political units. In such a transformation the party becomes personal to the voter, as were the notables whom it has displaced. The process of displacement and the related development of the party are gradual, and perhaps never complete, because personality always plays a role in politics, even in such party-oriented systems as that of Great Britain. Yet the efficient operation of a parliamentary system in a mass franchise environment ultimately depends on the ability of parties to engineer voter alignments and to construct parliamentary alignments that relate to them. The task of effecting this has been best achieved when parties have become ideologically identifiable and when voters have responded to them as distinct political units. It is largely because party growth has tended toward the realization of such parties that the parliamentary system has survived so well in Ceylon.

FROM PERSONAL TO SOCIAL PARTIES

Personal Parties

For the most part it was the response of political notables to the institution of a parliamentary system in 1947 that stimulated the emergence of parties in Ceylon. An example is the United National party. The notables who joined in its formation were well aware that a permanently aligned majority would be needed to make the new parliamentary system work, and the U.N.P. was organized explicitly to obtain that majority. However, the U.N.P. was constructed not only to make the new system work, but also to secure positions in Parliament, by combining their individual strengths, for those same notables who under the State Council system had been able to bargain for power independently. Some parties were formed by dissidents whose aspirations had been frustrated by their colleagues in the parties with which they had at first associated. The Sri Lanka Freedom party was organized by notables alienated from the U.N.P., while the Federal party was formed by dissidents who defected from the Tamil Congress. As time went on, other notables joined one or the other of these parties because it was useful to their political careers to do so.

While the origin of the other parties is not as intimately bound to the institution of Parliament as is that of the U.N.P., the S.L.F.P., and the F.P., all parties were profoundly affected by it. The T.C. and the Ceylon Indian Congress had originally been formed as communal pressure groups by notables who had the confidence of their respective communities. Both parties were highly personal organizations composed of notables who related to these minority communities in much the same way as U.N.P. notables related to the Sinhalese community. Once the parliamentary system was introduced, both parties were employed to bring like-minded notables into power-oriented and ambitious combinations in Parliament. The Marxist parties also had an extraparliamentary origin, though they too were highly personal organizations whose goal was the attainment of power for the notables who led them. The organizations of the Marxist parties themselves provided structural arenas in which competition for power between leaders took place, and in some ways this competition was similar to that between notables for power within Parliament. Marxist notables used their personal influence with the party members to mobilize factions against others in the party, and each used personally organized trade union affiliates of the party as a personal power base. Once the parliamentary system was introduced, Marxist notables put their parties into service in Parliament as power-oriented organizations, and their behavior was basically much the same as that of other notables.

The fact that parties were formed by notables to help them obtain power made them into organizations that were primarily notable-determined. The structure of non-Marxist parties was characterized by a central organization dominated by the party caucus and by election committees controlled by party candidates. The centralization of power in the party caucus followed naturally from the decentralization of the party's organizational extensions into the electorate. Almost the entire fabric of party organization consisted of an elaborate and intricate network of personal-influence structures which related the voter and interest groups to the party through the myriad links of party notables. For the most part, parties relied organizationally upon their notables and their affiliations with interest groups for contact with voters. The development of a formal party organization was not pushed, both because it was not needed and because party notables, whose influence in parties derived largely from the viability of their own personally committed organization and influence structure, actively discouraged it. The Marxist parties were much better organized than those of parliamentary origin and each had an efficient formal organization as well as blocs of ideologically committed voters. However, the formal organization of all the Marxist parties consisted of a combination of personal organizations committed to various party notables. Trade unions, electoral committees, youth branches, and the regular party cadre were personally controlled by party notables, who, in addition, secured election for themselves primarily through their own influence. The more powerful party notables usually were in both the party caucus and the top organ of the formal party organization. In these ways the organization of Marxist parties was as personal and informal as was that of other parties.

Party ideologies during the initial period of party development were also largely determined by party notables. No party at its origin was an ideologically clear and consolidated unit. Within the ranks of some parties there was perhaps a broad ideological consensus, but it was limited and vague. It was rarely an element of sufficient cohesion to contain the personal ambition of party members. The vague and inclusive character of party ideology was permissible, even necessary. Initially, the people voted for notables whom they knew and trusted, and it was the association of a party with notables that brought it electoral strength.

Parties, therefore, could be ideologically vague and unconcerned about projecting an image that would be clearly visible to the voter. More than that, ideological imprecision was necessary in mobilizing a wide variety of notables and interest groups. A vague or inclusive ideology made parties accessible to ideologically disparate groups and individuals, and parties depended for their life on this. Ideological imprecision was especially of service to political notables, because it facilitated their movement from party to party in search of the party association most profitable to their own career advancement. At the same time, ideological imprecision permitted parties to court prominent notables of dissimilar views. The ideology of Marxist parties was almost as inclusive as that of other parties. Arguing ideological questions was the sport of party intellectuals, and ideology was employed mainly to rationalize power conflicts between various leaders and personal factions within Marxist parties. While tactical questions concerning voters were involved, ideological disputes in Marxist parties were largely personal affairs, and the ideology of Marxist parties was no more voter-determined than that of other parties.

The initial period in the growth of parties in Ceylon was thus characterized by the operation of notable-determined parties. A party functioned as a power-oriented organization directed by notables on the basis of their own interest; party organization was highly personalized, informal, and notable-controlled; and party ideology was determined by party notables without consultation with voters. All this suited the interests of the notables well, because it allowed them maneuverability in Parliament and permitted them to retain their personal influence and personal organizations within their constituencies. This is not to suggest that parties were completely disconnected from their social bases. Every party had relations to some pressure groups that influenced its ideological orientation and both facilitated and rationalized its operation in Parliament as a party. The T.C. and the C.I.C. were communal pressure groups turned parties, the U.N.P. emerged from a coalition of pre-existing organizations and with the active support of business and Westernized elements, the S.L.F.P. had other organizational roots and social connections, and the Marxist parties, of course, had their trade unions. Affiliations of this sort had their influence on party ideology and certainly on the actions of notables linked directly to them. For the most part, however, the social base of parties was not politically activated on the basis of ideology, and parties relied for the mobilization of voters mainly on their notables.

Toward Social Parties

A second stage in the growth of parties in Ceylon began in 1956, when, under the pressure of voters, parties moved from their almost exclusive courtship of notables to a more intimate association with the people. In this stage of development parties became the property of the voter as well as of the notable, and the public became the molder of parties. As a result of this popular association parties undertook structural transformation in order to relate directly to the people. In pursuit of this goal they adopted more popular ideologies, became more ideologically precise and consolidated, and proceeded thereby to clarify their image for the voter. They developed organizational extensions into the electorate over and above those personal links under the command of their notables, constructed a more active formal organization, and functioned as more cohesive units. They became less dependent upon a network of notables and personal influence structures, and instead came under the command of the people. It was at this stage that the party in Ceylon became a clearly identifiable and socially responsive unit.

The shift into the second stage of development in Ceylon was generated by the appeal to voters on the basis of policy rather than of personal influence. Neither in this stage nor in the preceding one did the mass franchise act as a catalytic agent for party growth, as Max Weber suggested that it did in his analysis of party growth in Great Britain.[2] Ceylon had the mass franchise as early as 1931, and while parties emerged because of it, none survived. This was because the institutional arrangement of the State Council made the party unnecessary to the political career of elected members. When parties formed in 1947, it was in response to the introduction of Parliament, not to the franchise, because while the party was meaningful in Parliament, elections were still personal affairs. The experience of Ceylon, therefore, reveals that the mass franchise does not automatically bring about the emergence of parties and that it only does so when voters use it purposely to control parties.

The process by which the voter became directly linked to a party and began to remold it to fit his own ambitions was gradual in Ceylon. Neither in 1947 nor in 1952 was more than a fraction of the electorate party oriented. The affluent pressure groups, the vested interests, and certain elements in cultural and communal societies had a stake in the return of the U.N.P. Trade union members and some groups directly and unfavorably affected by a U.N.P. government, on the other hand, were enthusiastic supporters of Marxist or other parties. These voters, however, were not a great many, and most voters cast their ballot for notables in the elections of 1947 and 1952. The real beginnings of party consciousness in the voter came after 1952, when the mounting discontent was intentionally directed against the Government and the U.N.P. by the combined efforts of a wide variety of opposition groups. In essence, the process involved a polarization of political forces and eventuated in a division between voters that reflected and coincided with the parliamentary division between Government and Opposition. This involved, first, the growth of discontent and the generation of opposition in the electorate that paralleled the discontent and opposition in Parliament, and, second, the organization of the parliamentary and electoral opposition to the U.N.P. The most important force in organizing the electoral opposition and mobilizing it on behalf of the parliamentary opposition was the peramunas and balavegayas, or "fronts," composed of influential social and cultural elements directly and adversely affected by the U.N.P. rule. These organizations activated interests that initially had been dormant and focused public attention on the U.N.P. as the unit responsible for the problems faced by many groups in Ceylon. The opposition parties were prompt to react to the political opportunity offered by the mass protest organized by the peramunas. They organized in an electoral coalition, formed an alliance with discontented pressure groups, and sought through them to mobilize voters on the basis of issues rather than personalities. The M.E.P. coalition of 1956 was the first "party" whose ideology was voter-determined, and the M.E.P. government was the first elected on a promise to implement legislation specifically responsive to popular demand. Thus the party became a meaningful political unit to the voter, and once this had occurred, all Sinhalese parties began to seek an ideological image that reflected more of the aspirations of the people and was more in line with the demands of voters.

It was the opposition parties, therefore, in combination with the peramunas, that induced the voter into the party system, made the party a meaningful political unit to the voter, and ultimately compelled parties, as well as notables, to compete for votes. Once parties had entered the voter's awareness as relevant to his needs, and once they had to compete for votes as units, they undertook structural transformations intended to link them directly to the voter. The ideological adjustments and organizational construction undertaken by parties in Ceylon represented an attempt to adopt profitable ideologies and to present a clear image to the voter. It was at this stage of development that the ideologies of parties became voter-determined and their organizations became voter-oriented. The S.L.F.P. image was originally designed with the voter in mind, and after 1956 all the Sinhalese parties sought to emulate it. As Marshall Singer has observed, since 1956 "virtually every major party in Ceylon (save the Tamil parties) has remolded itself, if not into the S.L.F.P. image, at least into the Sinhalese nationalist-socialist image."[3] This has been true of Marxist parties as well as of the U.N.P. and others.

The adoption of communalism by the Marxist parties occurred despite the inevitable tension it introduced into their ranks, particularly with respect to their Tamil members. The acceptance of communalism by both the L.S.S.P. and the C.P. is a clear case of voters determining the ideology of doctrinal parties whose ideological orientations had previously been determined exclusively by the party members. Even doctrinal parties, therefore, become voter-determined when they adopt parliamentary and electoral tactics to obtain power. Such tactics were adopted by Marxist parties in Ceylon because a revolutionary orientation had become unprofitable and unrealistic. Marxist parties adopted the ideology of both parliamentary reformism and communalism because it was profitable and politically relevant to do so. The same opportunism has characterized every party in Ceylon since 1956 and is, as Allan P. Sindler suggests, characteristic of parties in general, because the "material drives of party tend to be more enduring than any commitment in the abstract to ideology or to any particular policy position."[4]

The induction of the voter into the party system also led to organizational changes by parties. In an attempt to link themselves intimately to the people and in order to popularize their images, parties in Ceylon developed formal organizational extensions to the voter. Aroused by its defeat in 1956, the U.N.P. took the initiative in building an effective formal organization. The S.L.F.P., primarily because it retained power until 1965, was slower to develop its organization. As in the case of the U.N.P., the S.L.F.P. had to suffer defeat before organizational development was undertaken in earnest. The effect of such organizational growth was to initiate the depersonalization of parties in Ceylon. As formal organizations became effective electorally, parties were less dependent upon the personal organizations of their notables, and this in turn transferred more authority to regular party members whose work had become essential to the party.

It was not until the voter intruded upon the party system, therefore, that parties in Ceylon became socially responsive units. When this occurred, the party performed a social, as well as a self-promoting function. The adoption of profitable ideologies released the party from its dependence on a network of notables, but it also brought the party under the command of the people and transformed it into a social, as well as a personal organization. This made the self-promoting and social functions of party mutually dependent, because the party could not realize its goal of power without performing a function for the larger society as well. At this stage the party acts to obtain power for both political notables and voters, its ideology is determined by consultation with voters, and its organization intimately links the party to voters. The experience of Ceylon supports the contention that when such a social orientation is achieved by the party, it is able to function best as a bridge or a link between the people and the institutions of government.

A REPLACEMENT THEORY OF PARTY GROWTH

The development of parties in Ceylon suggests that the dynamic of party growth is primarily the ambition of those involved in politics as a vocation. Parties initially are formed to help realize the ambitions of political notables, and they later change and develop for much the same reason. The growth of parties is basically due to an organizational response by notables to the needs of advancement in the political vocation, and parties neither form nor change unless the situation in which such notables operate demands it. Fundamentally, therefore, the party is the ambitions of notables organized. The growth of parties, however, while engendered by the needs of political notables, inevitably leads to the displacement of such notables as self-sufficient and viable political units.[5] This is the irony of party growth. In the formative period of party growth in Ceylon, the party replaced the independent as a viable political unit in Parliament because party association became vital for career advancement at that level. Once the party developed ideological identity and organizational linkage to the voter, it began to replace the independent as a viable political unit electorally. The replacement of notables as independent political units, therefore, coincides with the transformation of parties from personal to social organizations. Parties are personal when they serve purely as the parliamentary organizations of notables. Parties become social when they serve as the electoral associations of notables as well.

The growth of a party, therefore, can be measured by the extent to which it is able to replace notables as viable political units; the party may be said to reach maturity when it becomes a self-sufficient political unit. What the party seeks is to become a notable in its own right; to become ultimately as personal to the voter as were the notables whom the party replaces. The process of party growth and the related displacement of political notables involve a transfer of functions from notable to party. In the first stage the function of obtaining power is transferred from the independent to the party. In the second stage the function of securing election becomes a function of the party rather than of notables. The process of replacement is gradual, and the characteristics of the party system at any time are indicative of the extent to which the party has secured the replacement of notables. Many of the features of Ceylon's party system can be explained by the incomplete but developing replacement of notables by parties.

The Parliamentary Displacement of Notables

Before the emergence of parties in Ceylon, political notables were completely self-sufficient political units. Their personal influence and local reputation served to secure their election, as people voted for men of local prominence whom they both knew and trusted. Organizationally, notables were self-reliant, as friends and relatives helped them campaign and personally committed influence structures were employed to mobilize voters. Once elected, notables were able to secure their own place by co-option and personal maneuvers in a state council system specifically designed to accommodate independent notables. Parties did not form during this period because notables could derive no political or electoral profit from their formation. This changed when the parliamentary system was introduced, and parties were then formed as career-promoting organizations designed to function as power-oriented combinations in Parliament. But at the same time that parties promoted, or were intended to promote, the parliamentary career of those who joined them, they severely limited the political careers of those who did not. The main effect of party formation on the political vocation was the displacement of the independent as a self-reliant and viable political unit within the elected institution of government. While posts could be obtained in the State Council through personal co-option, the parliamentary system made association with a party essential for personal gain. The independent necessarily became an anomaly because without the organized support of a party behind him, he carried little influence in Parliament. The party had become the vehicle best able to provide advancement in politics, and consequently the political history of Ceylon since 1947 has witnessed the gradual decline of the independent in Parliament.

However, the replacement of the independent by the party in Parliament was retarded by the electoral independence of notables, which permitted them a great deal of independence and maneuverability in Parliament. In spite of party formation, elections remained essentially personal affairs in which candidates ran on their own merits, stressed their own qualities, and depended for success on their own resources and personal reputation. At the electoral level, the party was not at first a meaningful political unit because to the voter party meant nothing as a distinct entity apart from the notable who ran under its label. Even the Marxist parties, with their longer history, trade union affiliations, and organized blocs of committed voters, depended on the local influence of their notables. Party was therefore as much an anomaly in respect to the electorate as the independent was in Parliament, and in the initial phase of party evolution in Ceylon parties sought notables and notables sought party, and the strength of one was employed to compensate for the weakness of the other at the level of greatest deficiency.

The operating characteristics of the party system were determined by the uneven or partial development of parties and by the fact that neither party nor notable was a self-sufficient political unit. The behavior of both party and notable during this period confirms S. J. Eldersveld's contention that "the party is a mutually exploitative relationship—it is joined by those who would use it; it mobilizes for the sake of power those who would join it."[6] The influence of the party on notables derived from its parliamentary utility, while the influence of notables was a product of their electoral utility. Notables tended to gravitate naturally to the parties that appeared most capable of obtaining power in Parliament, while parties sought to recruit those notables who appeared most likely to succeed electorally. On the other hand, parties that seemed incapable of obtaining power in Parliament found the recruitment of notables difficult, and parties did not pursue potential candidates who were not electorally strong. It was a situation in which the rich sought the rich and in which, for a time at least, the rich got richer.

The electoral self-sufficiency of notables produced a highly fluid situation within Parliament, as elected members moved rather freely between parties. Self-sufficient as electoral units, and motivated primarily by personal ambition, notables joined parties, left them, and joined others in quest of party associations that would maximize their own opportunity for career advancement. For the most part, the influence that a notable had with a party in Parliament was measured by the electoral contribution he could make to that party. Every member in Parliament had some influence with his party because each had secured his own election and represented a certain electoral strength. However, a party member whose electoral strength went beyond his own constituency obtained more power than did those whose influence was locally confined. Power flowed naturally to the party members who were provincially or nationally prominent, or who led important cultural or other interest groups on the island. This is not to deny that more personal reasons such as caste, family background, and personal rivalries or feuds, played their part in the relations of men and party in Parliament, enhancing the careers of some and hindering the careers of others. In general, however, electoral power was translated into parliamentary power. Factions within parties were built around the more prominent and electorally influential members, and the ability to manipulate such personally committed blocs augmented the parliamentary influence of prominent leaders. It was such leaders who could found parties or move blocs of M.P.'s from party to party. Thus because of electoral independence and party accessibility, notables were still able to secure position on the basis of personal co-option despite the introduction of Parliament and the formation of parties.

The emerging parties in Ceylon, therefore, did not entirely displace notables in Parliament, because initially they were unable to displace notables electorally. The emergence of party makes party association essential for career advancement in Parliament, but the permeability of parties and the electoral independence of notables makes for a constant movement of notables between parties. This flow cannot be contained or retarded, and the displacement of notables at the level of Parliament cannot be completed, until the party can replace notables electorally.

The Electoral Displacement of Notables

The replacement of notable by party at the electoral level requires the organizational and ideological development of parties in the direction of image visibility to the voter. The notables, resisting the intrusion of the party into a direct association with their constituents and their resulting displacement, therefore often inhibit the further development of their own parties. They intentionally hamper the organizational growth of the party by discouraging the expansion and vitality of formal party organization, and they conduct personalized election campaigns, the effect of which is to inhibit the popularization of party images. In this way notables seek, consciously or not, to perpetuate the personal-influence structures on which their parties were originally constructed. There is little doubt that an informal personal-influence structure is essential to the origin of parties. They could hardly form otherwise, as a party label is meaningless unless the party is identifiable and its identity is confirmed by reputation, which takes time to evolve. The reputation of notables who are associated at the apex of a party and their local influence structures give the party meaning electorally. Yet this very personal-influence structure that is initially so vital and from which a party draws strength, eventually becomes the very obstacle it must overcome for its further development.

It is not until a party becomes a distinct political entity to the voter that the process of displacing notables as self-sufficient units at the electoral level begins. In Ceylon, it was the events of 1956 that made the voter aware of the relevance of party to his own interests and first acquainted him with the party as a distinct political unit. From 1956 on, the party label was politically meaningful to the voter, and while notables continued to compete with notables in elections, in most cases the party label meant the difference between victory and defeat. This made notables and parties mutually dependent because both were able to attract votes, but only by their combination could election be won. Because of this, notables had a personal stake in the development of their parties into profitable electoral units that could successfully compete with others for votes. The initial action taken by notables in an effort to construct a vote-getting identity for their party was to develop an ideology. All parties after 1956 consciously sought to build ideological images that would maximize their voter appeal. Party notables were willing to assist in the development of their parties into profitable electoral units through ideology because this did not obviously challenge the viability of their own personal-influence structures in their constituencies. Notables profited from associating with a party whose image was attractive to the voter, and he could encourage this without undermining his own influence because he still controlled the electoral organization of his party. This is why the ideological development of most parties in Ceylon preceded their organizational growth.

The S.L.F.P. was the first party to develop a profitable popular image, and this obviated the need to develop a viable formal organization. The U.N.P., on the other hand, had incurred an unprofitable image, and the party had to undertake a sustained effort to convey a renovated and more profitable image to the voter. For this reason, the U.N.P. spent a great deal of effort to develop a formal organization that would bring the party into intimate association with the voter and communicate to him the new image of the party. Similarly, the defeat of the S.L.F.P. in 1965 generated its organizational growth, as it sought to counter the great organizational strength exhibited by the U.N.P. in 1965. The party notables have no choice but to support this organizational growth, because their own election now depends upon the electoral ability of their party. The demands of political competition thus compel political notables to push the organizational growth of their party and to impress upon the voter a favorable view of it. The result of this is to make the party a distinct entity to the voter, to give it a clear and identifiable image, to give it, in other words, the personal quality of a notable with whom the voter feels well acquainted. The ultimate effect of this, as voters begin to cast their ballots for parties rather than for personalities, is to displace notables electorally. The process takes time. Parties must develop a reputation, as well as an ideological image and an organizational attachment, before they can fully replace notables electorally. Image visibility is a product not only of ideology, which verbalizes commitment, but also of performance, which makes it real and gives party a personal reputation to the voter. People tend to vote for that candidate whom they know and trust, for someone who has proven his devotion. When a party can obtain such a reputation then it becomes as personal to the voter as were the political notables before it. It is at this point that a party can replace notables electorally.

Parties in Ceylon have not yet reached such a state of development. Individuals are still electorally powerful, and a party cannot fully control the parliamentary behavior of its elected members until it can dispense with the votes which it still obtains by running notables. Elections are close in Ceylon, and since notables control a personally committed vote in their constituencies, parties must seek them if they want to return a parliamentary majority. Notables, however, have also become electorally dependent on parties. Few independents can win seats in their own right, and party association has become essential to election as well as to advancement in Parliament. This is an indication of the extent to which party has developed in Ceylon.

PARTY AND THE PARLIAMENTARY SYSTEM

Sigmund Neumann suggested in 1956 that the "development of a responsible party system could well be the secret of a successful transition from colonialism to political self-rule."[7] The history of the new states would seem to confirm Neumann's contention, for wherever the party system has not worked, the democratic system has also failed. In many new states the development of a competitive party system has been inhibited by the operation of monolithic nationalist parties, while in others an extremely proliferated party system has led to political instability and the assumption of power by the military. Ceylon has had none of this political instability, and it has experienced the operation of an efficient and competitive party system.[8] The parliamentary system has worked well in Ceylon because of this. Endowed with a responsible party system and competent and dedicated leaders, Ceylon has made the transition to self-rule perhaps better than any other new state.

The development of a responsible party system has been essential to the viability of a parliamentary system in Ceylon because it was through parties that both the political elite and the people were effectively related to Parliament. The formation of parties allowed adaptation of the operations of politics and of political figures to the operating methods of Parliament and so permitted it to function, while the transformation of parties from organizations of notables to voter-determined units, made Parliament function as a socially responsive institution. In the initial phase of their development parties functioned primarily as organizations in Parliament that served the political ambitions of elected notables. The U.N.P. at its origin was little more than an association of ambitious notables, but it provided the majority alignment essential to the formation of a government in the parliamentary system. It was because of this that the newly instituted Parliament was able to work. The organization of a parliamentary opposition took time to realize, and it was not until the formation of the S.L.F.P. in 1951 that the Opposition began to function with a fair degree of unity in Parliament, at least on occasion. Neither parties nor Parliament, however, had a direct link to the voter at this time. The voter was linked to both party and Parliament only indirectly through the notables whom he elected. This meant that the parliamentary division between Government and Opposition was meaningful only to the member of Parliament whose career was affected by his relation to that division. Parliamentary alignments, therefore, did not reflect voter alignments, and this prevented Parliament from functioning as a socially responsive institution. Notables were elected because of their local reputation, they associated with parties in Parliament as their ambition dictated, and they supported or opposed policy on the basis of a personal judgment relatively free from direct voter scrutiny.

It was the ambitions of political notables, as combined through the agency of party, that altered this and brought Parliament under direct voter control. The M.E.P. coalition of 1956 linked the parliamentary opposition to an electoral opposition, and for the first time parliamentary alignments reflected voter alignments. After this, policy decisions taken in Parliament more accurately represented the preferences of the voters, and the people were able to see their aspirations realized through the institutions and workings of Parliament. Parliament, as well as party, became real and meaningful to the voter, because both responded directly to his will. It was then that the parliamentary division into Government and Opposition became relevant to the voter as well as to political notables, and it was then that the construction of parliamentary alignments was determined primarily by voter alignments rather than exclusively by alignments of notables. It was this that made Parliament in Ceylon a socially responsive institution and it is because of this that Parliament has endured so well in Ceylon.

The viability of parliamentary government in Ceylon, therefore, has been largely due to the effectiveness of the party as an intermediary between the people and their political institutions. Parties have been socially responsive in Ceylon, and the predominant dispositions of its people have ideologically and naturally shaped the party system. This has in turn made parliament a "mirror of the will of the people," which through the implementation of policy responds to the demands of voter alignments. The effectiveness of Parliament in this regard largely discourages popular recourse to other methods of solving problems. The response of party and Parliament to popular pressure in 1956 pacified a potentially revolutionary situation and demonstrated the utility of election, party, and Parliament in effecting needed political and social change. The experience of Ceylon has revealed, therefore, that when parties become socially oriented and when their careers are linked to the aspirations of the people, they not only effectively relate Parliament to the people, but they make it a viable political institution as well.

It is manifest that the responsible nature of Ceylon's party system and its consequent contributions to the success of parliamentary government in Ceylon, has been due to the vitality of opposition parties and the ability of the party system to produce alternative governments. Fatma Mansur, among others, has observed that an essential weakness of most non-Western party systems has been the lack of an "opposition party which can become an alternative government."[9] In many new states this is due to the political monopoly that monolithic nationalist parties enjoy there, as well as to a fractionalized opposition that is unable to work in concert against the government party. Ceylon has had neither a monolithic nationalist party nor a fragmented opposition incapable of forming an anti-Government coalition, and this has been essential to the way the party system in Ceylon has evolved.

At bottom, the growth of a party system in Ceylon has involved a series of individual, organizational, and ideological responses to environmental and institutional pressures. In the process of response and adaptation, conditions indigenous to Ceylon have played their part: the independence struggle, the nature of politics during the preindependence period, the communal texture of Ceylonese society, and others. But at the same time, the growth of a party system in Ceylon has seen the natural maneuver and shifting of men and parties in their struggle for position in the game of politics. The ambition and opportunism inherent, to various degrees, in the political vocation have been behind most of the adjustments, alterations, and adaptations that have marked the careers of men and parties in Ceylon since independence.

List of Parties and Leaders / Notes / Bibliography / Index

ANNOTATED LIST OF MAJOR POLITICAL
PARTIES AND LEADERS

PARTIES

CEYLON COMMUNIST PARTY (C.P.)

The main Communist party in Ceylon. While it has had little strength in Parliament, the C.P. controls the largest trade unions of any party in Ceylon except the Ceylon Democratic Congress.

CEYLON COMMUNIST PARTY–CHINA WING (C.P.-CHINA)

Small Marxist party formed by dissidents from the C.P. in 1963. Its trade union membership is small, and it has elected none of its members to Parliament.

CEYLON DEMOCRATIC CONGRESS (C.D.C.)

Formerly the Ceylon Indian Congress, formed in 1939 as the political organization for the Indian minority in Ceylon. While the disfranchisement of most of the Indians in 1949 limited the ability of the congress to operate as a party, the massive trade unions it directs enable it to function as a politically influential pressure group.

FEDERAL PARTY (F.P.)

Tamil party formed in 1947 by S. J. V. Chelvanayakam and other Tamil notables who espoused a federal solution to the communal question. Since 1956 it has been the most powerful Tamil party in Ceylon.

LANKA SAMA SAMAJA PARTY (L.S.S.P.)

Marxist-socialist party that describes itself as Trotskyist. It is the oldest and strongest of the several Marxist parties in Ceylon.

LANKA SAMA SAMAJA PARTY–REVOLUTIONARY (L.S.S.P.-R.)

Party formed by radical members of the L.S.S.P. who broke from the party in 1964 when the L.S.S.P. entered into a coalition government with the S.L.F.P.

VIPLAVAKARI LANKA SAMA SAMAJA PARTY (V.L.S.S.P.)

Marxist party formed by Philip Gunawardena in 1950 when he broke from the L.S.S.P. In 1956 the V.L.S.S.P. entered a coalition to form the M.E.P. government. Subsequent to the breakup of the coalition in 1959 Gunawardena took its name for his party.

MAHAJANA EKSATH PERAMUNA (M.E.P.)

The first M.E.P. was the coalition that defeated the U.N.P. electorally in 1956 and ruled Ceylon from 1956 to 1959. The second M.E.P. is a small socialist party led by Philip Gunawardena that controls a considerable number of important trade unions.

SRI LANKA FREEDOM PARTY (S.L.F.P.)

Sinhalese socialist party formed by S. W. R. D. Bandaranaike and other dissidents from the U.N.P. in 1951. During its career the S.L.F.P. has developed from a moderate to a more radical socialist party.

TAMIL CONGRESS (T.C.)

Communal party formed by G. G. Ponnambalam in 1944 to unite Tamils politically. Its association with the U.N.P. from 1947 to 1956 caused the party to lose favor with the Tamils when communal discord erupted in Ceylon.

UNITED NATIONAL PARTY (U.N.P.)

Conservative "socialist" party formed in 1946 by prominent notables throughout Ceylon, most of whom had been active in preindependence politics and the movement for independence. Originally a pro-Western, conservative party, the U.N.P. sought after 1956 to attain a more popular image by adopting "democratic socialism" as its ideology and promising to implement progressive measures if it became the Government.

LEADERS

FELIX BANDARANAIKE

Cabinet minister in S.L.F.P. governments from 1960 to 1964. Nephew of S. W. R. D. Bandaranaike.

S. W. R. D. BANDARANAIKE

A leading member of the U.N.P. and cabinet minister from 1947 to 1951, founder of the S.L.F.P. in 1951, and Prime Minister of Ceylon from 1956 until he was assassinated in 1959.

MRS. SIRIMAVO BANDARANAIKE

Leader of the S.L.F.P. since 1960 and Prime Minister of Ceylon from 1960 to 1965. Widow of S. W. R. D. Bandaranaike.

S. J. V. CHELVANAYAKAM

Founding and leading member of the L.S.S.P.

W. DAHANAYAKE

Cabinet minister in the M.E.P. government from 1956 to 1959, Prime Minister of Ceylon from the assassination of S. W. R. D. Bandaranaike in September, 1959, until the election of March, 1960, and cabinet minister in the National (coalition) government formed in 1965.

C. P. DE SILVA

Cabinet minister in the M.E.P. and S.L.F.P. governments of 1956 to 1959 and 1960 to 1964, founder of the S.L.F.S.P. after his defection from the S.L.F.P. in 1964, and cabinet minister in the National government formed in 1965.

COLVIN R. DE SILVA

A founding and leading member of the L.S.S.P.

LESLIE GOONEWARDENE

Founding and leading member of the L.S.S.P.

PHILIP GUNAWARDENA

Founding member of the L.S.S.P., leader of the V.L.S.S.P. from 1950 to 1959, leader of the M.E.P. (party) and cabinet minister in the National government formed in 1965.

SIR JOHN KOTELAWALA

Leader of the U.N.P. and Prime Minister of Ceylon from 1953 until 1956.

PIETER KUENEMAN

A founding member and the secretary of the C.P.

N. M. PERERA

Founding member and main leader of the L.S.S.P., Leader of the Opposition from 1949 to 1952, and cabinet minister in the S.L.F.P.-L.S.S.P. government in 1964.

G. G. PONNAMBALAM

Founder and leader of the Tamil Congress, cabinet minister from 1948 to 1954, and in the National government formed in 1965.

EDMUND SAMARAKKODY

A founding and leading member of the L.S.S.P. until 1964, when he organized the L.S.S.P.-R.

D. S. SENANAYAKE

Main leader of the independence movement, founder of the U.N.P., and Prime Minister of Ceylon from 1947 until his death in 1952.

DUDLEY SENANAYAKE

Leader of the U.N.P., Prime Minister of Ceylon from 1952 to 1953, 1960, and from 1965. Son of D. S. Senanayake.

DR. S. A. WICKREMASINGHE

A founding member and the president of the C.P.

NOTES

Introduction

1. Quoted in the *New York Times,* May 7, 1952.
2. W. Howard Wriggins, *Ceylon: Dilemmas of a New Nation,* p. 68.
3. International Bank for Reconstruction and Development, *The Economic Development of Ceylon,* p. 144. At that time the rupee was worth 21 U.S. cents at the official rate of exchange.
4. Department of Census and Statistics, *Statistical Abstract of Ceylon,* p. 19.
5. *Ibid.*
6. Sir Ivor Jennings, *The Economy of Ceylon,* p. 126.
7. Department of Census and Statistics, *Abstract,* p. 160.
8. See statistics, *ibid.,* pp. 22–23.
9. Jennings, *Economy,* p. 144.
10. Department of Census and Statistics, *Abstract,* p. 113.
11. *Sessional Paper XIII of 1952.*
12. N. K. Sarkar and S. J. Tambiah, *The Disintegrating Village,* Table 3.
13. See B. H. Farmer, *Pioneer Peasant Colonization in Ceylon.*
14. Department of Census and Statistics, *Abstract,* pp. 32–33.
15. Planning Secretariat, *Six-Year Programme of Investment,* p. 157.
16. Wriggins, *Ceylon,* p. 53.
17. Jennings, *Economy,* p. 28.
18. Wriggins, *Ceylon,* p. 58.
19. *Ibid.,* p. 56.
20. International Bank for Reconstruction and Development, *Economic Development,* p. 209.
21. Department of Census and Statistics, *Abstract,* p. 25.
22. *Ibid.*
23. *Ibid.,* p. 28.
24. *Ibid.*
25. *Ibid.*

26. Quoted in Sir Charles Jeffries, *Ceylon: The Path to Independence,* p. 126.

27. *Ibid.,* p. ix.

28. Quoted in John R. Owens and P. J. Staudenraus, eds., *The American Party System* (New York: The Macmillan Co., 1965), p. 25.

29. *Political Parties: Their Organisation and Activity in the Modern State,* trans. Barbara and Robert North (London: Methuen & Co., 1962), p. xxiii.

30. For a criticism of Duverger's methodology see Aaron B. Wildavsky, "A Methodological Critique of Duverger's *Political Parties," Journal of Politics,* XXI (1959), 303–18.

31. See his "Toward a Theory of Political Parties," *World Politics,* VI (July, 1954), 549–63. For a review of the writings on political parties prior to this century see Austin Ranney and Willmoore Kendall, *Democracy and the American Party System* (New York: Harcourt, Brace and Co., 1956), pp. 116–54. For a review of more recent writings see Frederick C. Engelmann, "A Critique of Recent Writings on Political Parties," *Journal of Politics,* XIX (1957), 423–40; Neil A. McDonald, "Party Perspective: A Survey of Writings," in Harry Eckstein and David E. Apter, eds., *Comparative Politics* (New York: Free Press of Glencoe, 1963), pp. 332–50 and his *The Study of Political Parties* (New York: Random House, 1955). For good collections of readings on parties see Owens and Staudenraus, *American Party System,* and William J. Crotty, Donald M. Freeman and Douglas S. Gatlin, eds., *Political Parties and Political Behavior* (Boston: Allyn and Bacon, 1966).

32. Sigmund Neumann, ed., *Modern Political Parties: Approaches to Comparative Politics* (Chicago: The University of Chicago Press, 1956), p. 2. See also his "Toward a Comparative Study of Political Parties," *ibid.,* pp. 395–421.

33. "Political Parties: Introduction," in Eckstein and Apter, *Comparative Politics,* p. 329.

34. "The Place of Parties in the Study of Politics," *American Political Science Review,* LI (December, 1957), 943–54. See also his *Parties and Politics* (New York: Alfred A. Knopf, 1958).

35. "Politics as a Vocation," in H. H. Gerth and C. Wright Mills, eds., *From Max Weber: Essays in Sociology* (New York: Oxford University Press, Galaxy Books, 1958), pp. 77–128.

36. Duverger, *Political Parties,* pp. xxiii–xxiv.

37. "The Modern Party State," *Canadian Journal of Economics and Political Science,* XIV (May, 1949), 156.

38. *The Web of Government,* rev. ed. (New York: The Free Press, 1965), p. 157.

39. *Party Government* (New York: Farrar and Rinehart, 1942).

40. *Parties and Politics in America* (Ithaca, N.Y.: Cornell University Press, 1960), p. 67.

41. See also Otto Kirchheimer, "The Party in Mass Society," *World Politics,* X (October, 1957–July, 1958), 289–94.

42. *Permanent Revolution* (New York: Frederick A. Praeger, 1965), p. 118.

43. *Ibid.*

44. "Letter to Francis Hopkinson," in A. Koch and W. Pede, eds., *The Life and Selected Writings of Thomas Jefferson* (New York: Modern Library, 1944), p. 460.

45. For a criticism of their view see J. H. Meisel, *The Myth of the Ruling Class* (Ann Arbor: The University of Michigan Press, 1958).

46. (London: Macmillan, 1902). See also the more recent work by R. T. McKenzie, *British Political Parties* (London: William Heinemann, 1963), as well as Duverger, *Political Parties.*

47. *Political Parties* (New York: Dover Publications, 1959). See also C. W. Cassinelli, "The Law of Oligarchy," *American Political Science Review,* XLVII (1953), 773–84.

48. "What Is a Party," *Political Science Quarterly,* II (1896), 68.

49. "Party Systems in the United Kingdom and the Older Commonwealth: Causes, Resemblances and Variations," *Political Studies,* VII (1959), 12.

50. *Web of Government,* p. 156.

51. *Modern Political Parties,* p. 396.

52. In Eckstein and Apter, *Comparative Politics,* p. 384.

53. Gabriel Almond and G. Bingham Powell, Jr., *Comparative Politics: A Developmental Approach* (Boston: Little, Brown and Company, 1966), pp. 114–27. See also Gabriel Almond and James Coleman, eds., *The Politics of the Developing Areas* (Princeton, N.J.: Princeton University Press, 1960).

54. "Some Reflections on the Sociological Character of Political Parties," *American Political Science Review,* XXI (November, 1927), 765.

55. "Class, Status, Party," in Gerth and Mills, *From Max Weber,* p. 195.

56. *Political Parties,* p. 422.

57. In Gerth and Mills, *From Max Weber,* p. 87.

58. *Political Parties in the United States* (New York: St. Martin's Press, 1966), p. 8.

59. *Ibid.,* p. 9.

60. Eckstein and Apter, *Comparative Politics,* p. 329.

61. *Political Parties: A Behavioral Analysis* (Chicago: Rand McNally & Company, 1964), p. 6.

62. *Political Parties in the United States,* p. 8.

63. *Ibid.,* p. 9.

64. Eckstein and Apter, *Comparative Politics,* p. 330.

65. See Rupert Emerson, *From Empire to Nation* (Cambridge, Mass.: Harvard University Press, 1960).

Chapter 1

1. For the administrative setup during this period and earlier, see Sir Charles Collins, *Public Administration in Ceylon,* pp. 1–56 and Colvin R. de Silva, *Ceylon under the British Occupation, 1795–1833.*

2. Quoted in Sir Charles Jeffries, *Ceylon: The Path to Independence,* pp. 19–20.

3. The first council consisted of the Commander-in-Chief, the Chief Justice, and the Chief Secretary.

4. W. M. G. Colebrooke, *Report . . . upon the Administration of the Government of Ceylon,* p. 15.

5. *Ibid.,* p. 21.

6. *Ibid.,* pp. 24–25.

7. Legislative Council of Ceylon, *Addresses Delivered by Governors of the Colony Together with the Replies of the Council,* I (1833–60), 5.

8. His instructions in 1834 said that the unofficial members were "to be selected from and out of the principle merchants and the higher classes of natives, not holding any such office." *Ibid.,* p. 7.

9. *Ibid.,* II (1860–77), 49.

10. "To the President of the Legislative Council of Ceylon (Enclosure 2), September 26, 1864," in *Copies of Dispatches and Memorandum on Ceylon Military Expenditures,* pp. 45–48.

11. *Ibid.,* p. 48.

12. For further information see the series of articles in the *Ceylon Daily News* (Colombo), 1918, by J. R. Weinman, reprinted in 1947 as *Our Legislature,* especially pp. 34–42. See also the pertinent sections of B. R. Blaze, *The Life of Lorenz.*

13. Newspapers played an active role in the politics of Ceylon throughout the British period. Unfortunately, no history of the press in Ceylon exists. For the only record available see H. A. J. Hulugalle, *The Life and Times of D. R. Wijewardene,* especially pp. 83–96. Also, Hilaire Jansz, *Quaint Gaunt Saint,* and his series of articles in the *Ceylon Observer* (Colombo), 1960.

14. No comprehensive social history of Ceylon exists. For social developments in the nineteenth century I have relied primarily upon educational and economic statistics. Brief mention of this period can be found in G. C. Mendis, *Ceylon under the British;* Collins, *Public Administration,* pp. 81–109; Jeffries, *Ceylon,* pp. 33–39; Fr. S. G. Perera, *History of Ceylon,* pp. 198–203; and the fine introduction to I. D. S. Weerawardana, *Government and Politics in Ceylon, 1931–1946.* For a conceptual analysis of the

process of indigenous elite emergence, see Fatma Mansur, *Process of Independence.*

15. Mendis, *Ceylon under the British,* p. 127.

16. See S. J. Tambiah, "Ethnic Representation in Ceylon's Higher Administrative Services, 1870–1946." See also A. J. Wilson, "The Public Services in Ceylon," especially pp. 9–17.

17. The society was founded by W. A. de Silva and Ananda K. Coomaraswamy, future leaders of the nationalist movement. For the manifesto of the society see the *Ceylon National Review,* I, 3.

18. L. O. B., "United Ceylon," p. 67.

19. "Reform of the Legislative Council." See also A. Padmanabha, "Reform of the Ceylon Legislative Council."

20. The memorandum is reproduced in the *Ceylon National Review,* III, No. 9 (March, 1910), 178–82.

21. *Ibid.,* p. 179.

22. *Ibid.,* p. 181.

23. Colebrooke, *Report,* p. 24.

24. For his views on the reform, see W. T. Keble and D. S. Sena, *Life of Sir James Peiris,* pp. 40–49.

25. D. S. Senanayake was one of them.

26. Kalmane, *India and Ceylon,* p. 67. Also, Ponnambalam Arunachalam, *Speeches and Writings of Sir Ponnambalam Arunachalam,* p. 84.

27. Hulugalle, *D. R. Wijewardene,* p. 24.

28. Arunachalam, *Speeches,* p. 53. A short-lived journal, the *Ceylonese National Review,* was started at the same time, as an organ of protest. In its first issue (June, 1916, p. 1) it stated that it advocated only "two methods of political work: constitutional political propaganda and sincere, friendly cooperation with the Government."

29. *Speeches,* p. 24.

30. *Ibid.,* p. 44.

31. Joint Committee of the Ceylon National Association and the Ceylon Reform League, *Case for Constitutional Reform in Ceylon,* p. 7.

32. Arunachalam, *Speeches,* pp. 59–60.

33. S. W. R. D. Bandaranaike, ed., *The Handbook of the Ceylon National Congress, 1919–1928,* p. 177.

34. Arunachalam, *Speeches,* p. 130. For more information on Arunachalam, see *Ponnambalam Arunachalam, 1853–1924.*

35. Arunachalam, *Speeches,* p. 135.

36. A more radical approach was taken by the Young Lanka League, a youth organization that was formed in 1918 to agitate for immediate relief of social problems, as well as political reform. It was ephemeral, however, and its leaders joined the congress. Its head, A. E. Gooneshina, led a radical bloc in the congress and later formed unions and the Labour party.

For its original manifesto see J. A. W., "The Birth of a New Ceylon," *Young Lanka,* I, No. 1 (July, 1918), 5.

37. See A. J. Wilson, "The Crewe-McCallum Reforms, 1912–1921."

38. Bandaranaike, *Handbook,* pp. 231–32.

39. For details see *ibid.,* pp. 564–73.

40. For details of this scheme see Donoughmore Commission, *Report of the Special Commission on the Constitution,* p. 15.

41. *Times* (London), March 14, 1945.

42. In an incisive article, G. C. Mendis relates communal conflict in Ceylon to the middle-class struggle for posts vacated by the British. "The Causes of Communal Conflict in Ceylon."

43. J. A. Halangoda, "Our Right for Special Consideration in the Reconstruction of the Empire after the War." That job competition was a factor is shown in his "Ceylonese and Government Employment."

44. The Kandyan Association, *Monthly Letter,* No. 2 (November, 1920).

45. J. A. Halangoda, *Kandyan Rights and Present Politics* (Kandy: Miller and Co., 1920), p. 5.

46. *Ibid.,* p. 3.

47. These were made at the annual sessions after 1925. See Bandaranaike, *Handbook, passim.* In 1924 the congress passed a resolution deprecating "the introduction of caste and religion in connection with elites . . ." *Ibid.,* p. 608.

48. Donoughmore Commission, *Report,* p. 103.

49. G. E. P. de S. Wickramaratne, comp., *Towards a New Era,* p. 51.

50. Donoughmore Commission, *Report,* pp. 90–101. In the Legislative Council the Tamils, like all other minorities, voted against the reform. Legislative Council of Ceylon, *Debates,* 1929, p. 1823.

51. See his remarks on constitutional reform, State Council, *Debates,* 1939, II, 887–964 and 975–1009. His argument for communal electorates was opposed by a Tamil youth group which wanted territorial electorates in order to permit a class-based party system to evolve. The Youth Congress, *Communalism or Nationalism.*

52. See remarks in State Council, *Debates,* 1945, II, 6988–95.

53. House of Representatives, *Debates,* Vol. V, col. 499.

54. See "Objects of Association," in the association's *Quarterly Bulletin,* I, No. 1 (July, 1927), iii.

55. *The Serendib,* IV, No. 1 (1932), 3. For its constitution, see *ibid.,* pp. 3–7.

56. *Proceedings of the 18th Annual Sessions of the Ceylon Muslim League* (August 13, 1944), p. 15.

57. *Report,* p. 31.

58. See, for instance, Gooneshina's resolutions on the 1924 reforms, in Bandaranaike, *Handbook,* p. 605.

59. Legislative Council, *Debates,* 1929, p. 1662. This negative view was

held by the majority of the C.N.C. leadership, but not by all. W. A. de Silva, for instance, favored universal suffrage. *Ibid.*, pp. 1070–80. For the full testimony of the C.N.C., see Bandaranaike, *Handbook*, pp. 815–46.

60. In 1944 Bandaranaike succeeded in getting the State Council to pass, over Senanayake's protest, the "Free Lanka" bill calling for a constitution of the dominion type. State Council, *Debates*, 1944, II, 2624–2707. The motion carried by a vote of 26 to 3 with 6 abstentions.

61. *Times* (London), July 11, 1945.

62. *Ibid.*, December 27, 1942. He was also angry because of the acceptance of a Communist element into the C.N.C.

63. Sir Ivor Jennings, "D. S. Senanayake and Independence."

64. The fact that India was to be granted independence also had great bearing.

65. As Sir Ivor Jennings says, the "Ceylon National Congress, unlike the Indian National Congress, under Mahatma Gandhi's inspiration, never succeeded in arousing the enthusiasm of the common people." "Nationalism and Political Development in Ceylon," p. 76.

66. In addition to groups already mentioned there were the Dutch Burgher Union (1908), Burgher Association of Ceylon (1933), Muslim League (1922), All-Ceylon Malay Association (1922), All-Ceylon Moors' Association (1921), Catholic Union (1933), All-Ceylon Buddhist Congress (1918), and others, such as the Jaffna Association.

67. Keble and Sena, *Peiris*, pp. 45–49, and Arunachalam, *Speeches*, p. 17.

68. See N. S. G. Kuruppu, "Labour and the Rise of Capitalism."

69. The Donoughmore Commission noted "a complete absence of any party system among the elected representatives." *Report*, p. 19.

70. *Ibid.*, p. 20.

71. *Ibid.*, p. 24.

72. Bandaranaike, *Handbook*, p. 685.

73. *Report*, p. 18.

74. *Ibid.*, p. 31.

75. *Ibid.*, pp. 31 and 39.

76. *Ibid.*, p. 41.

77. *Ibid.*, p. 42.

78. *Ibid.*, p. 41.

79. *Ibid.*, p. 42.

80. This had been the original recommendation of the Secretary of State for Colonies at the beginning of the Donoughmore hearings. He recommended the creation of a legislative structure that discouraged party and cabinet government because he felt that there was "not only no immediate prospect of the appearance of a party system, but also the danger of the formation of groups based on racial or religious differences." Quoted in S. Namasivayam, *The Legislatures of Ceylon, 1928–1948*, p. 99.

81. For a discussion of these powers, see Jeffries, *Ceylon*, pp. 61–65.

82. These were the Departments of Home Affairs, Agriculture and Lands, Local Administration, Health, Labor, Industry and Commerce, Education, Communications, and Works.

83. The official members were the Chief Secretary, the Attorney-General, and the Financial Secretary.

84. "The Ceylon General Election of 1947," p. 134.

85. In some constituencies candidates ran uncontested, and in four the elections were boycotted. In all, 37 seats were contested.

86. Ceylon Daily News, *State Council, 1931* (Colombo: Associated Newspapers of Ceylon, 1931), p. 2.

87. *Ibid.,* p. 3.

88. *An Asian Prime Minister's Story,* p. 24.

89. The campaigns were evidently quite expensive, as later a bill was introduced to restrict expenditures. State Council, *Debates,* 1936, I, 402–6.

90. Sir John Kotelawala stressed this. *Story,* pp. 24–28.

91. Ceylon Daily News, *State Council, 1931,* p. 3.

92. *Times of Ceylon* (Colombo), July 1, 1931.

93. The elected candidates included 16 C.N.C. members, 10 Liberal League, 3 Labour, 1 Unionist, 1 Independent Liberal and 15 independents.

94. One member of the State Council, S. de Fonseka, was soon to argue that "dissatisfaction with the compromising policies which are inherent in any system of Committee Government have greatly accentuated the need and the growth of a party system." State Council, *Debates,* 1935, I, 512.

95. *Sessional Paper VIII of 1937,* p. 14.

96. *Ibid.,* pp. 13–14.

97. I. D. S. Weerawardana, *Government and Politics in Ceylon (1931–1946),* pp. 138–39.

98. *Ceylon Observer* (Colombo), March 12, 1936.

99. *Times of Ceylon,* January 20, 1936.

100. Quoted in Weerawardana, *Government and Politics,* p. 138.

101. *Times of Ceylon,* April 29, 1936.

102. State Council, *Debates,* 1936, I, 19. Some opinion in England used this to deny the value of the State Council. The London *Times* (March 26, 1936) argued that the "power, prestige and patronage thus conferred upon each individual member of the State Council is so great—and is so desired —that it constitutes an almost irresistable inducement to candidates for election or re-election to appeal to racial prejudices and to the worst passions of the electorate."

103. *Times* (London), May 15, 1932.

104. The minorities abstained, and the nominated members formed the opposition. See State Council, *Debates,* 1937, I, 903–82.

105. See State Council, *Debates,* 1938, III, 3685–721. The Tamils joined the nominated members in opposing the motion. The Governor was later overruled by the Supreme Court.

106. State Council, *Debates,* 1939, II, 977.

Chapter 2

1. See *Sessional Paper XXII of 1947* and *SP III of 1948*. For an analysis see Sir Ivor Jennings, *The Constitution of Ceylon*.

2. Soulbury Commission, *Report of the Commission on Constitutional Reform*, p. 50. It noted, for instance, the disproportionate ratio of Tamils and Burghers in the government service. *Ibid.*, p. 49.

3. For an analysis see A. J. Wilson, "Minority Safeguards in the Ceylon Constitution."

4. Soulbury Commission, *Report*, p. 69.

5. S. W. R. D. Bandaranaike estimated that none of the parties could have won more than ten or fifteen seats. *The United National Party*, a pamphlet written for the U.N.P. by Bandaranaike and reprinted in his *Speeches and Writings*, p. 128.

6. *Ibid.*, p. 114.

7. *Ibid.*

8. See, for instance, *ibid.*, pp. 117, 128, 139, 220–21; and House of Representatives, *Debates*, Vol. X, col. 698.

9. *Speeches*, p. 114.

10. United National party, *Manifesto and Constitution* (1947), arts. 3, 9.

11. Senator U. P. Jayasundera, ed., *United National Party* (1949).

12. *Ibid.*, p. 19.

13. *Ibid.*, p. 27.

14. House of Representatives, *Debates*, Vol. X, col. 698. See also his presidential address to the annual session of the S.M.S. in 1948, in Bandaranaike, *Speeches*, p. 117.

15. The need to compete with Marxist elements for trade union leadership later confirmed Gooneshina's conservatism.

16. N. S. G. Kuruppu, "Labour and the Rise of Capitalism," p. 145.

17. Leslie Goonewardene, *A Short History of the Lanka Sama Samaja Party*, p. 15.

18. *Twenty Years of the Ceylon Communist Party*, p. 3.

19. For details in regard to its first manifesto see Goonewardene, *A Short History*, p. 4.

20. For more information see my "The Trotskyite Movement in Ceylon" and Hector Abhayavardhana, "Categories of Left Thinking in Ceylon."

21. For opposite views on this see Keuneman, *Twenty Years*, and Goonewardene, *A Short History*.

22. For a brief description of the Tamil attitude at this time see W. Howard Wriggins, *Ceylon: Dilemmas of a New Nation*, pp. 143–47.

23. See P. Naguleswaran, "The Problem of Indian Immigrant Labour in the Nineteenth Century."

24. House of Representatives, *Debates*, Vol. V, col. 519.

25. Ceylon Labour party, *Policy and Programme*, pp. 2–4.

26. Jayasundera, *United National Party* (1949), p. 27.

27. Sir John Kotelawala, "How Much Is Peace Worth to You," in Senator U. P. Jayasundera, ed., *The United National Party* (1951), p. 173. For a review of the organization of the U.N.P. in 1947 see *ibid.*, pp. 161–62.

28. *Ibid.*, p. 161.

29. *Ibid.*

30. *Times of Ceylon*, March 6, 1947.

31. R. A. De Mel, *Manifesto*, p. 4.

32. *Times of Ceylon*, February 15, 1947.

33. It was estimated that 25,000 copies of *Sama Samajist Bhikkhu* were printed in Sinhalese and 2,000 in English. *Ibid.*

34. See column by Dharmika, January 4, 1947.

35. *Times of Ceylon*, January 24, 1947.

36. March 4, 1947.

37. *Times of Ceylon*, January 3, 1947.

38. See *Manifesto of the L.S.S.P. (Ceylon-Unit, B.L.P.I.)*, arts. 1–10.

39. "The Ceylon General Election of 1947," p. 133.

40. *Ibid.*, p. 136.

41. See his column in the *Times of Ceylon*, August 4, 1947.

42. See his column, June 7, 1947.

43. *Times of Ceylon*, August 5, 1947.

44. House of Representatives, *Debates*, Vol. I, col. 57.

45. *Ibid.*, cols. 55–64.

46. *Times of Ceylon*, August 4, 1947.

47. "Ceylon General Election," p. 150.

48. House of Representatives, *Debates*, Vol. I, col. 383.

49. See column by Dharmika, *Times of Ceylon*, January 25, 1947.

50. *Times of Ceylon*, September 10, 1947.

51. N. M. Perera had predicted during the election that Ponnambalam would eventually enter into a U.N.P. cabinet.

52. On the Cabinet, see S. Namasivayam, *Parliamentary Government in Ceylon, 1948–1958*, pp. 34–43, and W. A. Wiswawarnapala, "Composition of Cabinets 1948–1960."

53. House of Representatives, *Debates*, Vol. I, col. 73.

54. *Ibid.*, col. 74.

55. *Ibid.*, cols. 106–14, 127–57.

56. *Ibid.*, col. 60.

57. *Ibid.*, col. 398.

58. *Ibid.*, col. 43.

59. *Ibid.*, cols. 436–37.

60. Reproduced, *ibid.*, Vol. V, col. 602.

61. See additional remarks of Senanayake in Namasivayam, *Parliamentary Government*, pp. 38–39. For the opinion of the minister involved see House of Representatives, *Debates*, Vol. VIII (1950), col. 3272.

62. Bandaranaike never admitted this publicly, but it was the opinion

of those close to him. See, for instance, the remarks in House of Representatives, *Debates,* Vol. X, col. 1424.

63. See his address to the S.M.S. in 1946, in Bandaranaike, *Speeches,* pp. 113–15.

64. See articles by Andrew Roth, *Times of Ceylon,* April 27 and 28, 1947.

65. *Times of Ceylon,* September 15, 1947.

66. These are reproduced in Bandaranaike, *Speeches,* pp. 122–29.

67. *Ibid.,* pp. 117–21.

68. The correspondence covering this is reproduced *ibid.,* pp. 133–37.

69. *Ibid.,* pp. 138–40.

70. *Times of Ceylon,* June 9, 1951.

71. For Bandaranaike's explanation of his action see his *Speeches,* pp. 143–47 and his speech in the House of Representatives reproduced in G. E. P. de S. Wickramaratne, comp., *Towards a New Era,* pp. 3–6.

72. "Additional Notes on the General Election of 1952."

Chapter 3

1. S. W. R. D. Bandaranaike, *Speeches and Writings,* p. 138.

2. *Ibid.,* p. 153.

3. In regard to the "Independence Bill," an amendment removing the word rejoice from the main motion was defeated by a vote of 59 to 39. The main motion was carried by a vote of 59 to 11, with 29 abstentions. House of Representatives, *Debates,* Vol. I, cols. 735, 738.

4. See the remarks of Pieter Keuneman, *ibid.,* cols. 447–67.

5. See the remarks of S. J. V. Chelvanayakam, *ibid.,* col. 479, and *ibid.,* Vol. V, col. 709. See also the view of the Ceylon Indian Congress, *ibid.,* Vol. I, col. 476.

6. *Ibid.,* col. 195.

7. *Ibid.,* col. 365.

8. *Ibid.,* cols. 363–64.

9. *Ibid.,* col. 182.

10. *Ibid.,* col. 199.

11. *Ibid.,* Vol. IV, col. 1938.

12. *Ibid.,* Vol. I, col. 116.

13. See the remarks of S. W. R. D. Bandaranaike, *ibid.,* col. 378.

14. *Ibid.,* cols. 488–89. In 1951 the U.N.P. argued that the main weakness of the parliamentary system in Ceylon was its lack of "a democratic Opposition." Parliamentary democracy, it argued, "needs a healthy Opposition, but this does not mean that a revolutionary opposition can be encouraged." Senator U. P. Jayasundera, ed., *The United National Party* (1951), p. 162.

15. House of Representatives, *Debates,* Vol. IV, col. 1740.

16. *Ibid.,* Vol. V, col. 504. A leader of the C.I.C. answered that it was a defensive organization that would disappear when it was no longer required. *Ibid.,* col. 519.

17. Colvin R. de Silva, for example, gave grounds for such a judgment when he said, "We struggle not merely for an alternative Government. We struggle for an alternative State, and it is on the road to that alternative State that so many of us struggle to put in an alternative Government." *Ibid.,* Vol. I, col. 191.

18. *Ibid.,* col. 95.

19. For the debate on the bill, see State Council, *Debates,* 1946, cols. 1935–2025. For an analysis by a Marxist organization, see S. S. Sahabandu, "The Public Security Ordinance No. 25 of 1947."

20. These included the Citizenship Act of 1948, the Emigration Act of 1948, the Parliamentary Elections Act of 1948, the Indian Residents (Citizenship) Act of 1948, and the Parliamentary Elections (Amendment) Act of 1949–50.

21. House of Representatives, *Debates,* Vol. IV, col. 1820.

22. Bandaranaike, however, had immediately referred to Perera as Leader of the Opposition. *Ibid.,* Vol. I, col. 378.

23. *Ibid.*

24. *Ibid.,* col. 380. See also cols. 378–83.

25. *Ibid.,* Vol. X, col. 171.

26. Quoted in I. D. S. Weerawardana, "The General Elections in Ceylon, 1952," p. 118.

27. Quoted *ibid.*

28. Quoted *ibid.,* p. 121.

29. "Additional Notes on the General Election of 1952," p. 208.

30. Sir John Kotelawala, who organized the propaganda of the U.N.P. at the time, mentions this as the main issue in his *An Asian Prime Minister's Story,* p. 82. Bandaranaike, because his party split the "democratic vote," was referred to as "the Judas or Devadatta of democracy in Ceylon." *Times* (London), April 28, 1952.

31. J. R. Jayewardene, *Buddhism and Marxism.*

32. *Ibid,* p. 22.

33. *Ibid.*

34. *Ceylon Observer* (Colombo), November 5, 1952.

35. "Additional Notes," p. 201.

36. House of Representatives, *Debates,* Vol. I, col. 141.

37. *Ibid.,* Vol. V, col. 494.

38. *Ibid.,* Vol. VII, col. 425.

39. *Ibid.,* Vol. X, col. 117.

40. *Ibid.,* Vol. IX, col. 468.

41. "Additional Notes," p. 199.

42. House of Representatives, *Debates,* Vol. IX, col. 782.

43. *Ibid.,* col. 785.
44. "Additional Notes," p. 204.
45. House of Representatives, *Debates,* Vol. X, col. 171.
46. *Ibid.,* Vol. XXI, col. 161.
47. *Ibid.,* Vol. XI, col. 376.
48. *Ibid.,* col. 385.
49. *Ibid.,* Vol. XII, col. 120.
50. *Ibid.,* col. 154.
51. *Ibid.,* Vol. XI, col. 385.
52. *Ibid.,* Vol. XVII, col. 1135.
53. Colvin R. de Silva, *Their Politics—and Ours,* p. 28.
54. *Ibid.,* p. 25.
55. *Ibid.,* p. 27.
56. House of Representatives, *Debates,* Vol. XIV, col. 25.
57. *Ibid.,* Vol. XV, col. 2368.
58. *Ibid.,* Vol. XXI, col. 157.
59. *Ibid.,* Vol. XX, col. 4349. In reference to the Ceylon Democratic Congress, successor to the C.I.C., the U.N.P. condemned it as "the spearhead of the new colonialism of an Asian power." Quoted in the *Tribune* (Colombo), May 15, 1954, p. 10.
60. *Ceylon Observer,* May 23, 1955.
61. S. Namasivayam, *Parliamentary Government in Ceylon, 1948–1958,* p. 108.
62. Remark by Pieter Keuneman quoted *ibid.*
63. House of Representatives, *Debates,* Vol. XVII, col. 1126.
64. *Ibid.,* Vol. XXI, col. 177.
65. *Ibid.,* Vol. XV, col. 566.

Chapter 4

1. *Morning Times* (Colombo), March 3, 1955.
2. House of Representatives, *Debates,* Vol. XVII, cols. 1181–82. The Prime Minister said that the only impropriety in this was that it should have read as coming from the Leader of the U.N.P. rather than from the Prime Minister. *Ibid.,* col. 1187.
3. May 24, 1955. See also House of Representatives, *Debates,* Vol. XXI, cols. 179–80.
4. *Ibid.,* col. 180.
5. *Ibid.,* col. 240.
6. *Ibid.,* col. 242.
7. *Ibid.,* col. 212.
8. *Ibid.,* Vol. XIX, cols. 629–31.
9. See the manifesto of the United National party in the *Morning Times,* March 3, 1956.

10. *Morning Times,* February 19, 1956.

11. *Ceylon Daily News* (Colombo), February 8, 1956.

12. *Ceylon Observer* (Colombo), March 25, 1956.

13. *Morning Times,* April 3, 1956.

14. *Ceylon Observer,* March 25, 1956.

15. *Ibid.,* and *Ceylon Daily News,* April 4, 1956.

16. *Morning Times,* April 4, 1956.

17. *Ceylon Observer,* March 25, 1956.

18. *Ibid.,* March 12, 1956.

19. *Morning Times,* March 27, 1956.

20. *Ibid.,* March 24, 1956.

21. *Ceylon Daily News,* March 24, 1956.

22. *Ceylon Observer,* February 20, 1956.

23. Quoted in I. D. S. Weerawardana, *Ceylon General Election 1956,* pp. 72–75. See also the manifesto of the L.S.S.P. in the *Ceylon Daily News,* March 12, 1956.

24. *Morning Times,* March 20, 1956.

25. *Ceylon Observer,* February 2, 1956.

26. *Morning Times,* March 28, 1956.

27. *Ceylon Observer,* February 9, 1956.

28. For its manifesto see the *Morning Times,* March 21, 1956.

29. Quoted in Weerawardana, *General Election 1956,* p. 204.

30. *Ibid.,* pp. 200–204.

31. *Morning Times,* March 21, 1956.

32. Denzil Peiris, *1956 and After,* p. 10.

33. In 1952 a pamphlet, *The Premier Stakes,* appeared, describing the struggle in the U.N.P. over the succession. No author was given, but it is believed that it was ghost-written for Sir John Kotelawala. Sir John referred to the contents of the pamphlet as "distorted but substantially correct." See his *An Asian Prime Minister's Story,* pp. 72–92. The text of *The Premier Stakes* is reprinted in the *Tribune,* July 15, 1960, pp. 5–11.

34. See his explanation, House of Representatives, *Debates,* Vol. XIII, col. 26.

35. *Ibid.,* Vol. XX, col. 635.

36. *Ibid.,* col. 640.

37. *Morning Times,* May 11, 1954.

38. See his remarks on resignation, House of Representatives, *Debates,* Vol. XIX, col. 484.

39. See his remarks in the *Ceylon Daily News,* June 21, 1955.

40. A special committee appointed by the U.N.P. in 1956 to investigate the reasons for its defeat cited R. G. Senanayake as a major factor. See its report reprinted in the *Ceylon Observer,* July 28, 1956.

41. *Ceylon Observer,* May 11, 1956.

42. *Morning Times,* January 14, 1956.

43. *Ceylon Daily News,* February 10, 1956.

44. See the view of the Matara branch of the U.N.P., for instance. *Ceylon Observer,* February 12, 1956.

45. *Ceylon Daily News,* October 9, 1952.

46. *Morning Times,* February 4, 1953.

47. *Ibid.,* November 21, 1953.

48. *Ibid.,* September 4, 1954.

49. *Ibid.,* October 19, 1953.

50. *Ibid.,* October 21, 1953.

51. *Ibid.,* October 24, 1953.

52. *Ibid.,* March 1, 1955.

53. Leslie Goonewardena in the *Ceylon Daily News,* March 4, 1955.

54. *Morning Times,* November 21, 1953.

55. *Ibid.,* May 5, 1954.

56. *Ibid.,* July 6, 1953.

57. *Ceylon Daily News,* June 8, 1955.

58. *Ceylon Observer,* March 30, 1954.

59. *Ceylon Daily News,* January 20, 1956.

60. Originally the Labour party also was in the M.E.P., but Gooneshina withdrew when the M.E.P. entered into a no-contest pact with Marxist parties. *Ceylon Observer,* February 24, 1956. R. E. Jayatilleke, also of the Labour party, remained in the M.E.P. B. H. Aluwihare, a longtime associate of Bandaranaike and a Kandyan notable, resigned as a result of the pact. *Morning Times,* February 28, 1956.

61. Of these seats the S.L.F.P. won 38, the V.L.S.S.P. 5, the B.P. 4, and the independents 5.

62. *Morning Times,* February 24, 1956.

63. For the details of the negotiation see Weerawardana, *General Election 1956,* pp. 19–26.

64. The S.L.F.P. 4, the B.P. 5, the V.L.S.S.P. 2, and 1 independent.

65. [D. C. Vijayavardhana], *The Revolt in the Temple.*

66. *Ceylon Observer,* August 12, 1954.

67. Buddhist Committee of Inquiry, *The Betrayal of Buddhism,* Foreword.

68. *Ibid.,* pp. 1–39.

69. *Morning Times,* March 21, 1956.

70. *Ibid.,* March 12, 1956.

71. *Sessional Paper XVIII of 1951.*

72. See also *Sessional Paper XIII of 1952.*

73. Ministry of Home Affairs, *A Plan for the Rehabilitation of the Kandyan Peasantry in Central and Uva Provinces, 1955-56—1959-60,* p. 7.

74. *Ibid.,* pp. 17–101.

75. House of Representatives, *Debates,* Vol. VIII, col. 481.

76. *Ibid.,* Vol. IX, col. 1344.

77. Ivor Jennings, "The Languages of Ceylon," p. 1. See also S. J. Tambiah, "Ethnic Representation in Ceylon's Higher Administrative Services 1870–1946." See also William Ames Coates, "The Languages of Ceylon 1946–1953."

78. As far back as 1937 there was a resolution introduced for this purpose. State Council, *Debates*, 1937, I, 148. For the debate on the motion see *ibid.*, pp. 148–66, 175–89.

79. State Council, *Debates*, 1944, I, 745–70, 807–16. The motion was amended to include Tamil, and carried.

80. House of Representatives, *Debates*, Vol. IX, col. 1302.

81. *Ceylon Daily News*, January 7, 1955.

82. For the organization of language associations see Peiris, *1956 and After*, pp. 1–7 and Weerewardana, *General Election 1956*, pp. 1–15.

83. The figure was probably higher. See W. Howard Wriggins, *Ceylon: Dilemmas of a New Nation*, p. 349.

84. For population figures see Department of Census and Statistics, *Ceylon Year Book*, p. 38.

85. See editorials in the *Ceylon Observer*, July 15, 1954, and the *Morning Times*, June 8, 1954.

86. *Ceylon Daily News*, February 20, 1954.

87. *Morning Times*, February 28, 1956.

88. See also Wriggins, *Ceylon*, pp. 326–71.

89. *Ceylon Daily News*, April 17, 1956.

90. *Ibid.*, June 12, 1956. The purpose of both the C.P. and the L.S.S.P. was to liquidate what was left of the U.N.P.

91. See the *Ceylon Observer*, April 17, 1956.

92. *Morning Times*, April 18, 1956, and April 20, 1956.

93. See statements by Jinasena in the *Times of Ceylon* (Colombo), September 29, 1956 and by Sir Razik Fareed in the *Ceylon Daily News*, December 28, 1956.

94. *Times of Ceylon*, April 27, 1956.

95. *Ibid.*, May 2, 1956.

96. House of Representatives, *Debates*, Vol. XXV, col. 1674.

97. *Ceylon Daily News*, May 5, 1957.

98. House of Representatives, *Debates*, Vol. XXVIII, col. 55.

99. *Ibid.*, cols. 92–93.

100. *Times of Ceylon*, January 18, 1957.

101. Reprinted in the *Ceylon Daily News*, January 19, 1957.

102. *Times* (London), June 2, 1959.

103. *Morning Times*, August 12, 1956.

104. *Ceylon Daily News*, December 21, 1956. He was disgruntled over the failure of the Government to give full trade union rights to public servants. See debate on it in House of Representatives, *Debates*, Vol. XXX, cols. 3178–3204.

105. *Ceylon Observer*, September 30, 1956.

106. *Ibid.*, January 2, 1958.

107. House of Representatives, *Debates*, Vol. XXVIII, col. 833.

108. *Ibid.*, Vol. XXV, col. 1593.

109. *Ibid.*, col. 1601.

110. *Ibid.*, cols. 1688–89.

111. *Ibid.*, col. 1695.

112. *Ibid.*, Vol. XXVIII, col. 579.

113. *Ibid.*, col. 672.

114. *Ibid.*, Vol. XXX, cols. 4698–708.

115. *Ibid.*, Vol. XXXI, col. 1162.

116. *Ibid.*, Vol. XXVIII, col. 671.

117. *Times of Ceylon*, February 27, 1958.

118. *Ceylon Observer*, February 7, 1958.

119. *Ibid.*, February 9, 1958.

120. *Ceylon Daily News*, March 8, 1958.

121. *Ibid.*, March 9, 1958.

122. *Morning Times*, March 14, 1958.

123. *Ceylon Observer*, July 1, 1958.

124. *Ibid.*, August 6, 1958.

125. *Ceylon Daily News*, April 24, 1959.

126. *Ibid.*, May 8, 1959.

127. *Ceylon Times*, May 16, 1959.

128. *Ceylon Observer*, May 17, 1959.

129. *Ibid.*, May 18, 1959.

130. House of Representatives, *Debates*, Vol. XXXV, cols. 23–57.

131. *Ibid.*, col. 58.

132. These were the votes of Philip Gunawardena, De Silva, L. Rajapaksa, Panasuriya, D. F. Hettiarch, and K. Gunawardena. *Ceylon Daily News*, May 19, 1959.

133. They were H. Fernando, Jinadasa, P. Tennekoen, M. P. Herat, M. S. Themis, and Nimal Karunatilleke. *Times of Ceylon*, May 20, 1959.

134. *Ceylon Observer*, May 28, 1959.

135. House of Representatives, *Debates*, Vol. XXXV, col. 113.

136. Other motions of regret were defeated by votes of 50–28–14, 89–2–1, 70–8–13, 50–27–14 and 52–22–17. See House of Representatives, *Debates*, Vol. XXXV, cols. 108–623.

137. *Ceylon Daily News*, September 11, 1959.

138. See debate on the motion, House of Representatives, *Debates*, Vol. XXXVII, cols. 950–1126.

139. *Ceylon Daily News*, October 21, 1959.

140. *Ceylon Observer*, November 2, 1959.

141. See House of Representatives, *Debates*, Vol. XXXVII, cols. 1599–762.

Chapter 5

1. House of Representatives, *Debates,* Vol. XXIV, col. 25.
2. *Ibid.,* Vol. XXV, col. 129.
3. *Ibid.,* col. 1593.
4. *Ibid.,* Vol. XXIV, col. 85.
5. *Times of Ceylon* (Colombo), May 28, 1956.
6. This led the Muslim League to withdraw its support from the F.P. *Ceylon Daily News* (Colombo), August 5, 1956.
7. *Times of Ceylon,* May 26, 1957.
8. *Ceylon Daily News,* May 29, 1957.
9. House of Representatives, *Debates,* Vol. XXVIII, col. 126.
10. All quotes from the *Times* (London), May 28, 1957.
11. *Morning Times* (Colombo), February 5, 1958.
12. *Ceylon Daily News,* February 5, 1958.
13. See his remarks and subsequent debate, House of Representatives, *Debates,* Vol. XXIX, cols. 2202–310.
14. *Times of Ceylon,* April 6, 1957.
15. House of Representatives, *Debates,* Vol. XXVII, col. 169.
16. Text of the pact is reprinted in the *Ceylon Observer* (Colombo), August 12, 1957.
17. *Ibid.,* August 4, 1957.
18. *Times* (London), August 12, 1957.
19. *Morning Times,* April 10, 1958.
20. *Ceylon Daily News,* April 11, 1958.
21. See Bandaranaike's remarks, House of Representatives, *Debates,* Vol. XXXI, cols. 9–22.
22. He also said that he realized that the U.N.P. had taken steps purposely to foment communal rioting. *Ibid.,* cols. 32–33.
23. *Ibid.,* cols. 9–22.
24. *Ibid.,* col. 464.
25. *Ibid.,* col. 468.
26. *Ibid.,* col. 925.
27. See N. M. Perera's remarks, *ibid.,* col. 1938.
28. See, for instance, *ibid.,* Vol. XXXIII, cols. 484–747.
29. See debate, *ibid.,* cols. 1898–2026.
30. *Ceylon Daily News,* September 6, 1958.
31. *Times* (London), September 5, 1958.
32. *Ibid.,* October 27, 1958.
33. See House of Representatives, *Debates,* Vol. XXXIV, cols. 823–50 and 1850–2018. See also the remarks of Bandaranaike made on Radio Ceylon and reprinted in his *The Government and the People,* pp. 88–90.
34. *Times of Ceylon,* January 21, 1960.
35. *Ceylon Observer,* January 24, 1960.
36. *Ibid.,* January 25, 1960. The public services backed the Opposition,

and the Government Clerical Service Union asked its 10,000 members not to carry out any undemocratic or illegal orders. *Ceylon Daily News,* February 27, 1960.

37. *Times of Ceylon,* January 31, 1960.

38. *Ceylon Daily News,* February 16, 1960.

39. *Ceylon Observer,* January 16, 1960.

40. *Times of Ceylon,* February 17, 1960.

41. *Ceylon Daily News,* December 31, 1959.

42. *Ibid.,* March 2, 1960.

43. *Times of Ceylon,* January 17, 1960.

44. *Ibid.,* April 2, 1958.

45. *Ceylon Observer,* July 1, 1958.

46. *Ceylon Daily News,* December 15, 1959.

47. *Times of Ceylon,* August 9, 1959.

48. *Ibid.,* December 14, 1959.

49. Text in *Ceylon Daily News,* December 28, 1959.

50. See his statement, *Times of Ceylon,* February 4, 1957.

51. *Ceylon Daily News,* February 23, 1958.

52. *Times of Ceylon,* January 10, 1960.

53. *Ibid.,* March 10, 1960.

54. *Ibid.,* March 11, 1960.

55. For text see *Ceylon Daily News,* March 11, 1960.

56. *Ibid.,* March 16, 1960.

57. See its manifesto, *ibid.,* December 28, 1959.

58. See text of the L.S.S.P. manifesto, *ibid.,* January 9, 1960.

59. For the manifesto of the S.M.P. see the *Ceylon Observer,* January 1, 1960; for that of the B.B.P., see the *Ceylon Daily News,* December 15, 1959; for the U.P., see the *Times of Ceylon,* December 14, 1959; for the S.J.S., see the *Ceylon Observer,* January 1, 1960.

60. For these and other aspects of its program see the statement of Ponnambalam in the *Ceylon Observer,* March 11, 1960.

61. Quoted in the *Tribune,* July 28, 1956.

62. A total of 278 candidates, not counting independents, had to forfeit their deposits for not polling a minimum vote. The following are the party figures: L.P.P. 79, L.S.S.P. 48, M.E.P. 39, S.M.P. 35, C.P. 33, S.L.F.P. 15, C.I.C. 4, S.J.S. 4, U.P. 12, B.R.P. 3, U.N.P. 3, T.C. 2, F.P. 1. *Ceylon Observer,* March 21, 1960.

63. *Ceylon Daily News,* March 21, 1960.

64. *Ibid.,* March 22, 1960.

65. *Times of Ceylon,* March 24, 1960.

66. *Ceylon Daily News,* March 22, 1960.

67. *Ibid.,* April 4, 1960. See also Senanayake's summary, House of Representatives, *Debates,* Vol. XXXVIII, col. 875.

68. House of Representatives, *Debates,* Vol. XXXVIII, cols. 202–6.

69. *Ibid.*, col. 315.

70. *Ibid.*, col. 898.

71. *Ceylon Observer*, April 9, 1960.

72. *Ibid.*, March 28, 1960.

73. *Times of Ceylon*, March 29, 1960.

74. *Ceylon Daily News*, April 5, 1960.

75. *Times of Ceylon*, April 15, 1960.

76. *Ceylon Daily News*, April 18, 1960.

77. See remarks by Dr. Wickremasinghe in House of Representatives, *Debates,* Vol. XXXVIII, col. 183.

78. Chelvanayakam later explained that his support was given in the expectation that the S.L.F.P. would carry out the policy of the late Prime Minister, which he felt was in the interests of the Tamils. *Ceylon Daily News,* June 1, 1960.

79. House of Representatives, *Debates,* Vol. XXXVIII, col. 871.

80. *Ibid.*, cols. 327–28. Wickremasinghe and N. M. Perera argued along the same lines. *Ibid.*, cols. 178–80 and *Ceylon Daily News*, April 5, 1960.

81. House of Representatives, *Debates,* Vol. XXXVIII, col. 897. See entire debate, *ibid.*, cols. 179–897.

82. *Times of Ceylon*, April 3, 1960. See an analysis of the constitutional issue in A. J. Wilson, "The Governor-General and the Two Dissolutions of Parliament."

83. *Ceylon Observer*, April 24, 1960.

84. "The Governor-General," p. 207.

85. *Ceylon Observer*, May 22, 1960.

86. *Ceylon Daily News*, April 21, 1960.

87. They cited the infiltration of L.S.S.P. youths into the leagues. *Times of Ceylon,* May 22, 1960.

88. He was also disgruntled at not getting his party's nomination for the Galagedera seat. *Ibid.*, May 19, 1960.

89. *Ibid.*, June 12, 1960.

90. *Ceylon Observer*, May 3, 1960.

91. *Ceylon Daily News*, May 14, 1960.

92. *Ceylon Observer*, May 14, 1956.

93. *Ibid.*, May 17, 1960.

94. *Ceylon Daily News*, May 3, 1960.

95. *Ibid.*, June 14, 1960.

96. *Ceylon Observer*, June 1, 1960.

97. See the remarks of Mrs. Bandaranaike, *Times of Ceylon,* June 8, 1960.

98. See the text of the pact in the *Ceylon Observer*, June 23, 1960.

99. *Ibid.*, June 5, 1960.

100. *Ibid.*, May 29, 1960.

101. *Times of Ceylon*, May 22, 1960.

102. See, for instance, the *Ceylon Daily News,* July 16, 1960.

103. *Ceylon Observer,* May 22, 1960.

104. *Ceylon Daily News,* July 18, 1960.

105. *Ceylon Observer,* May 30, 1960.

106. *Ibid.,* June 5, 1960.

107. *Ibid.,* May 8, 1960.

108. See text of press release in the *Times of Ceylon,* May 26, 1960, and the *Ceylon Daily News,* May 17, 1960.

109. *Ceylon Daily News,* June 14, 1960.

110. *Ceylon Observer,* June 25, 1960.

111. See its press release in the *Ceylon Daily News,* June 14, 1960.

112. *Times of Ceylon,* July 20, 1960.

113. *Ceylon Daily News,* July 20, 1960.

114. *Ceylon Observer,* July 21, 1960.

115. From a copy of the English version of the throne speech presented to the audience at the time of the Governor-General's address.

116. *Ceylon Observer,* July 31, 1960.

117. House of Representatives, *Debates,* Vol. XL, col. 245.

118. *Ceylon Daily News,* August 5, 1960.

119. *Ibid.*

120. *Times of Ceylon,* August 7, 1960.

121. *Ceylon Daily News,* October 17, 1960.

122. House of Representatives, *Debates,* Vol. XL, col. 18.

123. *Times of Ceylon,* April 3, 1961.

124. *Ceylon Daily News,* November 14, 1961.

125. *Ceylon Observer,* November 16, 1961.

126. *Ibid.,* November 27, 1961.

127. *Ceylon Daily News,* December 1, 1961.

128. *Ibid.,* December 25, 1961.

129. *Ceylon Observer,* December 21, 1961.

130. *Ibid.,* April 19, 1961.

131. *Ceylon Daily News,* October 5, 1961.

132. *Ibid.,* January 30, 1962.

133. *Ibid.,* March 3, 1962.

134. *Ibid.,* February 14, 1962.

135. *Ibid.,* February 3, 1962.

136. *Ceylon Observer,* February 16, 1962.

137. See press release of the L.S.S.P. in the *Times of Ceylon,* February 17, 1962.

138. *Ceylon Daily News,* April 7, 1962.

139. *Ceylon Observer,* July 13, 1963.

140. The speech carried by a vote of 80 to 64.

141. See press release in the *Ceylon Daily News,* July 24, 1962.

142. *Ceylon Observer,* October 7, 1960.

143. *Times of Ceylon,* November 12, 1960. See also the remarks of J. R. Jayewardene in the *Ceylon Observer,* November 12, 1961.

144. *Times of Ceylon,* November 7, 1961.

145. *Ibid.,* May 2, 1962.

146. *Ibid.,* November 6, 1962.

147. See text in the *Ceylon Observer,* December 16, 1962.

148. *Sunday Times of Ceylon* (Colombo), February 17, 1963.

149. *Ceylon Observer,* March 18, 1963.

150. *Ceylon Daily News,* May 20, 1963.

151. See United Left Front, *Joint Manifesto of the L.S.S.P., M.E.P., and C.P.*

152. See the view of Pieter Keuneman, "Towards Unity of the Working Class." For an L.S.S.P. view see editorial in the *Young Socialist,* II, No. 4, 179–81. For its interpretation of Left unity on the basis of theoretical communism, see "From the Arsenal of Marxism," *ibid.,* III, No. 1, 37–44.

153. *Ceylon Observer,* May 12, 1963.

154. *Ceylon Daily News,* May 28, 1964.

155. *Ceylon News* (Colombo), June 11, 1964.

156. See text in the *Sri Lanka,* June 20, 1964.

157. Information on the U.N.P. Youth League was obtained by means of a personal interview with Mr. Iriyagolle. Much of what he told me was confirmed by other sources, including members of the S.L.F.P. and the Marxist parties.

158. March 25, 1965.

159. See the English translation of the manifesto of the S.L.F.P. in the *Ceylon News,* February 25, 1965.

160. *Ibid.*

161. *Ibid.,* March 18, 1965.

Chapter 6

1. Quoted in the *Tribune* (Colombo), July 28, 1956.

2. See interview in the *Ceylon Observer* (Colombo), July 14, 1963, p. 9.

3. Senator U. P. Jayasundera, ed., *United National Party* (1949), p. 19.

4. Senator U. P. Jayasundera, ed., *The United National Party* (1951), p. 179.

5. *Ceylon General Election 1956,* p. 48.

6. Jayasundera, *United National Party* (1949), p. 27.

7. Jayasundera, *United National Party* (1951), p. 185.

8. *General Election 1956,* p. 48.

9. *Ceylon: Dilemmas of a New Nation,* p. 113.

10. Jayasundera, *United National Party* (1951), p. 134.

11. Weerawardana, *General Election 1956,* p. 48.

12. Sir John Kotelawala, *This Is For You.*

13. *General Election 1956*, p. 89.

14. *Ibid.*, p. 35.

15. *Ibid.*, p. 36.

16. *Ibid.*

17. *Ibid.*, p. 37.

18. *Ibid.*, p. 214.

19. *Ceylon*, p. 114.

20. *General Election 1956*, p. 38.

21. *Ceylon Observer*, February 12, 1956, and *Ceylon Daily News* (Colombo), March 2, 1956.

22. Quoted in Weerawardana, *General Election 1956*, p. 37.

23. United National party, *Manifesto and Constitution* (1947).

24. *Ceylon*, p. 113.

25. See "Report of the Special Committee of the United National Party," *Ceylon Observer*, July 28, 1956.

26. *Ceylon Daily News*, February 23, 1958.

27. *Times of Ceylon* (Colombo), January 10, 1960.

28. *The Manifesto of the United National Party* (1960), p. 2.

29. See above, p. 143.

30. *Ceylon Observer*, July 14, 1963, p. 9.

31. See United National Party, *Constitution* (1962).

32. *Ceylon Observer*, July 28, 1956.

33. *Constitution* (1962), p. 2.

34. *Ibid*, p. 6.

35. *Ceylon Daily News*, September 30, 1965.

36. *Constitution* (1962), p. 7.

37. *Ceylon Observer*, April 30, 1960.

38. *Ceylon Daily News*, December 29, 1952.

39. *Ceylon News* (Colombo), May 20, 1965.

40. This expense compelled Bandaranaike to take out a mortgage on his home at Rosemead Place.

41. See *Manifesto and Constitution* (1951) of the Sri Lanka Freedom party, pp. 17-23.

42. *General Election 1956*, p. 217.

43. *Ibid.*, p. 29.

44. *Ibid.*, pp. 39–40.

45. *Ibid.*, pp. 36–37.

46. *Ceylon News*, June 17, 1965.

47. *Ceylon Observer*, June 30, 1963.

48. The *Times of Ceylon* (March 25, 1965) noted that the S.L.F.P. had well-organized district campaigns in almost all the constituencies.

49. *Sri Lanka Freedom Party: The Constitution, 1963–1964.* (A private and unofficial translation into English from the original Sinhalese by a language expert in Ceylon.)

50. Sri Lanka Freedom party, *Manifesto and Constitution* (1951), p. 8.

51. *Ibid.*, pp. 6–7.

52. House of Representatives, *Debates,* Vol. 43, col. 938.

53. *Constitution, 1963–1964.*

54. Denzil Peiris, *1956 and After*, p. 15.

55. *Ibid.*, p. 17.

56. Lanka Sama Samaja party, *For a Sama Samaja Government*, p. 2.

57. *Ceylon News*, June 11, 1964.

58. Leslie Goonewardene had cited its lack of rural support in 1959 as the greatest weakness of the L.S.S.P. and had advocated propaganda and other work in rural areas.

59. Peiris, *1956 and After*, p. 17.

60. *Ceylon*, p. 138.

61. *Administration Report of the Commissioner of Labour for 1960–61,* p. F109.

62. *Ceylon Daily News,* December 28, 1959.

63. *Ceylon Observer*, February 28, 1959.

64. *Ceylon Daily News,* June 6, 1959.

65. *Ceylon Observer*, March 1, 1959.

66. Parliament of Ceylon, "Trade Unions (Amendment) Act, No. 18 of 1956," p. 776.

67. Leslie Goonewardene, *A Short History of the Lanka Sama Samaja Party*, p. 36.

68. Weerawardana, *General Election 1956*, p. 214.

69. *Ceylon Observer*, March 16, 1964.

70. *Ceylon Daily News,* June 5, 1964.

71. *Morning Times,* October 19, 1953.

72. Wriggins, *Ceylon*, p. 138.

73. See article in *Ceylon Daily News*, April 4, 1964.

74. *Sunday Times*, April 28, 1964.

75. *Ceylon Observer*, May 8, 1964.

76. See the account of the nine-point program presented by the centrists and those points accepted by Perera in the *Ceylon Observer*, May 11, 1964.

77. *Ibid.*, May 29, 1964.

78. I have observed that Pieter Keuneman bows more ceremoniously to the mace when he enters the House of Representatives than any other M.P.

79. *Ceylon News,* February 6, 1964.

80. *Ceylon Daily News,* October 28, 1963.

81. *Ibid.,* June 6, 1964.

82. *Ibid.,* October 28, 1964.

83. *Forward*, March 13, 1964.

84. October 28, 1965.

85. *Ceylon News*, January 25, 1968.

86. *Administration Report of the Commissioner of Labour for 1960–61,* p. F109.

87. "Manifesto of the Federal Party," in Ceylon Daily News, *Parliaments of Ceylon 1960.*

Chapter 7

1. *Times of Ceylon,* February 15, 1947.
2. *Sessional Paper XX of 1966,* p. 8.
3. "Ceylon Parliamentary Elections (Amendment) Act, No. 11 of 1959," p. 9.
4. *Ibid.,* p. 19.
5. Government of Ceylon, "Ceylon (Parliamentary Elections) Order in Council 1946 as revised in 1956," in *Legislative Enactments,* p. 790.
6. *Sessional Paper II of 1962,* p. 125.
7. In his *Political Parties* (London: Methuen and Co., 1962), p. 217. For a criticism of Duverger's thesis, see Colin Leys, "Models, Theories, and the Theory of Political Parties," *Political Studies,* VII, No. 2 (1959), 127–46. See also Leslie Lipson, "Party Systems in the United Kingdom and the Older Commonwealth: Causes, Resemblances, and Variations," *Political Studies,* VII, No. 1 (1959), 12–31.
8. *Sessional Paper XIII of 1946,* p. 8. For the electoral districts prior to independence, see *SP XI of 1930* and *SP XVII of 1935.*
9. *Sessional Paper XIII of 1946,* p. 7.
10. *Sessional Paper XV of 1959,* p. 10. Italics added.
11. The idea of using area weightage to increase the number of seats for backward areas was taken into account before independence. See *Sessional Paper XI of 1930,* p. 4, and *SP XVII of 1935,* p. 11.
12. G. E. P. de S. Wickramaratne, comp., *Towards a New Era,* p. 148.
13. *Sessional Paper XIII of 1946,* p. 19.
14. *Ibid.,* p. 163.
15. *Sessional Paper XV of 1959,* p. 10.
16. Wickramaratne, *Towards a New Era,* p. 149.
17. House of Representatives, *Debates,* Vol. 33, col. 2491.
18. *Sessional Paper XV of 1959,* p. 10.
19. In 1935 a delimitation commission noted that it "was argued that the underdeveloped and sparsely inhabited areas of the dry zone require, and should be given, more representation in Council than the highly developed and thickly populated areas of the wet zone." *Sessional Paper XVII of 1935,* p. 11.
20. *Sessional Paper XIII of 1946,* p. 162.
21. *Ibid.,* p. 24.
22. *Ibid.*
23. *Sessional Paper XV of 1959,* p. 10.
24. *Ibid.,* p. 13.
25. All the statistics for this analysis were derived from information contained *ibid., passim.*

26. *Ibid.,* p. 107.
27. *Ibid.,* p. 84.
28. *Ibid.,* p. 14.

Conclusion

1. "Why Study Political Parties," in Sigmund Neumann, ed., *Modern Political Parties* (Chicago: The University of Chicago Press, 1956), p. 6.

2. See his "Politics as a Vocation," in H. H. Gerth and C. Wright Mills, eds., *From Max Weber: Essays in Sociology* (New York: Oxford University Press, Galaxy Books, 1958), pp. 77–128.

3. Marshall R. Singer, *The Emerging Elite,* p. 145. The Delimitation Commission noted in 1959 that the people "have not yet learnt to think sufficiently in terms of principles and policies in preference to race, caste or religion, but they are rapidly developing a political consciousness which tends to what is called a polarization towards the right, center or left." *Sessional Paper XV of 1959,* p. 13.

4. *Political Parties in the United States* (New York: St. Martin's Press, 1966), p. 8.

5. For a discussion of the relationship between party emergence and the decline of independent candidates in Great Britain see R. T. McKenzie, *British Political Parties* (London: William Heinemann, 1963), pp. 1–18; Sir Ivor Jennings, *Party Politics: The Growth of Parties* (Cambridge: Cambridge University Press, 1961); and Samuel H. Beer, "Great Britain: From Governing Elite to Organized Mass Parties," in Neumann, *Modern Political Parties,* especially pp. 9–16.

6. *Political Parties: A Behavioral Analysis* (Chicago: Rand McNally & Company, 1964), p. 5. Eldersveld suggests that in situations where parties are highly receptive to the inclusion of any applicants at the higher and lower echelons, problems of discipline and party cohesion naturally arise. He contends that where "adaptation is maximal, internal managerial control is difficult, factional pluralism multiplied, operational efficiency likely to be impaired, and goal orientations and ideological consensus highly noncongruent." *Ibid.,* p. 5.

7. Sigmund Neumann, "Toward a Comparative Study of Political Parties," in Harry Eckstein and David E. Apter, eds., *Comparative Politics* (New York: The Free Press of Glencoe, 1963), p. 367.

8. Fred R. von der Mehden is inaccurate in his contention that Ceylon has a one party dominant party system. *Politics of the Developing Nations* (Englewood Cliffs, N.J.: Prentice-Hall, Inc., 1964), p. 63.

9. Fatma Mansur, *Process of Independence,* p. 160. See also Lucien Pye, "Party Systems and National Development in Asia," in Joseph LaPalombara and Myron Weiner, eds., *Political Parties and Political Development* (Princeton, N.J.: Princeton University Press, 1966), pp. 369–98; and David E. Apter, *Some Conceptual Approaches to the Study of Modernization* (Englewood Cliffs, N.J.: Prentice-Hall, 1968), pp. 72–87.

BIBLIOGRAPHY

BOOKS AND PAMPHLETS

Amarasingam, S. P. *Rice and Rubber: The Story of China-Ceylon Trade.* Colombo: Ceylon Economic Research Association, 1953.

Annamalay, V. *Report of the General Secretary, Ceylon Workers' Congress.* Colombo, 1963.

Arunachalam, Ponnambalam. *Speeches and Writings of Sir Ponnambalam Arunachalam.* Colombo: H. W. Cave & Co., 1936.

Bailey, Sydney D. *Ceylon.* London: Hutchinson's University Library, 1952.

——. *Parliamentary Government in Southern Asia.* New York: International Secretariat, Institute of Pacific Relations, 1953.

Bandaranaike, S. W. R. D. *The Foreign Policy of Ceylon.* Colombo: Government Press, 1959.

——. *The Government and the People.* Colombo: Government Press, 1959.

——. *Speeches and Writings.* Colombo: Government Press, 1963.

——, ed. *The Handbook of the Ceylon National Congress, 1919–1928.* Colombo: H. W. Cave & Co., 1928.

Blaze, B. R. *The Life of Lorenz.* Colombo: Associated Newspapers of Ceylon, 1948.

Bolshevik-Leninist Party of India. *Manifesto of the L.S.S.P. (Ceylon-Unit, B.L.P.I.).* 1947.

Buddhist Committee of Inquiry. *The Betrayal of Buddhism.* Balangoda: Dharmavijaya Press, 1956.

Catholic Union of Ceylon. *Education in Ceylon according to the Buddhist Commission Report: A Commentary.* Colombo: Catholic Press, 1957.

Ceylon Burgher Association. *Constitution.* Colombo: Jubilee Printing Press, 1960.

Ceylon Daily News. *State Council, 1931.* Colombo: Associated Newspapers of Ceylon, 1931.

——. *The State Council of Ceylon, 1936.* Colombo: Associated Newspapers of Ceylon, 1936.

——. *Parliament of Ceylon, 1947.* Colombo: Associated Newspapers of Ceylon, 1947.

————. *Parliament of Ceylon, 1956.* Colombo: Associated Newspapers of Ceylon, 1956.

————. *Parliaments of Ceylon, 1960.* Colombo: Associated Newspapers of Ceylon, 1960.

————. *Parliament of Ceylon, 1965.* Colombo: Associated Newspapers of Ceylon, 1965.

Ceylon Labour Party. *Policy and Programme.* Colombo: Metro Printers, 1949.

Ceylon Muslim League. *Proceedings of the 18th Annual Sessions.* August 13, 1944.

Ceylon's Uplift. Colombo: Associated Newspapers of Ceylon, 1939. (Authors identified only as "medical men.")

Codrington, H. W. A. *A Short History of Ceylon.* Rev. ed. London: Macmillan & Co., 1947.

Collins, Sir Charles. *Public Administration in Ceylon.* London: Oxford University Press, 1951.

Cook, Elsie K. *Ceylon: Its Geography, Its Resources and Its People.* 2d ed. Madras: Macmillan & Co., 1951.

Cooray, Joseph A. R. *The Revision of the Constitution.* Colombo: Ceylon Printers, 1957.

Crane, Robert I., and Burton Stein. *Aspects of Economic Development in South Asia.* New York: Institute of Pacific Relations, 1954.

De Mel, R. A. *Manifesto.* Maradana: Sadhu Press, 1947.

De Silva, Colvin R. *Left Disunity.* Colombo: Luxman Press, 1950.

————. *Ceylon under the British Occupation, 1795–1833.* 2 vols. Colombo: Colombo Apothecaries, 1953.

————. *Hartal!* Colombo: L.S.S.P., 1953.

————. *Their Politics—and Ours.* Colombo: L.S.S.P., 1954.

————. *Outline of the Permanent Revolution.* Colombo: L.S.S.P., 1955.

De Silva, G. B. *Has the Common Man Confidence in the U.N.P.?* Kandy: Sithumina Printing Works, 1959.

Desai, Maganbhai. *Our Language Problem.* Ahmedabad: Navajivan Publishing House, 1956.

Dharma Samaja Party. *Manifesto: The Choice before the Buddhists.* Colombo: Swadeshi Printers, 1959.

The Dutch Burgher Union of Ceylon: Its Foundation, Its Aims and Its Membership. Colombo: Times of Ceylon, n.d.

Employers' Federation of Ceylon. *Annual Report and Accounts 1962–1963.* Colombo: Mortlake Press, 1963.

Farmer, B. H. *Pioneer Peasant Colonization in Ceylon.* London: Oxford University Press, 1957.

————. *Ceylon: A Divided Nation.* London: Oxford University Press, 1963.

Ferguson's Ceylon Directory 1956. Colombo: Ceylon Observer Press, 1956.

Fernando, Sylvan E. J. *The Law of Parliamentary Elections in Ceylon*. Colombo: Daily News Press, 1947.

Goonewardene, Leslie. *The Third International Condemned*. Colombo: L.S.S.P., 1940.

———. *Differences between Trotskyism and Stalinism*. Colombo: L.S.S.P., 1950.

———. *A Short History of the Lanka Sama Samaja Party*. Maradana: Gunaratne & Co., 1960.

Hulugalle, H. A. J. *The Life and Times of D. R. Wijewardene*. Colombo: Associated Newspapers of Ceylon, 1960.

International Bank for Reconstruction and Development. *The Economic Development of Ceylon*. Baltimore: The Johns Hopkins Press, 1953.

Jansz, Hilaire. *Quaint Gaunt Saint*. Colombo: Associated Newspapers of Ceylon, Lake House, 1963.

Jayasundera, Senator U. P., ed. *United National Party (Independence Day Souvenir)*. Colombo, 1949.

———. *The United National Party (Souvenir)*. Colombo, 1951.

Jayewardene, J. R. *Buddhism and Marxism*. Colombo: M. D. Gunasena and Co., 1950.

Jeffries, Sir Charles. *Ceylon: The Path to Independence*. London: Pall Mall Press, 1962.

Jennings, Sir Ivor. *The Commonwealth in Asia*. Oxford: Clarendon Press, 1951.

———. *The Economy of Ceylon*. 2d ed. London: Oxford University Press, 1951.

———. *The Constitution of Ceylon*. 3d ed. London: Oxford University Press, 1953.

———. *The Approach to Self-Government*. Cambridge: Cambridge University Press, 1956.

Joint Committee of the Ceylon National Association and the Ceylon Reform League. *Case for Constitutional Reform in Ceylon*. Colombo, 1919.

Kalmane. *India and Ceylon: A Federation*. London: P. S. King and Son, 1932.

Karalasingham, V. *The Way Out for the Tamil Speaking People*. Colombo: Wesley Press, 1963.

Keble, W. T., and D. S. Sena. *Life of Sir James Peiris*. Colombo: Times of Ceylon, 1950.

Keuneman, Pieter. *The Fight for Left Unity*. Colombo: Communist Party, 1951.

———. *Twenty Years of the Ceylon Communist Party*. Colombo: Lanka Press, 1963.

Kotelawala, Sir John. *This Is for You.* Colombo: Daily News Press, 1952.
———. *An Asian Prime Minister's Story.* London: George G. Harrap & Co., 1956.
Lanka Sama Samaja Party. *For a Sama Samaja Government: Election Manifesto.* Maradana: Gunaratne and Co., 1960.
Low-Country Products Association of Ceylon, *Annual Report for 1963.* Wellawatte: Wembley Press, 1963.
Mahajana Eksath Peramuna. *Joint Programme of the M. E. P.* Colombo, March, 1956.
Mansur, Fatma. *Process of Independence.* London: Routledge & Kegan Paul, 1962.
Mendis, G. C. *Ceylon under the British.* 3d ed. Colombo: Colombo Apothecaries, 1952.
———. *The Early History of Ceylon.* Calcutta: Y.M.C.A. Publishing House, 1954.
———. *Ceylon Today and Yesterday: Main Currents of Ceylon History.* Colombo: Associated Newspapers of Ceylon, 1957.
———, ed. *The Colebrooke-Cameron Papers: Documents on British Colonial Policy in Ceylon 1796–1833.* 2 vols. London: Oxford University Press, 1956.
Mutukumara, Nemsiri, ed. *This Man Razik.* Colombo: Associated Newspapers of Ceylon, 1963.
Namasivayam, S. *The Legislatures of Ceylon, 1928–1948.* London: Faber & Faber, 1951.
———. *Parliamentary Government in Ceylon, 1948–1958.* Colombo: K. V. G. De Silva, 1959.
Oliver, Henry M., Jr. *Economic Opinion and Policy in Ceylon.* London: Cambridge University Press, 1957.
Peiris, Denzil. *1956 and After: Background to Parties and Politics in Ceylon Today.* Colombo: Associated Newspapers of Ceylon, 1958.
Perera, Fr. S. G. *History of Ceylon: The British Period and After.* Colombo: Associated Newspapers of Ceylon, 1959.
Pieris, Ralph. *Sinhalese Social Organization: The Kandyan Period.* Colombo: Ceylon University Press, 1956.
———, ed. *Some Aspects of Traditional Sinhalese Culture.* Peradeniya: Conference on Traditional Cultures, Ceylon University, 1956.
Planters' Association of Ceylon. *History of the Planters' Association of Ceylon 1854–1954.* Colombo: Times of Ceylon, 1954.
Ponnambalam, G. G. *Presidential Address, First Plenary Session, The All-Ceylon Tamil Congress.* Colombo, November 27, 1944.
Ponnambalam Arunachalam, 1853–1924. Colombo: Ceylon Printers, 1953.
Rajapakse, Sir Lalita. *Presidential Address (English version), All-Ceylon Buddhist Congress.* Colombo: Metro Printers, 1961, 1963.
Rao, P. R. Ramachandra. *India and Ceylon: A Study.* Bombay: Orient Longmans, 1954.

Ryan, Bryce. *Caste in Modern Ceylon: The Sinhalese System in Transition.* New Brunswick, N.J.: Rutgers University Press, 1953.

––––. *Sinhalese Village.* Coral Gables, Fla.: University of Miami Press, 1958.

Samarakkody, Edmund. *The Crisis of Local Government.* Maradana: L.S. S.P., 1955.

Sarkar, N. K., and S. J. Tambiah. *The Disintegrating Village.* Colombo: Ceylon University Press, 1957.

Senanayake, E. L. *Kandy Parliamentary Seat.* Kandy: Union Printing Works, 1960.

Singer, Marshall R. *The Emerging Elite: A Study of Political Leadership in Ceylon.* Cambridge, Mass.: The M.I.T. Press, 1964.

Sri Lanka Freedom Party. *Manifesto and Constitution.* Wellampitiya: Navajivana Press, 1951.

Tambiah, Henry W. *The Laws and Customs of the Tamils of Ceylon.* Colombo: Tamil Cultural Society of Ceylon, 1954.

Thondaman, Sri S. *Presidential Address (16th Annual Conference, Ceylon Workers' Congress).* Colombo: Times of Ceylon, 1957.

––––. *Presidential Address (19th Sessions, Ceylon Workers' Congress).* Colombo: Plate Printers, 1963.

Tresidder, Argus John. *Ceylon: An Introduction to the Resplendent Land.* Princeton, N.J.: D. Van Nostrand Co., 1960.

United Left Front. *Joint Manifesto of the L.S.S.P., M.E.P., and C.P.* Colombo: Lanka Press, 1963.

United National Party. *Manifesto and Constitution.* Colombo, 1947.

––––. *For Stable Government: Manifesto.* Colombo: Times of Ceylon, 1960.

––––. *Constitution.* Colombo, 1962.

––––. *The United National Party in Colombo.* Colombo: Metro Printers, 1962.

Vaidialingham, A. *Samasamajism.* Colombo: L.S.S.P., 1940.

[Vijayavardhana, D. C.] *The Revolt in the Temple.* Colombo: Sinhala Publications, 1953.

Vittachi, Tarzie. *Emergency '58: The Story of the Ceylon Race Riots.* London: A. Deutsch, 1958.

Weerawardana, I. D. S. *Government and Politics in Ceylon (1931–1946).* Colombo: Ceylon Economic Research Association, 1951.

––––. *The Senate of Ceylon at Work.* Colombo: Ceylon University Press, 1955.

––––. *Ceylon General Election 1956.* Colombo: Gunasena & Co., 1960.

––––, and M. I. Weerawardana. *Ceylon and Her Citizens.* Madras: Oxford University Press, 1956.

Weinman, J. R. *Our Legislature.* Colombo: Associated Newspapers of Ceylon, 1947.

Wickramaratne, G. E. P. de S., comp. *Towards a New Era: Selected*

Speeches of S. W. R .D. Bandaranaike Made in the Legislature of Ceylon, 1931–1959. Colombo: Department of Information, Government of Ceylon, 1961.

Wickremasinghe, S. A. *The Economic Crisis.* Colombo: Communist Party, 1953.

————. *The Way Ahead: An Economic Policy for Ceylon.* Colombo: Lanka Press, 1955.

Wijesekera, N. D. *The People of Ceylon.* Colombo: M. D. Gunasena & Co., 1949.

Wriggins, W. Howard. *Ceylon: Dilemmas of a New Nation.* Princeton, N. J.: Princeton University Press, 1960.

Youth Congress. *Communalism or Nationalism.* Chunnakam: Thirnmakal Press, 1939.

ARTICLES

Abhayavardhana, Hector. "Categories of Left Thinking in Ceylon." *Community,* No. 4, pp. 31–57.

L. O. B. "United Ceylon." *Ceylon Review,* II, Nos. 4, 5 (April, 1894), 67–72.

Coates, William Ames. "The Languages of Ceylon 1946–1953." *University of Ceylon Review,* XIX, No. 1 (April, 1961), 81–91.

De Mel, F. S. "Reform of the Legislative Council." *Ceylon National Review,* II, No. 4 (July, 1907), 32–38.

Editorial Board of Suriya Books. "Marxism in Sinhala." *Young Socialist,* III, No. 1, 33–36.

European Association. "Objects of Association." *Quarterly Bulletin,* I, No. 1 (July, 1927), iii.

Fernando, C. N. V. "Christianity and Ceylon in the Portuguese and Dutch Periods." *University of Ceylon Review,* VI, No. 4 (October, 1948), 267–88.

————. "Christianity and Ceylon in the British Period." *University of Ceylon Review,* VII, No. 2 (April, 1949), 135–41.

E. F. G. "The Ceylon Legislative Council." *Ceylon Review,* III, No. 1 (September, 1894), 6–12.

Gilbert, William H. "The Sinhalese Caste System of Central and Southern Ceylon." *Ceylon Historical Journal,* II, Nos. 3, 4 (1952), 295–366.

Halangoda, J. A. "Ceylonese and Government Employment." *The Kandyan,* II, No. 1 (March, 1905), 81–89.

————. "Our Right for Special Consideration in the Reconstruction of the Empire after the War." *Journal of the Kandyan Association,* I, No. 3 (May, 1918), 94–96.

Hensman, C. R., ed. "The Public Services and the People." *Community* (special issue), 1963.

Jennings, Sir Ivor. "The Emergency Procedure of the State Council." *University of Ceylon Review,* I, No. 1 (April, 1943), 8–23.

———. "The Declaration of His Majesty's Government on Constitutional Reform: The Precedents." *University of Ceylon Review,* I, No. 2 (November, 1943), 1–14.

———. "Race, Religion and Economic Opportunity in the University of Ceylon." *University of Ceylon Review,* II, Nos. 1, 2 (October, 1944), 1–24.

———. "The Appointment of the Soulbury Commission." *University of Ceylon Review,* III, No. 2 (November, 1945), 11–28.

———. "The Evolution of the New Constitution." *University of Ceylon Review,* V, No. 1 (April, 1947), 1–20.

———. "The Ceylon General Election of 1947." *University of Ceylon Review,* VI, No. 3 (July, 1948), 133–95.

———. "Ceylon's 1952 Election." *Eastern Survey,* XXI (December 3, 1952), 177–80.

———. "The Languages of Ceylon." *University of Ceylon Review,* XI, No. 1 (January, 1953), 1–9.

———. "Additional Notes on the General Election of 1952." *Ceylon Historical Journal,* II, Nos. 3, 4 (January, April, 1953), 193–208.

———. "Nationalism and Political Development in Ceylon." *Ceylon Historical Journal,* III, Nos. 1–4 (1953–54), 62–85, 99–114, 197–206.

———. "Politics in Ceylon since 1952." *Pacific Affairs,* XXVIII, No. 4 (December, 1954), 338–52.

———. "D. S. Senanayake and Independence." *Ceylon Historical Journal,* V, Nos. 1–4 (1955–56), 16–22.

Kandyan Association. *Monthly Letter,* No. 2 (November, 1920).

Keuneman, Pieter. "Towards Unity of the Working Class." *World Marxist Review,* VI, No. 12 (December, 1963), 10–14.

Kuruppu, N. S. G. "Labour and the Rise of Capitalism: An Outline to 1935." *Ceylon Historical Journal,* I, No. 2 (October, 1951), 129–46.

Mendis, G. C. "The Causes of Communal Conflict in Ceylon." *University of Ceylon Review,* I, No. 1 (April, 1943), 41–49.

———. "Adult Franchise and Educational Reform." *University of Ceylon Review,* II, Nos. 1, 2 (October, 1944), 37–44.

Naguleswaran, P. "The Problem of Indian Immigrant Labour in the Nineteenth Century." *Ceylon Historical Journal,* I, No. 3 (January, 1952), 230–41.

Padmanabha, A. "Reform of the Ceylon Legislative Council." *Ceylon National Review,* II, No. 6 (May, 1908), pp. 171–200.

Pieris, Ralph. "The Alienation of the Modern Intellectual." *Community,* No. 4, pp. 17–30.

Rees, Sir Frederick. "The Soulbury Commission (1944–1945)." *The Ceylon Historical Journal,* V, Nos. 1–4 (1955–56), 23–48.

Sahabandu, S. S. "The Public Security Ordinance No. 25 of 1947." *Young Socialist,* II, No. 4, 213–17.

Samarakkody, Edmund. "Dynamics of the Ceylon Revolution." *Young Socialist,* III, No. 1, 13–20.

Senanayake, D. S. "The Commonwealth and the Future." *Ceylon Historical Journal,* V, Nos. 1–4 (1955–56), 110–14.

Stein, Burton. "Problems of Economic Development in Ceylon." *Ceylon Historical Journal,* III, Nos. 3, 4 (January, April, 1954), 286–328.

Sulasinghe, Michael. "Whither Sinhala Drama?" *Young Socialist,* II, No. 4, 219–22.

Tambiah, S. J. "Ethnic Representation in Ceylon's Higher Administrative Services, 1870–1946." *University of Ceylon Review,* XIII, Nos. 2, 3 (April–July, 1955), 113–34.

Vaeravagn, P. "The Western-educated Elite." *Community,* No. 4, pp. 85–89.

J. A. W. "The Birth of a New Ceylon." *Young Lanka,* I, No. 1 (July, 1918), 5–8.

Weerawardana, I. D. S. "The Governor's Reserve Powers during the First State Council." *University of Ceylon Review,* VII, No. 1 (January, 1949), 41–56.

———. "The Minorities and the Citizenship Act." *Ceylon Historical Journal,* I, No. 3 (January, 1952), 242–50.

———. "The General Elections in Ceylon, 1952." *Ceylon Historical Journal,* II, Nos. 1, 2 (July, October, 1952), 111–78.

Wilson, A. J. "Minority Safeguards in the Ceylon Constitution." *Ceylon Journal of Historical and Social Studies,* I (January, 1958), 73–95.

———. "The Crewe-McCallum Reforms, 1912–1921." *Ceylon Journal of Historical and Social Studies,* II (January, 1959), 84–115.

———. "The Governor-General and the Two Dissolutions of Parliament. December 5, 1959 and April 23, 1960." *Ceylon Journal of Historical and Social Studies,* III, No. 2 (July–December, 1960), 187–207.

———. "The Public Services in Ceylon." *Community,* No. 3 (1963), pp. 9–17.

Wiswawarnapala, W. A. "Composition of Cabinets 1948–1960." *Young Socialist,* II, No. 5, 267–72.

Woodward, Calvin A. "The Trotskyite Movement in Ceylon." *World Politics,* XIV, No. 2 (January, 1962), pp. 307–21.

Wriggins, W. Howard. "Ceylon's Time of Troubles, 1956–1958." *Far Eastern Survey,* Vol. XXVIII (March, 1959).

PUBLIC DOCUMENTS

Ceylon

Administration Report of the Commissioner of Labour for 1960–61. Colombo: Government Press, 1962.

Administration Report of the Director of Education for 1960. Colombo: Government Press, 1962.

Department of Census and Statistics. *Ceylon Year Book.* Colombo: Government Press, 1961.

——. *Statistical Abstract of Ceylon.* Colombo: Government Press, 1962.

House of Representatives. *Parliamentary Debates.* Colombo: Government Press, 1948–68.

Legislative Council of Ceylon. *Addresses Delivered by Governors of the Colony Together with the Replies of the Council.* Vol. I (1833–60), Vol. II (1860–77), Vol. III (1877–1900), Vol. IV (1900–1905). Colombo: Government Printer.

——. *Debates.* 1905–31.

——. "To the President of the Legislative Council of Ceylon (Enclosure 2), September 26, 1864," in *Copies of Dispatches and Memorandum on Ceylon Military Expenditures.*

Ministry of Home Affairs. *A Plan for the Rehabilitation of the Kandyan Peasantry in Central and Uva Provinces, 1955-56—1959-60.* Colombo: Government Press, 1956.

Parliament of Ceylon. "Parliamentary Elections (Amendment) Act, No. 19 of 1948."

——. "Ceylon (Parliamentary Elections) Amendment Act, No. 48 of 1949."

——. "Ceylon (Parliamentary Elections) Amendment Act, No. 7 of 1952."

——. "Registers of Parliamentary Electors (Special Provisions) Act, No. 34 of 1952."

——. "Ceylon (Parliamentary Elections) Amendment Act, No. 19 of 1953."

——. "Ceylon (Parliamentary Elections) (Amendment) Act, No. 26 of 1953."

——. "Ceylon (Constitution) Amendment Act, No. 29 of 1954."

——. "Ceylon Constitution (Special Provisions) Act, No. 35 of 1954."

——. "Ceylon Parliamentary Elections (Amendment) Act, No. 16 of 1956."

——. "Trade Unions (Amendment) Act, No. 18 of 1956."

——. "Industrial Disputes (Amendment) Act, No. 14 of 1957."

——. "Industrial Disputes (Amendment) Act, No. 62 of 1957."

——. "Ceylon Constitution (Amendment) Act, No. 4 of 1959."

——. "Public Security (Amendment) Act, No. 8 of 1959."

——. "Ceylon Parliamentary Elections (Amendment) Act, No. 11 of 1959."

——. "Ceylon (Parliamentary Elections) (Amendment) Act, No. 26 of 1959."

——. "Ceylon Parliamentary Elections (Amendment) Act, No. 2 of 1960."

——. "Ceylon Parliamentary Elections (Amendment) Act, No. 72 of 1961."

——. "Industrial Disputes (Amendment) Act, No. 4 of 1962."

————. *The Reports of the Parliamentary Bribery Commission 1959–1960.* Parliamentary Series No. 28, 5th Parliament, 1st session. December, 1960.

Planning Secretariat. *Six-Year Programme of Investment.* Colombo: Government Press, 1955.

Sessional Paper XVII of 1935. Report of the Commission for the Revision of Boundaries of Electoral Districts.

Sessional Paper VIII of 1937. Report of Mr. F. C. Gimson on the General Election to the State Council, 1936.

Sessional Paper XIV of 1938. Report of the Select Committee on Election Law Procedures.

Sessional Paper XIII of 1946. Report of the First Delimitation Commission.

Sessional Paper XXII of 1947. The Independence of Ceylon.

Sessional Paper III of 1948. The Constitution of Ceylon.

Sessional Paper XXII of 1948. Correspondence Relating to the Citizenship Status of Indians Resident in Ceylon.

Sessional Paper XVIII of 1951. Report of the Kandyan Peasantry Commission.

Sessional Paper XIII of 1952. Report on the Survey of Landlessness.

Sessional Paper XV of 1959. Report of the Delimitation Commission.

Sessional Paper II of 1962. Report on the Parliamentary General Elections, March 19 and July 20, 1960.

Sessional Paper XX of 1966. Report on the Sixth Parliamentary General Election of Ceylon, 22nd of March, 1965.

State Council. *Debates.* 1931–47.

Great Britain

Ceylon: Report of the Special (Donoughmore) Commission on the Constitution. Cmd. 3131. London: HMSO, 1928.

Ceylon: Report of the (Soulbury) Commission on Constitutional Reform. Cmd. 6677. London: HMSO, 1945.

Colebrooke, Lieutenant-Colonel. *Report . . . upon the Administration of the Government of Ceylon.* London: HMSO, 1831.

INDEX

Agricultural production, 5–6
All-Ceylon Moors' Association.
   See Moors' Association
All-Ceylon Muslim League.
   See Muslim League
All-Ceylon Tamil Conference, 35
Almond, Gabriel, 16
Alternative governments, 103
Aluwihare, B. H., 34, 48
Appointed members, House of
   Representatives, 72–73, 256
Apter, David E., 13, 17, 19
Area weightage, 258–59, 262, 264
Arunachalam, Sir Ponnambalam,
   26, 29–30, 39

Banda, S. D., 112
Bandaranaike, Felix, 154, 161, 162, 209
Bandaranaike, S. W. R. D., 55, 66, 72, 86,
   97, 98, 115–16; and preindependence
   politics, 34, 37, 47, 48; in U.N.P.,
   54–55, 76–79, 80–81, 107–8; and
   S.L.F.P., 88–89, 91, 96, 112, 113,
   143–44, 194, 197–201, 207–9; and M.E.P.
   campaign, 102, 104, 105, 113, 122,
   128–29; as prime minister, 124, 127, 130,
   131, 134, 136–37, 139, 259, 261;
   death, 132, 201
Bandaranaike, Mrs. Sirimavo, 144, 153–54,
   157–58, 163, 164, 202, 203, 209
Bandaranaike, Sir Solomon Dias, 43
Bandaranaike-Chelvanayakam Pact, 136–37
Bandaranayake, S. D., 129, 130, 141
Beligammana, C. R., 130, 141
Bhasa Peramuna, 114, 120, 121, 124
Bolshevik-Leninist party (B.L.P.),
   60, 69, 70, 82, 87
Bolshevik-Leninist party of India
   (B.L.P.I.), 60
British occupation, 9–10

Buddhists, 9, 26, 115–17. *See also*
   Religion, in politics
Burghers, 8
Burke, Edmund, 13

Ceylon Communist party. *See*
   Communist party
Ceylon Daily News, 102, 136
Ceylon Federation of Labour, 60, 214
Ceylon Federation of Trade Unions,
   226, 227
Ceylon Indian Congress, 64–65, 70–71,
   81–88 *passim,* 272
Ceylon League, 24–25
Ceylon Muslim League. *See* Muslim League
Ceylon National Association, 29, 33
Ceylon National Congress, 30–39, 44, 45,
   47, 53, 54, 56, 61, 73
Ceylon National Review, 26
Ceylon News, 227
Ceylon Observer, 101, 136
Ceylon Reform League, 29, 33
Ceylon Social Reform Society, 26
Ceylon Trade Union Congress, 65
Ceylon Trade Union Federation,
   60, 225, 227
C.F.T.U. *See* Ceylon Federation of Trade
   Unions
Chandrasiri, Somaweera, 112, 114
Chelvanayakam, S. J. V., 35, 88, 92, 135,
   136, 148, 231
Christians, 9, 116. *See also* Religion, in
   politics
C.I.C. *See* Ceylon Indian Congress
Clokie, H. McD., 14
C.N.C. *See* Ceylon National Congress
Coalitions. *See* No-contest pacts
Colebrooke, Lt. Col., 23, 28
Colebrooke reforms of 1833, 22–23
Committee system, State Council, 43, 46
Communal competition, 31–32, 265–69

333

Communal groups, 6–9, 256–57
Communal parties, 81, 82, 86
Communist party: formation, 60–61;
  1947 election, 60, 69, 70, 72; and U.N.P.
  government (1947–52), 81, 82; alliance
  with V.L.S.S.P., 87, 111, 112; 1952
  election, 87, 88, 92; and U.N.P.
  government (1952–56), 97, 98; 1956
  election, 102, 103, 105, 106, 114;
  and M.E.P. government, 124–25, 126–27;
  1960 elections, 140–41, 142, 145, 147,
  149–52, 155, 156, 225; 1963 split, 225;
  and S.L.F.P. government, 157, 158–59,
  161, 162; 1965 election, 166, 167, 169,
  225–26; and National government, 170
Communist party (China wing), 168,
  225–26, 227
Constitution: S.L.F.P., 198–99, 205–6;
  U.N.P., 55, 56, 182, 189–90
Coomaraswamy, Sir Muttu, 26
Cooray, Archbishop Thomas, 91
Coup attempt, 161
C.P. *See* Communist party
Crowther, S. J. K., 70
C.T.U.F. *See* Ceylon Trade Union
  Federation

Dahanayake, W.: in State Council, 48;
  opposition to U.N.P., 112; and "Sinhala
  only," 114; and M.E.P. coalition, 124,
  130; as prime minister, 132–33, 139, 140;
  and L.P.P., 142, 145, 147, 170
Dalpatada, K. A., 66
D'Alwis, James, 26
Delimitation Commission: first, 256–57,
  264; second, 257, 261–62, 264–65,
  268–69
De Mel, F. S., 27
De Mel, R. A., 67
Deposit, for candidates, 237–38
De Silva, C. P., 129, 144, 164, 168, 170,
  204, 209, 210
De Silva, Colvin R.: in preindependence
  politics, 58, 60; 1947 election, 82; and
  English language, 119; and M.E.P.
  government, 136; July 1960 election,
  151; and S.L.F.P. government, 160; in
  L.S.S.P., 218–19, 220, 221
De Silva, P. H. William, 124, 131
De Silva, W. A., 37
De Zoysa, Francis, 41
De Zoysa, Stanley, 128, 129, 130
Dharma Samaja party (D.S.P.), 141–42,
  155

Disfranchisement, Indians, 85–86, 259–60,
  264
Dissawe, T. B. Pannabokke, 109
Dissolution of Parliament (1960), 148–49
Donoughmore Commission, 34, 36, 40–42
Dutch occupation, 10
Duverger, Maurice, 13, 14, 16–17, 18, 255

Economic conditions, 3–6, 120
Eksath Bhikku Peramuna, 117
Eldersveld, S. J., 17, 282
Election: of 1931, 44–45; of 1936, 46–47;
  of 1947, 52, 66–72; of 1952, 87–95;
  of 1956, 100–107, 113–15; of March
  1960, 140–47, 253–54; of July 1960,
  149–57, 254; of 1965, 165–70, 254
Elections: regulations, 237–39; two-way
  character, 249–53
Electoral districts, 140, 261
Electoral system, 255–65
Engelmann, F. C., 16
English language, 119
European Association, 35–36
European population, 8

Federal party, 230–31; formation, 88,
  271–72; 1952 election, 88, 91–92, 235;
  1956 election, 102, 105–6; and M.E.P.
  government, 134–35, 137, 138; 1960
  elections, 145–46, 147–48, 149, 152, 155;
  and S.L.F.P. government, 157, 158, 160;
  1965 election, 168–69; and National
  government, 170
Fernando, Hugh, 131
Fernando, Meryl, 213
Forward Bloc, S.L.F.P., 131, 201, 203
Fourth International, 59, 60
F.P. *See* Federal party
Funds: L.S.S.P., 223; S.L.F.P., 91, 199,
  206; U.N.P., 67, 89, 94, 176–77

Ginger Group, 204
Gooneshina, A. E.: in preindependence
  politics, 36, 37, 39–40, 43, 47, 48; and
  Trade Union Act, 57; 1947 election, 65;
  in U.N.P. government, 73
Goonetilleke, Sir Oliver, 3, 38, 137
Goonewardene, Leslie, 58, 218–19, 220, 221
Governor, powers, 21–22, 31, 42, 48–49
Governor-General, 108, 137–38, 148–49
"Governor's party," 48
Gunasekera, A., 60
Gunawardena, Philip: in State Council, 48;
  and L.S.S.P., 58, 60, 215–16; and

V.L.S.S.P., 87; in M.E.P. coalition, 114,
124, 128, 129–31, 201, 203; and
"Sinhala only," 120; and M.E.P. (party),
142, 144, 160, 228–30, 249; 1960
elections, 148, 150; and United Left
Front, 162; 1965 election, 168, 170
Gunawardena, Robert, 216

Halangoda, J. A., 33
Hindus, 9
Horton, Governor, 23
House of Representatives, membership,
51, 140, 256, 261

Ideology: C.P., 224–25, 228; F.P., 254;
Labour party, 65–66; L.S.S.P., 59, 60,
82, 210, 212–14; Marxist parties, 82, 91,
97, 254; M.E.P. government, 129; and
party development, 273–75; S.L.F.P., 91,
96, 207–11; U.N.P., 56–57, 67–68,
74–75, 90, 107–8, 110, 143, 188–89
Image: C.P., 224; L.S.S.P., 213; of party,
and notable, 283–86; S.L.F.P., 206–11,
277, 285; U.N.P., 173–74, 285
Independents: 1947 election, 70, 71, 72;
1952 election, 88, 93; 1956 election, 102,
106; 1960 elections, 141, 147, 153,
156–57; 1965 election, 169; decline in
politics, 232–41, 281
India, 7, 28–29, 83
Indians, 6–7, 62, 63–65, 85–86, 259–60, 264
Iriyagolle, I. M. R. A., 114, 119, 122, 127,
141, 142, 165

Jatika Vimukthi Peramuna (J.V.P.):
proscription (1958), 137; 1960 elections,
141, 152, 156, 242; proscription (1961),
160; 1965 election, 166, 168, 169, 242;
and U.N.P., 253
Jayasuriya, F. R., 137, 141
Jayewardene, J. R., 74, 83, 90, 110, 119, 148
Jefferson, Thomas, 15
Jeffries, Sir Charles, 11
Jennings, Sir W. Ivor, 43, 70, 71, 78, 90, 91,
93, 94, 149

Kandyan Association, 33
Kandyan National Assembly, 34
Kandyan Peasantry Commission, 118
Kandyans, 8–9, 32–34, 109, 117–18, 141,
264–65
Keuneman, Pieter: and Communist party,
82, 105, 111, 227; electoral strength, 226,
249; on L.S.S.P., 59, 112; and M.E.P.
government, 136, 138; and Parliament,

97, 224; and S.L.F.P. government,
160, 162
Kotelawala, Sir John: in preindependence
politics, 44; 1947 election, 67, 68; in
U.N.P. government (1947–52), 76–78,
108, 176; 1952 election, 94; as prime
minister, 97, 98, 109, 111, 183–84;
1956 election, 102, 103–4, 174, 179;
retirement, 186; March 1960 election, 147
Kumarasiri, P., 162

Labor unions. *See* Trade unions
Labour party, 37, 43, 44, 45, 47, 65–66,
95, 102
Landlessness, 4–5, 118
Language issue, 69, 100–101, 102–3, 105,
109, 119–20, 122, 135–36, 160
Lanka Prajathantrawadi Pakshaya: 1960
elections, 142, 145, 146–47, 152, 155,
156, 242; and S.L.F.P. government,
158–59; and U.N.P., 252–53
Lanka Sama Samaja party: formation, 47,
58–59; split (1939), 59; proscription,
59–60; 1947 election, 60, 69, 70;
merger and split (1950), 87, 95; 1952
election, 88, 92, 111; attempts at unity,
112; 1956 election, 102–6 *passim*, 114;
and M.E.P. government, 125, 126, 138,
139; 1960 elections, 141, 142, 144–45,
147, 148–52, 154–55, 156, 214; and
S.L.F.P. government, 157, 158–59, 160,
161, 162, 163–64; split (1964), 213;
coalition with S.L.F.P., 213, 221–22;
1965 election, 166, 167, 169, 213; and
National government, 170
Lanka Sama Samaja party (Revolutionary
Section), 164, 168, 213
Legislative Council: formation, 22–23;
opposition in, 23–24; reform of 1910,
27–28; reform of 1921, 30–31; and
responsible government, 40–41
Leiserson, Avery, 13
Liberal League, 43, 44, 47
Lipson, Leslie, 16
London *Times,* 136
Lorenz, Charles A., 24, 26
Low-country Sinhalese, 8–9, 264–65
L.P.P. *See* Lanka Prajathantrawadi
Pakshaya
L.S.S.P. *See* Lanka Sama Samaja party

MacIver, Robert, 14, 16
Mahadeva, A., 54
Mahajana Eksath Peramuna (coalition):

formation, 102, 114; 1956 election,
104–5, 106, 107, 121–23; Bandaranaike
government, 123–24, 126, 127–32,
134–39, 277; Dahanayake government,
132–33, 139–40
Mahajana Eksath Peramuna (party):
1960 elections, 142, 144, 147, 148, 149,
150, 152, 155, 156, 229; and S.L.F.P.
government, 159, 160; 1965 election,
166, 168, 169, 229; as personality party,
241
Mahindapala, H. L. D., 189
Malays, 7–8
Mansur, Fatma, 289
Marikkar, C. A. S., 129–30, 150
Marxist Left parties: origins, 57–58, 211;
1947 election, 52, 53–54, 61–62, 68–69,
72; and U.N.P. government (1947–52),
81–82, 84, 85, 86; 1952 election, 87, 91,
111; and U.N.P. government (1952–56),
95, 97, 98; 1956 election, 102; 1965
election, 166; attempts at unity, 111–12,
162, 211–12; and communalism, 278;
as personality parties, 272
Mass franchise, and party development,
275–76
Mendis, M. G., 58, 159, 226, 227
M.E.P. *See* Mahajana Eksath Peramuna
Mettananda, 137, 141, 142
Michels, Robert, 15, 16
Minority groups, and electoral system,
265–69
Mooloya Estate strike, 49, 58
Moonesinghe, Anil, 218–19
Moors, 7, 257
Moors' Association, 36, 54, 56, 184
Moraes, Frank R., 70, 71
Morning Times, 136
Morse, Anton D., 15–16
Mosca, Gaetano, 15
Motha, G. R., 64
Multimember districts, 257
Multipartism, 255
Muslim League, 36, 54, 56, 73, 184
Muslims, 9, 36, 237. *See also*
Religion, in politics

Nadesan, S., 54, 106
Natesa-Aiyar, K., 39, 64
National government (1965), 169–70
Nationalist movement, 26–39
Nehru, Jawaharlal, 64
Nell, Dr., 66
Neumann, Sigmund, 13, 14–15, 16, 270, 286

No-contest pacts, 114–15, 149–52, 155–56,
166, 251–52
Nominations: L.S.S.P., 223; S.L.F.P.,
199–200; U.N.P., 67, 110–11, 178–79,
181, 191–92
Notable-determined parties, 272–75
Notables: and party, 271–72, 280–86; in
U.N.P., 173–74. *See also*
Personal-influence structures

One-party trend (1956), 106–7
Opposition: in Legislative Council, 23–24;
in State Council, 49; to U.N.P.
(1947–52), 81–87, 111; to U.N.P.
(1952–56), 95–99, 111–13; to M.E.P.,
124–27, 138, 139–40; to S.L.F.P.,
158–59; to National government, 170
Opposition parties: and alternative
governments, 289; and voter influence,
276–77
Organization: C.P., 226–28; L.S.S.P., 58,
214–24; S.L.F.P., 113, 195–207, 278;
U.N.P., 55–56, 89, 110–11, 174–78,
189–94, 278
Ostrogorski, M. I., 15

Paddy Lands Act, 128, 144
Pareto, Vilfredo, 15, 16
Parliament: and intergroup conflict, 269;
notables in, 282–83; and party contest,
253–55
Parliamentary system, and party, 12–13,
271–72, 286–89
Parties: and democracy, 14–15; functions,
15–19; and personal ambition, 20; study
of, 13
Party formation, before independence,
40–43, 45–46
Party maturation, 171–72, 279–80
Peiries, Darrell, 66
Peiris, James, 27, 30, 39
Pereira, I. X., 64
Perera, E. W., 43–44, 46–47, 48
Perera, G. P., 219
Perera, N. M.: in State Council, 48; and
L.S.S.P., 58, 60, 212, 214, 218–19, 220,
247; 1947 election, 71; and U.N.P.
government (1947–52), 73, 74, 86; 1952
election, 94, 96; and U.N.P. government
(1952–56), 97–98; 1956 election, 102;
and attempts at Leftist unity, 111, 112;
and M.E.P. government, 125, 131, 132,
136, 137, 138; 1960 elections, 151, 152;